ST. LAURENCE HIGH SCHOOL

26076

P9-CAY-701

WORLD HISTORY BY ERA

The World Wars

VOLUME 8

WORLD HISTORY BY ERA

The World Wars

VOLUME 8

Other titles in the
World History by Era series:

WORLD HISTORY BY ERA

The World Wars

VOLUME 8

Myra H. Immell, *Book Editor*

Daniel Leone, *President*
Bonnie Szumski, *Publisher*
Scott Barbour, *Managing Editor*

Greenhaven Press, Inc., San Diego, California

Every effort has been made to trace the owners of copy-
righted material. The articles in this volume may have been
edited for content, length, and/or reading level. The titles
have been changed to enhance the editorial purpose.

No part of this book may be reproduced or used in any form
or by any means, electrical, mechanical, or otherwise, including, but not limited to, photocopy, recording, or any information storage and retrieval system, without prior permission
from the publisher.

Library of Congress Cataloging-in-Publication Data

The World Wars / Myra H. Immell, book editor.
    p. cm. — (World history by era ; v. 8)
    Includes bibliographical references and index.
    ISBN 0-7377-0769-0 (lib. : alk. paper) —
    ISBN 0-7377-0768-2 (pbk. : alk. paper)
    1. World War, 1914–1918. 2. World War, 1939–1945.
    3. History, Modern—20th century. I. Immell, Myra.
    II. Series.

D521 .W67 2002
940.3—dc21   2001050176

Cover inset photo credits (from left):
Corel Professional Photos; Photodisc; Corel Professional
Photos; Corel Professional Photos; Planet Art; Digital Stock;
Photodisc
Main cover photo credit: National Archives
Digital Stock, 261
Library of Congress, 35, 44, 84, 136, 184, 235

Copyright © 2002 by Greenhaven Press, Inc.
10911 Technology Place, San Diego, CA 92127

Printed in the USA

CONTENTS

Chapter 1: 1913–1918: When the Monarchies Ended

1. The Panama Canal Unites the Oceans

The Panama Canal, the waterway that links the Atlantic and Pacific Oceans, is the result of a herculean
effort by thousands of people lasting more than a
decade. Although one of the greatest engineering
achievements in the world, the canal—and the celebrations that should have accompanied its opening—was almost totally overshadowed by Germany's declaration of war.

2. Mass Production: A New Force in Industry

Henry Ford first brought mass production into the
automotive industry late in 1913 in Highland Park,
Michigan. Mass production became a major new
force in human affairs that changed industry forever and helped ring in a new era.

3. Marie Curie, Woman of Distinction

Marie Curie opened up a completely new field of
research—radioactivity—at a time when opportunities for women in the scientific arena were almost
nonexistent. When she helped show for the first
time in history that an element could be transmuted
into another element, she revolutionized chemistry.

4. Sarajevo: The Shot That Started a World War

When a nineteen-year-old terrorist killed a visiting
archduke and his wife in June 1914, it set off a
global war. Had it not been for the archduke's lack
of sensitivity to his subjects' state of mind, his desire
to give his wife a special anniversary gift, and a se-

ries of blunders, the assassination attempt probably would not have been successful.

dress, bobbed hair, made-up faces, and noncon-
formist behavior, were known as flappers.

Tutankhamen ruled Egypt more than three thousand years ago. When, in 1922, after a long and frus-
trating search, Howard Carter discovered Tutankhamen's long-hidden tomb, he unearthed a
multitude of treasures that awed all who saw them.

In 1922 Benito Mussolini choreographed a Fascist
march on Italy's capital city of Rome. Mussolini,
who had a high opinion of himself and his importance, promised the Italian people that fascism
would strengthen the nation and return it to its former position of world prominence.

Mustafa Kemal fought successfully to liberate his
nation from Ottoman rule. When he became the first
president of the republic of Turkey, he acted on his
belief that for a nation to be considered civilized it
had to be Westernized and embarked on a crusade
to Westernize Turkey.

During the last months of 1929, the stock market
went on a roller coaster ride that ended in a crash
on October 29. The crash, which resounded around
the world, resulted in the loss of billions of dollars
and ushered in a period of worldwide depression.

Chapter 3: 1930–1939: A Time of Trial and Change

When a worldwide depression set in in the 1930s,
each country blamed another country for what had
happened. Many people laid the responsibility on
the United States, pointing to the 1929 stock market
crash as the trigger.

Churchill made it clear that the British people would give their all to keep that from happening.

FOREWORD

T he late 1980s were a time of dramatic events worldwide. Tragedies such as the explosions of the space shuttle *Challenger* and the Chernobyl nuclear power plant shocked the world out of its complacent belief that humankind had mastered nature and firmly controlled its technological creations. In U.S. politics, scandal rocked the White House when several high-ranking officials in the Ronald Reagan administration were convicted of selling arms to Iran and aiding the Nicaraguan Contra rebels. In global politics, U.S. president Ronald Reagan and Soviet president Mikhail Gorbachev signed a landmark treaty banning intermediate-range nuclear forces, marking the beginning of an era of arms control. In several parts of the world—including Beijing, China, the West Bank and Gaza Strip, and several nations of Eastern Europe—people rose up to resist oppressive governments, with varying degrees of success. In American culture, crack cocaine and inner-city poverty contributed to the development of a new and controversial music genre: gangsta rap.

Many of these events were unrelated to one another except for the fact that they occurred at about the same time. Others were linked to global developments. Greenhaven Press's World History by Era series provides students with a unique tool for examining global history in a way that allows them to appreciate the seemingly random occurrences as well as the general trends of human progress. This series divides world history—from the time of ancient Greece and Rome to the end of the second millennium—into ten discrete periods. Each volume then presents a collection of both primary and secondary documents that describe the major events of the period in chronological order. This structure provides students with a snapshot of events occurring simultaneously in all parts of the world. The reader can then see the connections between events in far-flung corners of the world. For example, the Palestinian uprising (*Intifada*) of December 1987 was near in time—if not in character and location—to similar protests in Beijing, China; Berlin, Germany; Prague, Czechoslovakia; and Bucharest, Romania. While these events were different in many ways, they all involved ordinary citizens striving for self-autonomy and democracy against governments that were attempting to impose strict controls on their civil liberties. By making the connections between these events, students can see that they comprised a global movement for democracy and human rights that profoundly impacted social and political systems worldwide.

Each volume in this series offers features to enhance students' understanding of the era of world history under discussion. An introductory essay provides an overview of the period, supplying essential context for the readings that follow. An annotated table of contents highlights the main point of each selection. A more in-depth introduction precedes each document, placing it in its particular historical context and offering biographical information about the author. A thorough chronology and index allow students to quickly reference specific events and dates. Finally, a bibliography opens up additional avenues of research. These features help to make the World History by Era series an extremely valuable tool for students researching the rise and fall of civilizations, social and political revolutions, cultural movements, scientific and technological advancements, and other events that mark the unfolding of human history throughout the world.

AN ERA PLAGUED BY WAR AND CHANGE

Throughout every era of history, people in almost every part of the world have been confronted at one time or another with the devastation of war and the bewilderment and exhilaration of change. The people of the modern era that fell between the years 1913 and 1945 are no exception. Theirs was an era indelibly marked by war and the irrevocable change that it engendered. From a historical perspective, the thirty-two years of that era are not a lot of time. Yet, within that relatively short span of time, people suffered not one war but two—wars that devastated economies, left nations in ruins, and changed the geography of much of the world.

In many ways, the wars overshadowed almost everything for most of the era. But some extraordinary events not necessarily related to war occurred during those thirty-odd years. Between 1913 and 1918, for example, the United States completed the Panama Canal after more than ten years of successes and failures; American entrepreneur Henry Ford revolutionized the automotive industry by introducing the concept of mass production into his Michigan automobile plant; Nobel Prize–winning Polish-born scientist Marie Curie shared her research on radium and proved to the skeptical scientific world that a woman could excel in the sciences; and millions of Armenians in the Ottoman Empire died at the hands of the Turks.

Between 1919 and 1939, people had a respite from world war but not from suffering, despair, anger, or change. A short-lived influenza pandemic came out of nowhere and took the lives of mil-

lions of people in different parts of the world. Archaeologists discovered the three-thousand-year-old treasure-filled tomb of an
Egyptian boy-king. Turkey became a republic, and its first president set in motion a crusade to Westernize the nation. During the
same period of time, the New York Stock Exchange crashed, resulting in the loss of billions of dollars and a major worldwide economic depression unlike any experienced before or since. In the
midst of that Depression, Indian leader Mohandas K. Gandhi
preached nonviolent resistance to British rule and set followers on
a firm course toward independence; and in China, Mao Tse-tung
and his Red Army undertook a grueling six-thousand-mile trek to
northern China, bringing China a step closer to Communist rule.

By then, as the decade of the 1930s drew to an end, the rum-
blings of a second world war were growing louder. Much of the
world held their breath as the facade of world peace collapsed
and the prospect of war became a reality. World attention once
again focused on Europe as Adolf Hitler's Nazi storm troopers
overran and devoured Poland.

EUROPE ON THE PATH TO WAR

For much of the 1800s, Europe had been made up of individual
countries, some independent and some part of a vast empire.
Over time, a spirit of nationalism had taken seed and grown
within a number of the countries. The motivator was power. By
the end of the century, five European nations had emerged as the
most powerful—France, Germany, Britain, Austria-Hungary, and
Russia. All five of the powers harbored a desire for empire and
supported the concept of imperialism. As time went on, each became more militaristic. Coming to the conclusion that there was
strength in numbers and that simply building up its own armed
forces might not provide enough protection in case of a war, each
sought alliances with other states or nations.

By 1907, two powerful alliances had come into existence. One
was the Triple Alliance, made up of Germany, Austria-Hungary,
and Italy. The other was the Triple Entente, an alliance between
France, Russia, and Britain. At the heart of the alliance system
was the promise that each member nation would help the other
if one of them were attacked by another nation. The rivalry between the two alliances grew, fueled to a great extent by eco-
nomics, imperialism, and nationalism. By 1914, some Europeans
feared that what had started out as rivalry was dangerously close
to turning into armed conflict. Other Europeans retained an optimistic outlook, arguing that no one would be foolish enough to
threaten the current wave of prosperity by escalating a rivalry
into a major war.

THE DEATH OF AN ARCHDUKE: THE TRIGGER FOR WORLD WAR

Even those who ardently believed that war was not in the near future could not deny the undercurrents at play in Europe. The area of the Balkans, where three nations were playing a dangerous game of tug-of-war for control, was of particular concern. Both Russia and Austria-Hungary wanted to lay claim to the area, much of which was home to various groups of Slavs. At the same time, the small Balkan nation of Serbia had another agenda: to unite the Slavs in the Balkans and expand Serb territory. Serbia saw the acquisition of the southern part of Bosnia, which was part of Austria-Hungary's empire, as a step toward achieving the Serbian goal. Knowing that they could not take on Austria-Hungary without a strong ally to support them, the Serbs looked to Russia for help.

In 1914, the heir to the throne of Austria-Hungary, Archduke Franz Ferdinand of Austria, and his wife, Sophie, made an official visit to the Bosnian capital of Sarajevo. As they rode in an open car in a motorcade, a nineteen-year-old Bosnian student named Gavrilo Princip shot and killed them both. Princip, a fervent Serbian nationalist, was one of seven young and inexperienced members of a secret Serbian nationalist-terrorist society involved in the assassination plot. Within a month after Princip's bullets had found their mark, most of Europe was at war.

Austria-Hungary blamed Serbian leaders for Franz Ferdinand's death, using it as an excuse to declare war on Serbia. Russia jumped in and announced its intention of going to the aid of Serbia. Then Germany countered by proclaiming its support of Austria-Hungary and declaring war on Russia. Two days later, Germany declared war on France and sent troops into Luxembourg. German demands on neutral Belgium to permit German troops to pass through Belgian territory brought Britain into the war on the side of Russia and France. Other nations soon aligned themselves with one side or the other, creating two major alliances—the Allied Powers and the Central Powers. France, Russia, Britain, and Italy were the Allies, while Turkey, Germany, and Austria-Hungary were the Central Powers. Gradually, more nations took sides. Serbia, Belgium, and later Japan and Montenegro joined the Allies, while the Ottoman Empire and Bulgaria gave their support to the Central Powers.

WORLD WAR I: A NEW KIND OF WAR

Both the Allies and the Central Powers were sure not only that they could win the war but that they could do so pretty quickly.

Confidence and optimism prevailed, with each side convinced of its military prowess and certain of its superiority. History has shown, however, that in actuality neither side was really prepared for what was to come. Both anticipated a quick victory, not a war of attrition that would drag on for four years with naval battles fought all over the world and battlefields in the Middle East and Africa as well as in Europe. Neither had anticipated new weapons as powerful as the machine gun or as potent as the poison gases whose fumes killed many soldiers and permanently damaged the brains of others. And, certainly, no one was prepared for the bomb-carrying airplanes that dropped their lethal cargoes on soldier and civilian alike or the submarines that hid on the ocean floor lying in wait for enemy ships totally unaware of their presence. Neither side had anticipated the subsequent slaughter of so many civilians.

Early on in the war, it appeared that the Central Powers, who gained control of the richest part of France and most of Belgium, had the upper hand. But then the war on the western front came to a virtual standstill with neither side managing to make any headway against the other. The war became one of trench warfare, with soldiers on each side hunkered down in trenches dug during the dark hours of the night. From the Swiss border to the North Sea, the landscape was marked by two seemingly endless and unbroken lines of trenches that ran parallel to one another, each fortified by land mines and barbed wire. All that separated the soldiers huddled in one line of trenches from the enemy soldiers huddled in the other line was the fairly narrow strip of land between them known as no-man's-land.

Meanwhile, on the seas, the British maintained control, using their dominance to enforce a blockade against the Central Powers. In an effort to diminish British sea power, the Germans turned to submarine warfare. They prowled the Atlantic, on constant lookout for enemy ships. The Germans chose to ignore the rules of naval warfare, which dictated that a submarine had to give warning before using its torpedoes to sink a ship. If it received no reply and chose to sink the ship, naval rules dictated that it was also obligated to take on board any evacuees from the sunken ship. In spite of complaints and threats from the Allies, German submarines continued to attack without warning any ship the Germans thought might be carrying arms or supplies to the Allies.

Several years passed before the stalemate that had characterized the war came to an end. Two major events helped break the stalemate. One was Russia's decision, based primarily on the breakdown of military morale and discipline coupled with internal problems, to withdraw from the war. The other event was America's decision to enter the war after years of refusing to get caught up in what most Americans considered a European war to solve Europe's problems. Finally, in 1917, the United States declared war on Germany. The carefully maintained U.S. neutrality, as well as all peace efforts by American president Woodrow Wilson, came to an abrupt end when Germany announced that it would initiate unrestricted submarine warfare against all British shipping and any shipping to Britain. The 2 million American troops ultimately dispatched to Europe helped the war-weary Europeans turn the tide of the war.

In 1918, the Germans mounted a series of offensives in hopes of ending the war before American troops could arrive. Just when it appeared that they might achieve their goal, the Allies managed to stop them. The Allies clearly had the advantage now with a supply of strong reserves, an abundance of tanks, and the support of the 250,000 American troops arriving in France each month. The Germans had no more reserves and virtually no morale. Before the year was out, first Turkey and then Austria-Hungary surrendered to the Allies. German kaiser William II abdicated his throne and fled Germany, leaving the Germans to surrender and ending a four-year-long global war during which not one decisive battle had been fought.

THE CONSEQUENCES OF WAR

The cost of the war had been high. A shattered Europe, with 10 million soldiers dead and another 20 million wounded or disabled, was only part of the cost. Paying for the war had seriously damaged the economies of the participants. After the battlefield fighting had stopped and the armistice had been signed, the diplomatic maneuvering began in earnest. The Allies, who had cooperated on military strategies and the waging of war and had been so willing to bend and cooperate with one another, had differing views about what reparations should be part of the peace settlement. Before the war had ended, President Wilson had drawn up a peace plan—"Fourteen Points"—with terms meant to reward the victors without excessively punishing the losers. The British, French, and Italians, however, had other ideas. They thought victory entitled them to land that before the war had belonged to the defeated Central Powers. They also wanted Germany to pay them for the damage done to their countries during the war.

When the Allies finally negotiated the terms of the World War I Treaty of Versailles, they meted out the very punishment President Wilson had tried so hard to avoid. The treaty gave the British, French, and Italians land that belonged to the Central

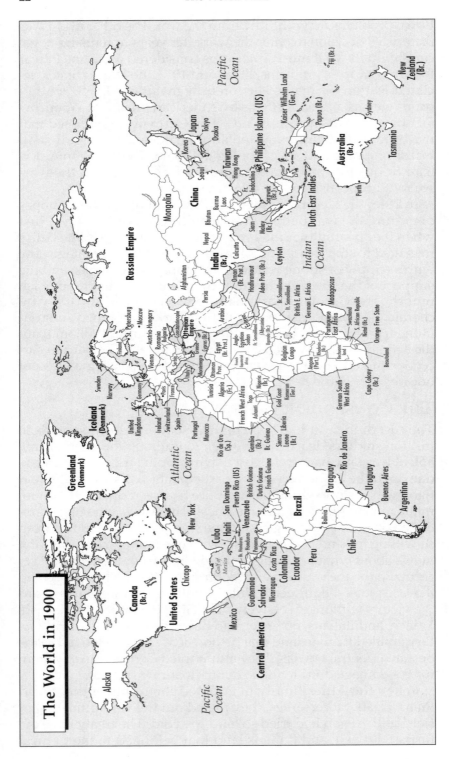

The World in 1900

Powers. Germany's colonies in Africa went to France and Britain, while its colonies in the Pacific were put under Japanese control. Austria-Hungary was split into four new countries—Austria, Hungary, Czechoslovakia, and Yugoslavia. The Allies singled out Germany as the one chiefly responsible and accountable for the war and imposed harsh penalties on the Germans. Not only did they insist that Germany pay huge sums of money in reparation for war damages, they forced the Germans to limit the size of their army and abolish their navy as well. The treaty did establish the world peace organization—the League of Nations—that President Wilson had envisioned in his Fourteen Points, but it ensured the league's failure by not giving it any powers of enforcement.

The war was over, peace treaties had been signed, battle-weary soldiers who had survived the war had returned home, and life had gone on. But nothing was the same as it had been before, nor would it ever be again. The way of life that had existed before the war was gone forever. So many had died or been scarred psychologically that an entire generation—the one that had fought in the war—came to be known as the "lost generation." Parts of Belgium and northern France had been destroyed; empires had collapsed; and gone was the era of dynasties, monarchies, and nobility. The economies of some European countries were as shattered as their cities and countryside. Some governments verged on bankruptcy. Most of the countries that had taken part in World War I had borrowed heavily to pay for their part in the war and were deeply in debt. Germany was in the worst shape of all. In addition to their staggering war debt, the Germans owed $35 million in reparations, which they had no hope of being able to pay. No jobs were available for many of the returning military, not even for those who had not been crippled physically or emotionally by the war, and there was no hope of producing the goods that would help restore a floundering economy. Not even the geography had remained the same. The war had resulted in the need to redraw the boundaries of parts of Europe, the Middle East, Asia, and Africa.

GOOD TIMES—AND BAD

For most of the world, the peace had come, but it was uneasy at best. So much had changed that people were not quite sure of what to do next or how to go about doing it. Some sought to restore normalcy, or normalcy as they had known it. Others turned their back on tradition and developed new styles in politics, society, and culture. Still others took advantage of the situation to further their own ambitions. Europeans were fighting hard times, trying to rebuild what the war had destroyed and overcome the disillusionment created by the war.

Americans, too, were tired of the strains of war. But their situation was different from that of the other Allies. By the time the United States had entered the war, the others had been fighting for several years and had already expended many of their resources—human and otherwise. While other countries and civilians had been scarred by fighting and weapons of war, not one battle had been fought in the United States. Instead of emerging from the war economically and humanly challenged, the United States had come out in a much stronger position with more influence in world affairs than ever before. Business boomed, and people had money to spend. The war had ushered in the Roaring '20s, a decade of prosperity when even the not-so-rich could afford a car, people bought all kinds of consumer goods on credit, and many young women rebelled by bobbing their hair, raising their hemlines, and partying. The automobile gave Americans a mobility they had never had before, broadening their horizons and changing the landscape. The stock market boomed, and many people made fortunes. People were optimistic and willing to take chances. A large number of investors invested more than they truly had, buying on the margin. Life was good—until 1929, when the stock market crashed. Within a few weeks, stocks had lost nearly half of their value. Those holding stock they had bought on the margin found themselves in the awkward position of having to pay for those stocks in full. They had known, but had ignored, the fact that buying on credit was risky. For many stockholders, bankruptcy proved inevitable.

By the end of 1929, an economic depression had set in. Factories kept closing, and millions of people lost their jobs. By 1932, the depression, which had spread to many parts of the globe and turned into the Great Depression, had reached its worst point. World trade had been cut by more than half, affecting business all over the world. Thousands of banks had closed because they did not have the funds to pay their depositors. People who had saved for years found the doors of their banks shut and their savings totally gone. In the United States, more than a quarter of the people were out of work. Manufacturers found the products they had produced did not sell because most of the people had no money to buy them. So they stopped producing as much and laid off more workers. Some businesses simply ceased to exist.

THE RISE AND THREAT OF TOTALITARIANISM

Bad feelings and discontent resulting from World War I were reinforced by flagging economies and the perceived unfairness of some of the World War I peace treaties. Some Europeans began to doubt the worth of their governments. Beginning in the 1920s, new leaders emerged. The political movements set in motion by these strong-willed dictators resulted in totalitarian governments that came to threaten world peace.

Russia was a case in point. Internal revolution had been a major factor in Russia's decision to withdraw from World War I. In 1917, its centuries-old czarist government had come to an abrupt end as Bolsheviks led by the Russian revolutionary Lenin achieved their goal of taking over the Russian government. Czar Nicholas II became the last czar to rule Russia. Many Russians had blamed the czar and his government for hardships and suffering they experienced during World War I. Social and political conditions had worsened continually, and Lenin had used the rapidly deteriorating conditions to his advantage. Lenin called for "Peace, Land, and Bread." He promised the Russian people that if the Bolsheviks were in charge, they would pull Russia out of the war, give the peasants land, and make sure the people received the food supplies they needed. Once in power, the Bolsheviks began to call themselves Communists and, with their supporters in Russia and in other parts of the world, they formed the Communist Party. Civil war broke out between the Communists and those who opposed them. By 1921, the Russian Communists had emerged victorious, and the following year Russia, now a Socialist state, officially became the Union of Soviet Socialist Republics (USSR). Lenin died in 1924, and Marxist revolutionary Joseph Stalin took control a few years later. By 1939, Stalin had established one of the most brutal dictatorships in history and ran the country with an iron hand.

Another nation that moved toward totalitarianism was Japan, which had not reaped the benefits it had expected for taking the side of the Allies during the war. Technically, Japan was ruled by an emperor, but, in fact, true control rested with the military. As a small island nation, Japan was totally dependent on other countries for raw materials, as well as for markets in which to sell its finished goods. The Japanese believed that they needed more land and natural resources to strengthen the national economy. With the understanding that they might have to go to war to get the land and resources, they built up their army. In 1931, Japanese soldiers overran Manchuria, the northwestern region of China; renamed it and declared it an independent country; and, despite China's protests, achieved what they had started out to do—control a territory rich in minerals.

Italy, too, underwent major change after the war, becoming the first Western nation to become a dictatorship. Even though the

Italians had been a victor in World War I, the postwar years had been anything but prosperous. Huge war debts remained to be paid, the economy was depressed, and the number of unemployed had continued to grow, as did social unrest. To further anger and embitter the Italians, they had not gotten all the land they had expected as a prize of war. Fascist leader Benito Mussolini took advantage of the situation, inflaming the people and building on their discontent and fear of communism. Once they were convinced that a democratic government could not solve their problems, Mussolini took control. In 1922, he established a Fascist government, proclaimed himself *Il Duce* ("the Leader"), and invested the state with absolute authority and the right to rule by force. Then, in accordance with Fascist philosophy, he set about through war and conquest to make good on his promise to make Italy a major world power and restore the glory that had once belonged to ancient Rome. In 1935, Mussolini's Fascist troops invaded and took control of the African nation of Ethiopia. Within a year, Ethiopia was formally annexed to Italy.

Spain also was experiencing radical governmental change. After centuries as a monarchy, the reigning king was forced to leave, and Spain became a republic, whose leaders vowed to modernize the nation. The move to a republican form of government and the changes taking place did not please everyone. Conservative groups wanted to return to the old ways. In 1936, conservative army chiefs in Spanish Morocco revolted against the republic, setting off a civil war that spread across Spain. Before long, what had begun as a civil conflict between Spanish conservatives—Nationalists—and Spanish republicans—Loyalists—turned into a confrontation between fascism and communism, with the Germans and Italians supporting the Nationalists and the Soviets supporting the Loyalists. Germany's Nazi leader Adolf Hitler, who had established a totalitarian government in Germany, saw his chance to use Spain as a testing ground for the new war techniques of the German air force and ground troops. When, after more than three years, the civil war came to an end, leaving much of Spain in ruins and hundreds of thousands of Spaniards dead, Spain emerged not as a republic or a monarchy but as a dictatorship with Nationalist leader army general Francisco Franco—*El Caudillo*—firmly in charge.

Nowhere was the discontent about the result of World War I stronger than in Germany, where the monarchy that had engineered World War I had been replaced by a republican form of government. The Germans had experienced bitter disappointment when the Treaty of Versailles was not based on Woodrow Wilson's original Fourteen Points as they had expected. Austrian-born soldier Adolf Hitler, still smoldering over Germany's defeat and its consequences, and supported by the fledgling National Socialist Party (Nazis), promised to make Germany strong again.

In an article he wrote in 1998, John Keegan, defense editor for the *Daily Telegraph*, explains just how much Hitler had been influenced by the events of World War I and how much Hitler's actions had influenced future events:

> The rise of Hitler was a direct result of the war [World War I] as well. Hitler's raw material—the disaffected ex-frontfighters who formed the Stormtroopers—was a product of the Great War, just as so many of Mussolini's original supporters were ex-soldiers resentful of how little Italy had gained at Versailles for its participation. . . . Mussolini was the first leader of a mass political movement to uniform his followers. Hitler took the militarisation of politics to its logical conclusion. His Nazi party mimicked an army at every level, ultimately by subjecting every organ of German life, from the law courts to the Lutheran church, to party control.

> Hitler himself regarded the war as "the supreme experience." Defeat in it supplied his motive for the seizure of power, and the achievement of power offered him the opportunity he set above all the others, that of reversing the verdict of 1918. "We do not pardon," he proclaimed in 1922. "No, we demand—Vengeance." What made his mission of vengeance all the more ghastly in its outcome was that those who joined him in it were a generation brutalised by mass combat and mass slaughter. Those who had survived the mass-production of corpses were men hardened to the process. What they learnt in the trenches they would repeat 20 years later in every corner of Europe. From their awful cult of death the continent is still recovering.[1]

Hitler, made chancellor of Germany in 1933, soon abolished the republic. Taking the title of *der Führer* ("The Leader"), he proclaimed himself dictator of Germany and proclaimed the new government the Third Reich, an empire that would last one thousand years. Hitler rebuilt the German army in defiance of the Treaty of Versailles, the terms of which he was determined to change or ignore or both. Once in power, he deprived Germany's Jews of their jobs and their legal rights, justifying his blatant anti-Semitism by claiming that the Jews had been responsible for most of Germany's troubles. Once again defying the terms of the Treaty of Versailles, he sent his Nazi troops into the Rhineland area of western Germany between Germany and France. Britain and France's failure to stop Hitler's takeover of the Rhineland spelled the end for the Versailles Treaty. Germany began rearming rapidly and in earnest. Next, Hitler annexed Austria and took control of the Sudetenland region of Czechoslovakia bordering Germany. Within a year, in complete contradiction of the promises he had made, he gobbled up the western part of Czechoslovakia and made the eastern part of the country a German puppet state. A shocked world stood by and watched as Hitler made inroads toward realizing his slogan—"Today, Germany, tomorrow, the world!"

WORLD WAR FOR THE SECOND TIME

When Hitler threatened to take over the Baltic port of Danzig and the Polish Corridor, Britain and France acted. They increased military spending and promised Poland they would help defend the border if Hitler attacked. Meanwhile, to avoid risking a fight on two fronts, Hitler signed a nonaggression pact with the Soviets, which also divided control of parts of Eastern Europe between Germany and the Soviet Union. On September 1, 1939, Hitler sent his troops into Poland. Two days later, Britain and France declared war on Germany.

For the second time in two decades, the Allies and Germany were at war. The devastation and number of deaths resulting from this war, which escalated rapidly into World War II, far exceeded those of World War I. This time, instead of the Central Powers, the Allies' enemy was the Axis—Germany, Italy, and Japan. By 1941, the list of European countries overrun and occupied by the Germans and the Italians included Albania, Poland, Denmark, Belgium, the Netherlands, Luxembourg, Norway, France, Romania, and Hungary. The Italians, meanwhile, had established a hold in North Africa, and the Soviets had occupied the eastern portion of Poland. France had been among the first to fall, forcing the British to take an even stronger stand against Germany. As expected, Hitler targeted Britain, trying first to bomb the British into submission and, when that did not work, starving them into submission by having German submarines sink any merchant ship carrying supplies to Britain. But Hitler underestimated the skill of the British Royal Air Force, the power of the British naval forces, and the resolve and tenacity of the British people. He also misjudged how far the American government would go to help the British.

When Hitler realized that he could not defeat Britain—at least for the time being—he turned on his ally, the Soviet Union. However, once again, Hitler underestimated his opponent. As soon as

German troops stepped onto Soviet territory, the Soviets moved farther into the interior, burning and destroying land, crops, livestock, personal property, anything they thought the Germans could use. No matter how hard the Germans pushed, the Russians kept resisting and, no matter the suffering or loss, refusing to surrender.

At the same time the Germans and Italians were trying to conquer Europe, the Japanese were waging war in Asia. In line with their philosophy that Asia belonged to Asians and the Western powers had no right to control any part of the continent, the Japanese made plans to unite all of east and southeast Asia under their rule. At the same time, they strengthened their ties with Germany and Italy. By 1941, in control of much of China and the East Indies and all of Indochina, the Japanese turned their attention to the United States, the other major power in the Pacific. The Japanese viewed the American forces in the Philippines as a threat to their control of the Pacific. In addition, they resented the United States for protesting Japanese expansion in Asia by cutting off all exports. On December 7, 1941, while negotiations between the United States and Japan were being conducted, the Japanese launched a surprise attack on the American military base at Pearl Harbor in Hawaii, crippling much of the American fleet docked there. Pearl Harbor was the deciding factor for the Americans. The United States entered the war on the side of the Allies.

BRINGING THE WAR TO A CLOSE

The American entry into the war signaled new hope for the Europeans and major problems for the Axis. As the greatest industrial power in the world, the United States could turn out thousands of planes, tanks, and ships at a point in time when the Axis powers, who had been fighting for several years, were struggling to produce the war materials they needed to supply their forces. Russia was costing the Nazi cause a great deal. Invading the Soviet Union had been a major blunder, one Hitler compounded by refusing to pull his troops out even when no real hope of victory remained. Even some of the highest German officials were admitting secretly that the Soviet Union was proving to be too much for them—too big and too cold. By 1943, the tables had turned completely, with the Soviet forces attacking the Germans instead of the other way around. The Axis powers lost ground in Africa and Italy as well, and then in France. The Germans found themselves caught between the Soviets in the east and the Americans, British, French, and Canadians in the west. Finally, in 1945, Allied troops came together at the Elbe River in Germany. Unable to face the inevitable, Hitler, who had entrenched himself in a bunker in Berlin, committed suicide, leaving Grand Admiral Karl Doenitz no choice but to surrender.

Although the war in Europe was over, the war in the Pacific was not. Early victories in southeast Asia and the Pacific had expanded the Japanese empire so much that by 1942 it stretched from the Aleutian Islands near Alaska south to the Solomon Islands in the western Pacific, and from Wake Island west to Burma. Not until then did the Japanese suffer their first major defeats. The Americans, supported by Australians and, to some extent, the British, hopped from one Pacific island to another, driving off the Japanese and pushing their way relentlessly toward Japan.

But even with American planes bombing their homeland, the Japanese refused to surrender. Frustrated by Japan's continual refusal to end the war and fearful of the toll an all-out invasion of Japan would take on American lives, American president Harry S Truman ordered the use of a newly developed secret weapon—the atomic bomb. The Americans dropped the first bomb on August 6, 1945, on the Japanese city of Hiroshima, killing and maiming tens of thousands of people and destroying most of the city. When the Japanese still made no move to surrender, the Americans unleashed a second and larger bomb on the city of Nagasaki, creating even greater devastation and death. This time, the Japanese surrendered. World War II was over.

THE OUTCOMES OF WAR

World War II proved infinitely more damaging than World War I and, in terms of human and material resources, was the greatest war in history. Three-fourths of the world's population had been involved in the war. The death toll was staggering—more than 25 million military dead and 30 million or so civilians—not counting the approximately 6 million victims of the Nazi Holocaust. Much of Europe and Asia lay in ruins, including the factories, railroads, and highways, and millions of people of all ages were on the brink of starvation. Financially, too, the war exacted a heavy sum—more than all other wars combined. The atrocities committed by the Japanese and the Germans during the war were so inhumane and incomprehensible, even given the circumstance of war, that many former German and Japanese leaders were put on trial for war crimes. The trials resulted in death sentences for eleven top Nazi leaders and seven former Japanese leaders, with others sentenced to long terms in prison.

World War II, like World War I, had altered the map of the world, and, collectively, the two wars had decimated European economies. For many nations, the need to rebuild was overwhelming, as was the cost. Western nations that had depended on their Asian and African colonies to provide the raw materials and cheap labor that had bolstered their economies found themselves at a loss. By the time the war had come to an end in 1945, a number of those colonies had declared their independence and established their own governments.

The world power of Western European nations, already diminished by the First World War, was lessened yet again by the Second World War. New world leaders with diametrically opposing philosophies of government—the United States and the Soviet Union—emerged from the chaos. The United States, whose factories and farms produced more than any other country, was the world's leading industrial power and led all others in trade. The Soviet Union was the largest country in the world, with a vast array of natural resources and millions of workers. The Soviet Union had gained control in eastern Europe and set up Communist governments in almost all of the countries of the area, while the United States was recognized as the new leader of the Western world.

NOTES

1. John Keegan, "The Great Watershed," *Daily Telegraph*, November 9, 1998.

1913–1918: When the Monarchies Ended

CHAPTER 1

THE PANAMA CANAL UNITES THE OCEANS

DAVID MCCULLOUGH

The Panama Canal, considered by many the Eighth Wonder of the World, took more than thirty years to build. In 1913, at the height of the project, close to forty-four thousand people worked on the canal. By the time the Panama Canal was completed in 1914, it had cost the United States approximately $380 million and more than six thousand lives. In this excerpt from his highly acclaimed book, *The Path Between the Seas: The Creation of the Panama Canal 1870–1914*, award-winning writer, historian, lecturer, and teacher David McCullough focuses on the events that preceded the opening of the canal. He also explains why the canal's 1914 opening was anticlimactic and not the major event that the United States had anticipated.

F or all practical purposes the canal was finished when the locks [water-filled chambers] were. And so efficiently had construction of the locks been organized that they were finished nearly a year earlier than anticipated. Had it not been for the slides in the Cut [an artificially created channel], adding more than 25,000,000 cubic yards to the total amount of excavation, the canal might have opened in 1913.

READYING THE CUTS

The locks on the Pacific side were finished first, the single flight at Pedro Miguel in 1911, Miraflores in May 1913. Morale was at an all-time high. Asked by a journalist what the secret of success had been, [chief engineer Army Colonel George Washington]

Reprinted with the permission of Simon & Schuster from *"The Path Between the Seas,"* by David McCullough. Copyright © 1977 by David McCullough.

Goethals answered, "The pride everyone feels in the work."

"Men reported to work early and stayed late, without over-time," Robert Wood remembered. ". . . I really believe that every American employed would have worked that year without pay, if only to see the first ship pass through the completed Canal. That spirit went down to all the laborers."

The last concrete was laid at Gatun on May 31, 1913, eleven days after two steam shovels had met "on the bottom of the canal" in Culebra Cut. Shovel No. 222, driven by Joseph S. Kirk, and shovel No. 230, driven by D.J. MacDonald, had been slowly narrowing the gap all day when they at last stood nose to nose. The Cut was as deep as it would go, forty feet above sea level.

In the second week in June, it would be reported that the newly installed upper guard gates at Gatun had been "swung to a position halfway open; then shut, opened wide, closed and . . . noiselessly, without any jar or vibration, and at all times under perfect control."

On June 27 the last of the spillway gates was closed at Gatun Dam. The lake at Gatun had reached a depth of forty-eight feet; now it would rise to its full height.

Three months later all dry excavation ended. The Cucaracha slide still blocked the path, but Goethals had decided to clear it out with dredges once the Cut was flooded. So on the morning of September 10, photographers carried their gear into the Cut to record the last large rock being lifted by the last steam shovel. Locomotive No. 260 hauled out the last dirt train and the work crews moved in to tear up the last of the track. "The Cut tonight presented an unusual spectacle," cabled a correspondent for *The New York Times*, "hundreds of piles of old ties from the railroad tracks being in flames."

THE TEST RUN OF THE *GATUN*

Then on September 26 at Gatun the first trial lockage was made.

A seagoing tug, *Gatun,* used until now for hauling mud barges in the Atlantic entrance, was cleaned up, "decorated with all the flags it owned," and came plowing up from Colón in the early-morning sunshine. By ten o'clock several thousand people were clustered along the rims of the lock walls to witness the historic ascent. There were men on the tops of the closed lock gates, lean-ing on the handrails. The sky was cloudless, and in midair above the lower gates, a photographer hung suspended from the ca-bleway. He was standing in a cement bucket, his camera on a tri-pod, waiting for things to begin.

But it was to be a long, hot day. The water was let into the up-per chamber shortly after eleven, but because the lake had still

*A ship awaits passage through the Gatun Lock of the Panama Canal.
Gatun was the site of the canal's first trial lockage.*

to reach its full height, there was a head of only about eight feet
and so no thunderous rush ensued when the valves were
opened. Indeed, the most fascinating aspect of this phase of the
operation, so far as the spectators were concerned, was the quantity of frogs that came swirling in with the muddy water.

With the upper lock filled, however, the head between it and
the middle lock was fifty-six feet, and so when the next set of culverts was opened, the water came boiling up from the bottom of
the empty chamber in spectacular fashion.

The central control board was still not ready. All valves were
being worked by local control and with extreme caution to be
sure everything was just so. Nor were any of the towing locomotives in service as yet. Just filling the locks took the whole afternoon. It was nearly five by the time the water in the lowest
chamber was even with the surface of the sea-level approach out-

side and the huge gates split apart and wheeled slowly back into their niches in the walls.

The tug steamed into the lower lock, looking, as one man recalled, "like a chip on a pond." [Army engineer William Luther] Sibert, [engineer Edward] Schildhauer, young George Goethals, and their wives were standing on the prow. "The Colonel" and [lock designer Army engineer Harry F.] Hodges were on top of the lock wall, walking from point to point, both men in their shirt sleeves, Goethals carrying a furled umbrella, Hodges wearing glossy puttees and an enormous white hat. The gates had opened in one minute forty-eight seconds, as expected.

The tug proceeded on up through the locks, step by step. The gates to the rear of the first chamber were closed; the water in the chamber was raised until it reached the same height as the water on the other side of the gates ahead. The entire tremendous basin swirled and churned as if being stirred by some powerful, unseen hand and the rise of the water—and of the little boat—was very apparent. Those on board could feel themselves being lifted, as if in a very slow elevator. With the water in the lower chamber equal to that in the middle chamber, the intervening gates were opened and the tug went forward. Again the gates to the stern swung shut; again, with the opening of the huge subterranean culverts, the caramel-colored water came suddenly to life and began its rise to the next level.

It was 6:45 when the last gates were opened in the third and last lock and the tug steamed out onto the surface of Gatun Lake. The day had come and gone, it was very nearly dark, and as the boat turned and pointed to shore, her whistle blowing, the crowd burst into a long cheer. The official time given for this first lockage was one hour fifty-one minutes, or not quite twice as long as would be required once everything was in working order.

PRESIDENT WILSON PRESSES A BUTTON

That an earthquake should strike just four days later seemed somehow a fitting additional touch, as if that too were essential in any thorough testing-and-proving drill. It lasted more than an hour, one violent shudder following another, and the level of magnitude appears to have been greater than that of the San Francisco quake of 1906. The needles of a seismograph at Ancon were jolted off the scale paper. Walls cracked in buildings in Panama City; there were landslides in the interior; a church fell. But the locks and Gatun Dam were untouched. "There has been no damage whatever to any part of the canal," Goethals notified Washington.

Water was let into Culebra Cut that same week, through six

big drain pipes in the earth dike at Gamboa. Then on the afternoon of October 10, President Woodrow Wilson pressed a button in Washington and the center of the dike was blown sky-high. The idea had been dreamed up by a newspaperman. The signal, relayed by telegraph wire from Washington to New York to Galveston to Panama, was almost instantaneous. Wilson walked from the White House to an office in the Executive Building (as the State, War, and Navy Building had been renamed) and pressed the button at one minute past two. At two minutes past two several hundred charges of dynamite opened a hole more than a hundred feet wide and the Cut, already close to full, at once became an extension of Gatun Lake.

In all the years that the work had been moving ahead in the Cut and on the locks, some twenty dredges of different kinds, assisted by numbers of tugs, barges, and crane boats, had been laboring in the sea-level approaches of the canal and in the two terminal bays, where forty-foot channels had to be dug several miles out to deep water. Much of this was equipment left behind by the French; six dredges in the Atlantic fleet, four in the Pacific fleet, a dozen self-propelled dump barges, two tugs, one drill boat, one crane boat, were all holdovers from that earlier era. Now, to clear the Cut of slides, about half this equipment was brought up through the locks, the first procession from the Pacific side passing through Miraflores and Pedro Miguel on October 25.

The great, awkward dredges took their positions in the Cut; barges shunted in and out, dumping their spoil in designated out-of-the-way corners of Gatun Lake, all in the very fashion that Philippe Bunau-Varilla had for so long championed as the only way to do the job. Floodlights were installed in the Cut and the work went on day and night. On December 10, 1913, an old French ladder dredge, the *Marmot,* made the "pioneer cut" through the Cucaracha slide, thus opening the channel for free passage.

The first complete passage of the canal took place almost incidentally, as part of the new workaday routine, on January 7, when an old crane boat, the *Alexandre La Valley,* which had been brought up from the Atlantic side sometime previously, came down through the Pacific locks without ceremony, without much attention of any kind. That the first boat through the canal was French seemed to everyone altogether appropriate.

CLOSING UP SHOP

The end was approaching faster than anyone had quite anticipated. Thousands of men were being let go; hundreds of buildings were being disassembled or demolished. Job applications

were being written to engineering offices in New York and to factories in Detroit, where, according to the latest reports, there was
great opportunity in the automobile industry. Families were
packing for home. There were farewell parties somewhere along
the line almost every night of the week.

William Gorgas resigned from the canal commission to go to
South Africa to help fight an alarming surge of pneumonia
among black workers in the gold mines. The understanding was
that it would be a brief assignment, after which he was to be
made surgeon general of the Army.

Joseph Bucklin Bishop left to resume his literary career in
New York.

With the arrival of the new year the Isthmian Canal Commission was disbanded and President Wilson named Goethals the
first Governor of the Panama Canal, as the new administrative
entity was to be officially known. . . .

In Washington after a drawn-out, often acrimonious debate,
Congress determined that the clause in the Hay-Pauncefote
Treaty stipulating that the canal would be open to the vessels of
all nations "on terms of entire equality" meant that American
ships could not use the canal toll free, as many had ardently
wanted and as much of the press had argued for. American ships
would pay the same as the ships of every other nation, 90 cents
per cargo ton.

War Overshadows the Triumph

In Washington also, and in San Francisco, plans were being made
for tremendous opening celebrations intended to surpass even
those at the opening of the Suez Canal. More than a hundred
warships, "the greatest international fleet ever gathered in American waters," were to assemble off Hampton Roads on New
Year's Day, 1915, then proceed to San Francisco by way of
Panama. At San Francisco they would arrive for the opening of
the Panama-Pacific International Exposition, a mammoth world's
fair in celebration of the canal. The estimate was that it would
take four days for the armada to go through the locks.

Schoolchildren in Oregon wrote to President Wilson to urge
that the old battleship *Oregon* lead the flotilla through the canal.
The idea was taken up by the press and by the Navy Department. The officer who had commanded the ship on her famous
"race around the Horn" in 1898, retired Admiral Charles Clark,
hale and fit at age seventy, agreed to command her once again
and the President was to be his honored guest.

But there was to be no such pageant. The first oceangoing ship
to go through the canal was a lowly cement boat, the *Cristobal*,

and on August 15 the "grand opening" was performed almost perfunctorily by the *Ancon*. There were no world luminaries on her prow. Goethals again watched from shore, traveling from point to point on the railroad. The only impressive aspect of the event was "the ease and system with which everything worked," as wrote one man on board. "So quietly did she pursue her way that . . . a strange observer coming suddenly upon the scene would have thought that the canal had always been in operation, and that the *Ancon* was only doing what thousands of other vessels must have done before her."

Though the San Francisco exposition went ahead as planned, all but the most modest festivities surrounding the canal itself had been canceled.

For by ironic, tragic coincidence the long effort at Panama and Europe's long reign of peace drew to a close at precisely the same time. It was as if two powerful and related but vastly different impulses . . . had converged with eerie precision in August 1914. The storm that had been gathering over Europe since June broke on August 3, the same day the *Cristobal* made the first ocean-to-ocean transit. On the evening of the third, the French premier, Viviani, received a telephone call from the American ambassador who, with tears in his voice, warned that the Germans would declare war within the hour. The American ambassador was Myron T. Herrick, who had once been so helpful to Philippe Bunau-Varilla, and at the same moment in Panama, where it was still six hours earlier in the day, Philippe Bunau-Varilla was standing at the rail of the *Cristobal* as she entered the lock at Pedro Miguel, at the start of her descent to the Pacific, he being one of the very few who had come especially for the occasion.

Across Europe and the United States, world war filled the newspapers and everyone's thoughts. The voyage of the *Cristobal*, the *Ancon*'s crossing to the Pacific on August 15, the official declaration that the canal was open to the world, were buried in the back pages.

There were editorials hailing the victory of the canal builders, but the great crescendo of popular interest had passed; a new heroic effort commanded world attention. The triumph at Panama suddenly belonged to another and very different era.

THE CULMINATION OF THE DREAM

Of the American employees in Panama at the time the canal was opened only about sixty had been there since the beginning in 1904. . . .

Goethals, Sibert, Hodges, Schildhauer, Goldmark, and the others had been on the job for seven years and the work they performed was of a quality seldom ever known.

Its cost had been enormous. No single construction effort in American history had exacted such a price in dollars or in human life. . . . Taken together, the French and American expenditures came to about $639,000,000.

The other cost since 1904, according to the hospital records, was 5,609 lives from disease and accidents. No fewer than 4,500 of these had been black employees. The number of white Americans who died was about 350.

If the deaths incurred during the French era are included, the total price in human life may have been as high as twenty-five thousand, or five hundred lives for every mile of the canal. . . .

Technically the canal itself was a masterpiece in design and construction. From the time they were first put in use the locks performed perfectly.

Because of the First World War, traffic remained comparatively light until 1918, only four or five ships a day, less than two thousand ships a year on the average. And not until July of 1919 was there a transit of an American armada to the Pacific, that spectacle Theodore Roosevelt had envisioned so long before. Thirty-three ships returning from the war zone, including seven destroyers and nine battleships, were locked through the canal, all but three in just two days.

Ten years after it opened, the canal was handling more than five thousand ships a year. . . .

The creation of a water passage across Panama was one of the supreme human achievements of all time, the culmination of a heroic dream of four hundred years and of more than twenty years of phenomenal effort and sacrifice. The fifty miles between the oceans were among the hardest ever won by human effort and ingenuity, and no statistics on tonnage or tolls can begin to convey the grandeur of what was accomplished. Primarily the canal is an expression of that old and noble desire to bridge the divide, to bring people together. It is a work of civilization.

For millions of people after 1914, the crossing at Panama would be one of life's memorable experiences. The complete transit required about twelve hours, and except for the locks and an occasional community along the shore, the entire route was bordered by the same kind of wilderness that had confronted the first surveyors for the railroad. . . .

But for those on board a ship in transit, the effect for the greater part of the journey was of sailing a magnificent lake in undiscovered country. The lake was always more spacious than people expected, Panama far more beautiful. Out on the lake the water was ocean green. The water was very pure, they would learn, and being fresh water, it killed all the barnacles on the ship's bottom.

In the rainy season, storms could be seen long in advance, building in the hills. Sudden bursts of cool wind would send tiny whitecaps chasing over the lake surface. The crossing was no journey down a great trough in the continent, as so many imagined it would be, but a passage among flaming green islands, the tops of hills that protruded still above the surface. For years after the first ships began passing through, much of the shore was lined with half-drowned trees, their dry limbs as white as bones.

The sight of another ship appearing suddenly from around a bend ahead was always startling, so complete was the feeling of being in untraveled waters, so very quiet was everything.

In the Cut the quiet was more powerful, there being little if any wind, and the water was no longer green, but mud-colored, and the sides of what had been the spine of the Cordilleras seemed to press in very close.

Even in the locks there was comparatively little noise. Something so important as the Panama Canal, something so large and vital to world commerce, ought somehow to make a good deal of noise, most people seemed to feel. But it did not. Bells clanged on the towing locomotives now and again and there was the low whine of their engines, but little more than that. There was little shouting back and forth among the men who handled the lines, since each knew exactly what he was to do. The lock gates appeared to swing effortlessly and with no perceptible sound.

MASS PRODUCTION: A NEW FORCE IN INDUSTRY

ALLAN NEVINS AND FRANK ERNEST HILL

Automotive manufacturer and entrepreneur Henry Ford modified the American way of life with his Model T, "the universal cheap car." Equally important, he revolutionized industry as a whole when he "introduced" mass production into his automobile factories in late 1913 and early 1914. According to Pulitzer Prize–winning author and historian Allan Nevins and author-researcher Frank Ernest Hill, most people of the time defined mass production as large-scale production with the use of interchangeable parts. The authors explain that this is not mass production but simply quantity production, one of the seven different principles that make up the complex process of mass production. Nevins and Hill view mass production as an instrument of change responsible in great part for the dawn of a new era in industry in which the engineer, technician, and practical planner take control of industry from the financier, in whose hands control traditionally rested.

O f the many American activities that expressed industrial power, automotive manufacturing was becoming preeminent both in size and influence. Nonexistent twenty years earlier, a mere collection of sheds and shops in 1900, it had grown with the rage of Iowa corn in July and the solidity of an oak. Producing only 89,110 vehicles in 1910, it had multiplied that product tenfold (880,489 in 1915)—an output valued at

Reprinted and edited with the permission of Scribner, a division of Simon & Schuster, Inc., from *Ford: Expansion and Challenge, 1915–1933*, by Allan Nevins and Frank Ernest Hill. Copyright © 1957 by Allan Nevins; copyright renewed 1985 by Meredith Nevins Moyar and Anne Nevins Loftus.

$691,778,000. Another year, and the value would exceed a billion.

But the social and technological impacts of the industry had been even more remarkable than its rapid development. It had created a wholly new type of transportation. Some two and a half million Americans now possessed automobiles, and the life of the nation was changing because of this fact; for the motor vehicle was the first free-ranging form of inland transportation, not tied like locomotives to rails, or steamboats to piers. Remotely situated farmers, miners, or shop owners were no longer isolated economically because they were far from railroad stations or ports. Social isolation was disappearing. The complex of highways that served the nation was being replanned and expanded, with 2340 miles of new concrete-surfaced roads already built, and a vision growing of a future system of 4,000,000 miles.

DEFINING MASS PRODUCTION

The manufacture of motor cars had also made its contribution to the improvement of industrial tools and processes. "The real revolution in American consumption, involving not only radical changes in ways of living but also profound industrial consequences," wrote Ralph C. Epstein some years later, "is in large measure a function of the automobile." From the late eighteen-nineties, starting from the point reached by the successive advances of the arms, sewing machine, and bicycle industries, the automobile makers had taken over the development of machine tools. They had diminished the margin of tolerance for precision elements from a few hundredths of an inch to ten thousandths; they had experimented with alloy and heat-treated steels, immensely extended the possibilities of forgings and stampings, and developed the use of electricity to provide magnetos and batteries, self-starters and lighting systems. Their work in the provision of raw materials and spare parts, of factory layouts, and of mass production methods had been revolutionary.

We shall do well to note at this point the meaning of that term, "mass production." Had an ordinary American been asked in 1915 what was the greatest achievement of the Ford Company, he would erroneously have replied, "The universal cheap car, the Model T." Its most remarkable exploit was actually the creation of the womb in which modern industry was to be reshaped, mass production. If asked to define mass production, the ordinary citizen would again have replied erroneously, "It means large-scale production by the use of uniform interchangeable parts." Indeed, most people still confound mass production with quantity production, which is only one of its elements. Actually, as Henry Ford himself wrote, mass production is the focusing upon a manufacturing operation of seven different principles: power, accuracy, economy, continuity, system, speed, and repetition. When all seven are used to make a car, tractor, refrigerator, airplane, or other complicated commodity, then mass production throws open the door to plenty, low prices, and an improved standard of living. Arming a people in peace against want, in war against enemies, it becomes an instrument to alter radically the shape of civilization.

Henry Ford, pictured here, revolutionized the theory of mass production, making automobiles more affordable for people to buy. He eventually developed the Ford Motor Company.

By the end of 1915 the alteration had begun. Mass production had made its first appearance in the world at Highland Park, Michigan, in 1913–14. It was there that the seven principles named were combined in three great creative components. The first was the planned, orderly, and continuous progression of the commodity—the car—through the shop. The second was the systematic delivery of the work to the mechanic, instead of bringing the mechanic to his work. The third was the analysis of all the operations into their constituent parts, with a suitable division of labor and materials.

Each one of the components of mass production was in itself more complicated than any amateur student would suppose. We may instance the orderly and continuous progression of the growing commodity through the factory. The assembly line had to move at just the right speed, on just the right level, through just the right sequence of activities. Or, still more complex, we may instance the delivery of the work to the mechanic. This meant that a multitude of subsidiary assembly lines had to feed into the main assembly line at precisely the proper points and pace. A car-spring, for example, did not suddenly appear out of thin air beside the workman charged with fastening it to the chassis. No, the spring (which consisted of seven leaves) had itself passed through a variety of subordinate operations: punch press, bending machine, nitrate bath, bolt insertion, fastening of nuts on bolts, application of two clips, painting and inspection, every operation controlled by automatic gauges. This subsidiary line for providing springs (before long 50,000 a day) had to move without halt. It had to flow into the main assembly line as a small stream flows into a river. But a half-hundred other streams had to flow in, bearing each its vital part, at the same time; and the flow of every one had to be accurately controlled. The whole plant was in motion. Meantime, geared to this motion, every mechanic had his scientifically-ascertained fraction of the labor to perform; for the efficiency expert had found just how much he could best do, and what was the optimum time-allowance for doing it.

A kinetic plant!—moving, moving, moving; every segment—presses, furnaces, welders, stamps, drills, paint-baths, lathes—in use every minute; not an ounce of metal or a degree of heat avoidably wasted; and the economy in time and labor matching the economy in materials. Fascinating in its intricate intermeshing of activities, it meant a new era.

DAWN OF A NEW ERA

It meant a new era not only because mass production turned out far more goods at much lower prices than ever before, but for still larger reasons. It required the constant adoption of new methods and new machines, with the ruthless scrapping of all that was obsolete—even if it had cost a large sum but a few months earlier. It thus stimulated constant advances in the making of better machine-tools, and the installation of an ever-widening variety of single-purpose specialized machines. By lifting more of the load of work off men, and placing more of it on these complex mechanical tools, it reduced the really *hard* labor of the world. Samuel Butler had predicted a civilization in which machines would control men; but mass production implied that men constantly changed, improved, and more fully mastered machines

as their servants. Under mass production, if it were properly administered, more skilled artisans and more creative designers
would be needed than before; for every large factory would require busy departments devoted to invention, engineering, and
art. In a world moulded economically by mass production, the
control of industry would be more and more largely withdrawn
from the mere financier, and more fully placed in the hands of
the engineer, technician, and practical planner.

These were at any rate among the larger results which Henry
Ford hoped would flow from this tremendous new force in human
affairs. Another result he had already helped give reality. A rich
abundance of inexpensive mass-produced goods would require a
fast-expanding body of consumers. People must be given the
means to buy; and Ford had possessed the insight and the courage
to make high wages the concomitant of mass production. The five-
dollar day had rung in a new economic era as the moving assembly line had ushered in a new industrial age. All this, could men
but have seen it, was bound up in the Ford exhibit at the San Francisco Exposition, and, from that time forward, in most of the assembly lines of other automotive manufacturers.

MARIE CURIE, WOMAN OF DISTINCTION

NANNY FRÖMAN

The following selection is excerpted from a lecture given in 1996 at the Royal Swedish Academy of Sciences by Nanny Fröman, professor emeritus from the Department of Theoretical Physics of Uppsala University in Sweden. In Fröman's view, Marie Curie, a Polish immigrant living in Paris, France, was an exceptional woman who helped revolutionize chemistry. Fröman reveals how Curie's decision to conduct a systematic investigation of uranium rays led to the conclusion that radiation was linked not to how atoms were arranged in a molecule but to the interior of the atom itself. Fröman also describes Curie's successes, including the discovery (with her husband Pierre) of polonium and radium; the receipt of two Nobel Prizes, one in physics and the other in chemistry; and her appointment to teach at the Sorbonne, making her the first female ever appointed to the faculty of that university. She also provides insights into the challenges Marie Curie had to face, from the accidental death of her husband to public scandal concerning her private life to rejection by the Academy of Sciences.

M arie and Pierre Curie's pioneer research was again brought to mind when on 20 April, 1995, their bodies were taken from their place of burial at Sceaux, just outside Paris, France, and in a solemn ceremony were laid to rest under the mighty dome of the Panthéon. Marie Curie thus

Excerpted from "Marie and Pierre Curie and the Discovery of Polonium and Radium," by Nanny Fröman, lecture given at the Royal Swedish Academy of Sciences, Stockholm, Sweden, February 28, 1996. Reprinted by permission of the author.

became the first woman to be accorded this mark of honour on her own merit. . . .

FROM CHILDHOOD TO MARRIAGE

Marie Sklodowska, as she was called before marriage, was born in Warsaw in 1867. Both her parents were teachers who believed deeply in the importance of education. Marie had her first lessons in physics and chemistry from her father. She had a brilliant aptitude for study and a great thirst for knowledge; however, advanced study was not possible for women in Poland. . . .

It was not until she was 24 that Marie came to Paris to study mathematics and physics. . . . By then she had been away from her studies for six years, nor had she had any training in understanding rapidly spoken French. But her keen interest in studying and her joy at being at the Sorbonne with all its opportunities helped her surmount all difficulties. . . .

In 1894, there occurred an event that was to be of decisive importance in her life. She met Pierre Curie. He was 35 years old, eight years older, and an internationally known physicist, but an outsider in the French scientific community—a serious idealist and dreamer whose greatest wish was to be able to devote his life to scientific work. . . .

Marie, too, was an idealist; though outwardly shy and retiring, she was in reality energetic and single-minded. . . . In July 1895, they were married at the town hall at Sceaux, where Pierre's parents lived. . . .

In 1896, Marie passed her teacher's diploma, coming first in her group. Their daughter Irène was born in September 1897. Pierre had managed to arrange that Marie should be allowed to work in the school's laboratory, and in 1897, she concluded a number of investigations into the magnetic properties of steel on behalf of an industrial association. Deciding after a time to go on doing research, Marie looked around for a subject for a doctoral thesis. . . .

Marie decided to make a systematic investigation of the mysterious 'uranium rays'. She had an excellent aid at her disposal—an electrometer for the measurement of weak electrical currents, which was constructed by Pierre and his brother, and was based on the piezoelectric effect.

A REVOLUTIONARY DISCOVERY

Results were not long in coming. Just after a few days, Marie discovered that thorium gives off the same rays as uranium. Her continued systematic studies of the various chemical compounds gave the surprising result that the strength of the radiation did not depend on the compound that was being studied. It depended only on *the amount* of uranium or thorium. . . . Marie drew the conclusion that the ability to radiate did not depend on the arrangement of the atoms in a molecule, it must be linked to the interior of the atom itself. This discovery was absolutely revolutionary. *From a conceptual point of view it is her most important contribution to the development of physics. . . .*

Fascinating new vistas were opening up. Pierre gave up his research into crystals and symmetry in nature which he was deeply involved in and joined Marie in her project. . . . In a work they published in July 1898, they write, 'We . . . believe that the substance that we have extracted from pitchblende contains a metal never known before, akin to bismuth in its analytic properties. If the existence of this new metal is confirmed, we suggest that it should be called *polonium* after the name of the country of origin of one of us'. It was also in this work that they used the term *radioactivity* for the first time. After another few months of work, the Curies informed the *l'Académie des Sciences,* on 26 December 1898, that they had demonstrated strong grounds for having come upon an additional very active substance that behaved chemically almost like pure barium. They suggested the name of *radium* for the new element. . . .

In 1903, Marie and Pierre Curie were awarded half the Nobel Prize in Physics. . . .

A SECOND NOBEL PRIZE

On 19 April 1906, Pierre Curie was run over by a horse-drawn wagon near the Pont Neuf in Paris and killed. Now Marie was left alone with two daughters, Irène aged 9 and Ève aged 2. Shock broke her down totally to begin with. But even now she could draw on the toughness and perseverance that were fundamental aspects of her character. When she was offered a pension, she refused it: I am 38 and able to support myself, was her answer. She was appointed to succeed Pierre as the head of the laboratory, being undoubtedly most suitable, and to be responsible for his teaching duties. She thus became the first woman ever appointed to teach at the Sorbonne. After some months, in November 1906, she gave her first lecture. . . .

In 1908 Marie, as the first woman ever, was appointed to become a professor at the Sorbonne. She went on to produce several decigrams of very pure radium chloride before finally, in collaboration with André Debierne, she was able to isolate radium in metallic form. André Debierne, who began as a laboratory assistant, became her faithful collaborator until her death and then succeeded her as head of the laboratory. In 1911 she was awarded the Nobel Prize in Chemistry. The citation by the Nobel Committee was, 'in recognition of her services to the advancement of chemistry by the discovery of the elements radium and polonium, by the isolation of radium and the study of the nature and compounds of this remarkable element'. . . .

Some biographers have questioned whether Marie deserved the Prize for Chemistry in 1911. They have claimed that the discoveries of radium and polonium were part of the reason for the Prize in 1903, even though this was not stated explicitly. Marie was said to have been awarded the Prize again for the same discovery, the award possibly being an expression of sympathy for reasons that will be mentioned below. Actually, however, the citation for the Prize in 1903 was worded deliberately with a view to a future Prize in Chemistry. Chemists considered that the discovery and isolation of radium was the greatest event in chemistry since the discovery of oxygen. That for the first time in history it could be shown that an element could be transmuted into another element, revolutionized chemistry and signified a new epoque.

REJECTION AND SCANDAL

Despite the second Nobel Prize and an invitation to the first Solvay Conference with the world's leading physicists, . . . 1911 became a dark year in Marie's life. In two smear campaigns she was to experience the inconstancy of the French press. The first was started on 16 November 1910, when, by an article in Le Figaro, it became known that she was willing to be nominated for election to l'Académie des Sciences. . . . It turned out that it was not merit that was decisive. The dark underlying currents of anti-Semitism, prejudice against women, zenophobia and even anti-science attitudes that existed in the French society came welling up to the surface. . . . It was said that in her career, Pierre's research had given her a free ride. She came from Poland, though admittedly she was formally a Catholic but her name Sklodowska indicated that she might be of Jewish origin, and so on. A week before the election, an opposing candidate, Édouard Branly, was launched. The vote on 23 January 1911 was taken in the presence of journalists, photographers and hordes of the curious. The election took place in a tumultuous atmosphere. In the first round Marie lost by one vote, in the second by two. . . .

However, Marie's tribulations were not at an end. When, at the beginning of November 1911, Marie went to Belgium, being invited with the world's most eminent physicists to attend the first Solvay Conference, she received a message that a new campaign had started in the press. Now it was a matter of her private life and her relations with her colleague Paul Langevin, who had also been invited to the conference. He had had marital problems for several years and had moved from his suburban home to a small apartment in Paris. Marie was depicted as the reason. Both were described in slanderous terms. The scandal develops dramatically. Marie stands up in her own defence and manages to force an apology from the newspaper *Le Temps*. The same day she receives word from Stockholm that she has been awarded the Nobel Prize in Chemistry. However, the very newspapers that made her a legend when she received the Nobel Prize in Physics in 1903, now completely ignore the fact that she has been awarded the Prize in Chemistry or merely report it in a few words on an inside page. The Langevin scandal escalates into a serious affair that shakes the university world in Paris and the French government at the highest level. Madame Langevin is preparing legal action to obtain custody of the four children. With a burglary in Langevin's apartment certain letters are stolen and delivered to the press. Léon Daudet makes the whole thing into a new Dreyfus affair. Day after day Marie has to run the gauntlet in the newspapers: an alien, a Polish woman, a researcher supported by our French scientists, has come and stolen an honest French woman's husband. Daudet quotes Fouquier-Tinville's notorious words that during the Revolution had sent the chemist Lavoisier to the guillotine: 'The Republic does not need any scientists.' Marie's friends immediately back her up. Jean Perrin, Henri Poincaré and Émile Borel appeal to the publishers of the newspapers. Henri Poincaré's cousin, Raymond Poincaré, a senior lawyer who is to become President of France in a few years time, is engaged as advisor. But the scandal keeps up its impetus with headlines on the first pages such as 'Madame Curie, can she still remain a professor at the Sorbonne?' With her children Marie stays at Sceaux where she is practically a prisoner in her own home. Her friends fear that she will collapse. The drama culminates on the morning of 23 November when extracts from the letters are published in the newspaper *L'Oeuvre*. There is no proof of the accusations made against Marie. . . .

However, the publication of the letters and [a subsequent] duel are too much for those responsible at the Swedish Academy of Sciences in Stockholm. Marie receives a letter from a member, Svante Arrhenius, in which he . . . asks her to cable that she will not be coming to the Prize ceremony and to write him a letter to the effect that she does not want to accept the Prize until the Langevin court proceedings have shown that the accusations against her are absolutely without foundation. Of those most closely affected, the person who remains level-headed despite the enormous strain of the critical situation is in fact Marie herself. In a well-formulated and matter-of-fact reply, she points out that she had been awarded the Prize for her discovery of radium and polonium, and that she cannot accept the principle that appreciation of the value of scientific work should be influenced by slander concerning a researcher's private life. . . .

CONQUERING THE OPPOSITION

Marie called up all her strength and gave her Nobel lecture on 11 December in Stockholm. The lecture should be read in the light of what she had gone through. She made clear by her choice of words what were unequivocally her contributions in the collaboration with Pierre. She spoke of the field of research which 'I have called radioactivity' and 'my hypothesis that radioactivity is an atomic property', but without detracting from his contributions. She declared that she also regarded this Prize as a tribute to Pierre Curie. . . .

Marie had opened up a completely new field of research: radioactivity. Various aspects of it were being studied all over the world. . . .

When, in 1914, Marie was in the process of beginning to lead one of the departments in the Radium Institute established jointly by the University of Paris and the Pasteur Institute, the First World War broke out. Marie placed her two daughters, Irène aged 17 and Ève aged 10, in safety in Brittany. She herself took a train to Bordeaux, a train overloaded with people leaving Paris for a safer refuge. But Marie had a different reason for her journey. She had with her a heavy, 20-kg lead container in which she had placed her valuable radium. Once in Bordeaux the other passengers rushed away to their various destinations. She remained standing there with her heavy bag which she did not have the strength to carry without assistance. Some official finally helped her find a room where she slept with her heavy bag by her bed. The next day, having had the bag taken to a bank vault, she took a train back to Paris. It was now crowded to bursting point with soldiers. Throughout the war she was engaged intensively in equipping more than 20 vans that acted as mobile field hospitals and about 200 fixed installations with X-ray apparatus.

She trained young women in simple X-ray technology, she herself drove one of the vans and took an active part in locating metal splinters. . . .

After the Peace Treaty in 1918, her Radium Institute, which had been completed in 1914, could now be opened. It became France's most internationally celebrated research institute in the inter-war years. Even so, . . . the French state did not do much in the way of supporting her. In the USA radium was manufactured industrially but at a price which Marie could not afford. She had to devote a lot of time to fund-raising for her Institute. She also became deeply involved when she had become a member of the Commission for Intellectual Cooperation of the League of Nations and served as its vice-president for a time. . . .

MADAME CURIE TRIUMPHANT

Marie regularly refused all those who wanted to interview her. However, a prominent American female journalist, Marie Maloney, known as Missy, who for a long time had admired Marie, managed to meet her. This meeting became of great importance to them both. Marie told Missy that researchers in the USA had some 50 grams of radium at their disposal. 'And in France, then?' asked Missy. 'My laboratory has scarcely more than one gram', was Marie's answer. 'But you ought to have all the resources in the world to continue with your research. Someone must see to that', Missy said.'But whom?' was Marie's reply in a resigned tone. 'The women of America', promised Missy.

Missy, like Marie herself, had an enormous strength and strong inner stamina under a frail exterior. She now arranged one of the largest and most successful research-funding campaigns the world has seen. . . .

In the last ten years of her life, Marie had the joy of seeing her daughter Irène and her son-in-law Frédéric Joliot do successful research in the laboratory. She lived to see their discovery of artificial radioactivity, but not to hear that they had been awarded the Nobel Prize in Chemistry for it in 1935. Marie Curie died of leukemia on 4 July 1934.

SARAJEVO: THE SHOT THAT STARTED A WORLD WAR

EDMOND TAYLOR

On June 28, 1914, in Sarajevo, in the annexed Balkan province of Bosnia-Herzegovina, an assassin's bullet killed Francis Ferdinand, archduke of Austria-Este, and his wife, Sophie. The assassination triggered World War I. According to journalist and author Edmond Taylor, both Ferdinand and his nineteen-year-old assassin, Gavrilo Princip, were victims of the same revolutionary process: the decline and fall of the dynastic system in Europe and of the social structures it supported. In this article, Taylor explains that Ferdinand went to Sarajevo as much for personal reasons as for political ones. Taylor contends that, had the archduke been more sensitive to the public temper in Bosnia at the time, the outcome might have been very different. Taylor paints a vivid picture of the assassination—and of the miscommunication, lack of communication, and outright blunders that characterized the entire episode.

O ne of the last known photographs of the Archduke Francis Ferdinand of Habsburg, heir to the throne of his uncle, the octogenarian Emperor Francis Joseph of Austria-Hungary, shows him coming down the steps of the city hall in Sarajevo a few minutes after eleven on the morning of Sunday, June 28, 1914. Under the refulgent uniform topped with a plumed hat his stout body is rigid; his heavy features seem congested and his neck swollen above the tight-fitting collar; his

From *The Fall of the Dynasties: The Collapse of the Old Order, 1905–1922*, by Edmond Taylor. Copyright © 1963 by Edmond Taylor. Used by permission of Doubleday, a division of Random House, Inc.

thick, curling mustaches bristle like a wild boar's. Beside him walks his morganatic wife Sophie, the Duchess of Hohenberg, her plump face looking pinched and taut. They are just about to step into a waiting car. Both are clearly uneasy, but not yet really frightened. The local Bosnian dignitaries who line the steps, framing the doomed couple, are not frightened either; many of them are Moslems—paradoxically the only friends the Catholic Habsburgs have in this seething, semi-Oriental province, only recently freed from the Turkish yoke. . . .

In five minutes Francis Ferdinand and Sophie will be lying unconscious in their speeding car bleeding to death from an assassin's bullets: an ancient dynasty—and with it a whole way of life—will start to topple; then another and another and another. Close to nine million men fell in World War I as a direct result of those two shots fired in a dusty Balkan town. . . .

The view of Sarajevo as one approaches from the southwest is a lovely one. High but gently sloping mountains almost encircle it. The valley of the Miljacka, a shallow torrent that cuts the town in two, narrows at its eastern outskirts to a rugged gorge commanded by the ruined Turkish fort (serai) from which it takes its name. . . .

Francis Ferdinand's Misalliance

Though not a man normally sensitive to beauty, the archduke no doubt was gladdened by the scene. He demonstrated no more enthusiasm than he habitually displayed at the opera or at Court balls . . . but as he leaned stiffly against the leather-upholstered seat condescending to the view, his arrogant, morose face, with the sagging middle-aged jowls—he was fifty-one—seemed unusually cheerful. . . . The ceremonial visit to Sarajevo, promised, for all its tedium, to be even more satisfying; its timing had a private significance that in the Archduke's mind may possibly have overshadowed the political one. June 28 was the anniversary of the most important date in his life.

Fourteen years ago on that day, Archduke Francis Ferdinand of Austria-Este (as he preferred to call himself) had married Countess Sophie Chotek, a member of a noble but comparatively obscure Czech family. . . . Francis Ferdinand had been obliged to renounce all rights of rank and succession for his children before taking Sophie as his morganatic wife. He had never forgotten the humiliation. He loved Sophie enough to swallow it, but it rankled all the same. . . .

It was in part for Sophie's sake that the Archduke had organized the trip to Sarajevo, and she knew it.

In the stylized ballet of Vienna Court life, . . . there was no place for Sophie. . . . The Archduke's numerous enemies exploited every weapon in the armory of protocol to vex and humiliate her. . . . Eventually Francis Ferdinand, a brooding, vindictive man, burning with ill-concealed impatience for his uncle to die and given to black fits of depression and rages so violent that Sophie sometimes feared he was going insane, set up a kind of rival Court at his Belvedere Palace, on a hilltop overlooking Vienna. The great German and Magyar feudal families were but perfunctorily represented there; the Archduke particularly loathed the haughty Magyar nobles because of their independence, and surrounded himself with a paradoxical mixture of Slavs, reactionary clerics, and German Christian Socialists. This tended to split the aristocracy and officialdom of the empire into two factions. . . .

It was to punish his detractors and to atone to Sophie for all the times she had been forced to walk at the tail of some court procession while he had headed it with an Archduchess on his arm, that Francis Ferdinand in 1914 hatched up a kind of *protocol-putsch*. He would take advantage of his new office as Inspector General of the armed forces . . . to attend the forthcoming maneuvers in the recently annexed province of Bosnia-Herzegovina. While there he would pay an official visit to its capital, Sarajevo, in his military capacity rather than as heir to the throne. But of course he would have to be treated like royalty. And he would take Sophie with him—on their wedding anniversary. She would be received like the wife of an Inspector General who happened to be the royal heir—that is to say, like a queen.

A COMPLEX POLITICAL SITUATION

The political motivations back of the Archduke's visit to Sarajevo were no less convoluted than his private ones. . . . In many respects Austria and Hungary were less like nations than like two associated empires. In each a master race—in Austria, the Germans; in Hungary the Magyars—ruled more or less oppressively over a number of subject peoples. . . . Most of the submerged nationalities belonged to the Slavic race . . . but they stemmed from several different branches of it, and instead of being grouped in one area they were scattered throughout Austria-Hungary along with various ethnic minorities. . . . The Habsburgs, as the feudal overlords of this anachronistic hodge-podge of peoples naturally, had the most trouble with their biggest and proudest vassals, the Magyars; therefore, they tended to favor certain of their Slav subjects as a sort of counterweight to Magyar ambition or stubbornness. . . . Francis Ferdinand was undoubtedly more clearsighted than most high-ranking Austrian officials in recognizing the ominously growing strength of the nationalist movement among the empire's Slav minorities, particularly among its South Slavs. . . .

Bosnia had a significant, if ambivalent, relationship to all such schemes, and it was a major factor in the general Balkan imbroglio. Vienna had administered the provinces—together with its sister province of Herzegovina—since 1877. . . . Then in 1908 the old Emperor's ministers had persuaded him to sign a decree formally annexing the provinces to his empire. This irresponsible act had disturbed the great powers, enraged the pepper-patriots in free Serbia—who had hoped some day to annex Bosnia-Herzegovina themselves—and inflamed the pro-Serbian or Pan-Slav nationalism of the local population. . . .

A FATAL INSENSITIVITY

To most of the Bosnians who turned out to greet—or simply to stare at—their presumptive future monarch and his wife, the date marked a quite different sort of anniversary. June 28—actually June 15 by the Serbian Orthodox calendar—is the Vidovdan, the Feast of St. Vitus. To the Slav peoples of the Balkan Peninsula it is a holiday unlike any other. . . .

Francis Ferdinand, the least tactful of men and the most intrusive of all possible strangers, knew that the date he had picked for his first visit to Sarajevo was the Vidovdan. He was *also* aware that Bosnia and the Bosnian capital had remained under the Austro-Hungarian yoke what they had been under the Turkish—hotbeds of nationalist conspiracy and terrorism. . . .

The civil authorities both in Sarajevo and in Vienna had picked up warnings of a plot against the Archduke. . . . The civilian and the military authorities of the empire were simply not speaking to each other, or at least the latter were not paying any attention to what the former said. Francis Ferdinand had not wanted to give the official Court a pretext for interfering with his plans to honor Sophie; he insisted on treating the visit as a purely military matter. His pigheadedness infuriated the Court and the joint Austro-Hungarian Ministry of Finance, which was responsible for the civil administration in Bosnia. . . . The soldiers joined enthusiastically in the feud. Marshal Oskar Potiorek, the military governor of Bosnia . . . never reported to his nominal chief, the Finance Minister, that the visit had been arranged. . . .

A BOMB GOES OFF

The end result of this bureaucratic schizophrenia was that Potiorek assumed sole responsibility for the security of the Archduke's party without having the means to assure it. Many of his soldiers and gendarmes had been drawn away to take part in the field maneuvers, and a recklessly sparse cordon held back the crowd when the royal cortege—six motorcars with the Archduke's second—entered Sarajevo shortly after 10 A.M. on the Vidovdan.

The first portent came just after the royal car passed the Bank of Austria-Hungary on the avenue bordering the Miljacka embankment.

Franz, Count Harrach, the Archduke's aide-de-camp, was in the front seat next to the chauffeur. Sophie was in the back on the right-hand side, nearest the embankment; Francis Ferdinand next to her. Opposite them sat Potiorek. . . . He was showing them what the army had done for the arts in Sarajevo—the newly built Austrian barracks in mustard-colored bureaucratic baroque across the river. Where his finger pointed there was a gap in the crowd on the sidewalk and standing in the gap, a tall dark young man, who, exactly at that instant, made a queer gesture with his hands. There was a small sound, no louder than cork popping from a bottle; then odd, disconnected things began to happen. Harrach thought—mistakenly—that he had heard a bullet whistle near his head. Sophie definitely felt something graze the back of her neck and put up her hand to touch it. Potiorek saw a black object float away from the young man on the embankment and land somewhere behind the royal car. The front tire of the following one blew out with a loud noise, spilling officers into the street. One of them, Lieutenant Erich von Merizzi, Potiorek's aide-de-camp, could not understand at first why his face was suddenly dripping blood. On the embankment a confused scuffle broke out in the crowd and a tall figure raised a hand to its mouth, then jumped over the parapet into the bed of the stream. . . .

In the royal car the Archduke and his wife sat very straight. Potiorek, looking over their heads, reported that a bomb had gone off. . . . Potiorek reported further that an officer in the third car had been hurt. . . . Francis Ferdinand said to stop the car and look after him. Nobody protested this lunatic order, which was promptly obeyed. The lead car then halted, too. Down in the bed of the Miljacka several policemen were dragging along the dark young man—who now smelled of bitter almonds and vomit—while conscientiously beating him with the flats of their swords. His name, they were soon to discover, was Nedjelko Cabrinovic and he was a nineteen-year-old printer, born in Sarajevo. . . .

The car with the crumpled front wheel was quickly pushed off to the curb for whatever good that might do. Puzzling over the strange sequence of events, the military experts in the royal party came up almost at once with the right explanation. The first popping sound that had seemed to jar things off their course was the fuze cap or detonator of a small bomb or hand grenade blown off when the dark young man had purposely whacked it against a lamppost. Undoubtedly it was this fragment—too light to hurt anyone—that had grazed Sophie's neck. The bomb proper, merely charged by the initial detonation, had gone off twelve seconds later, thus explaining why it had hit the wrong car. . . . Potiorek lost no time in ordering the remaining cars of the cortege to resume their route—this time at a much faster pace—and not to stop until they reached the city hall. . . .

The brief reception by the city fathers at the *Rathaus,* a tasteless structure erected by the Austrians . . . was not a success. The mayor had hardly commenced his address of welcome when the Archduke furiously interrupted him.

"Mr. Mayor," he nearly shouted, "I come here on a visit and I get bombs thrown at me. It is outrageous."

It was only with difficulty that Francis Ferdinand was persuaded to make a short, extemporaneous speech in reply to the mayor's. . . .

While the reception was going on upstairs, in the city hall, Cabrinovic, the would-be assassin . . . was being questioned at the police station. He had information that could have saved the royal couple and his interrogators were not exactly gentle in trying to get it out of him, but he kept his mouth shut as long as was necessary. . . .

It was determined later that there had been only five or six or at most seven, assassins in the streets—all stationed at intervals along the embankment of the Miljacka in the quarter mile or so between the bank of Austria-Hungary and the city hall. In any event neither Potiorek nor the chief of police, who was present at the impromptu conference, at first thought it advisable to cancel the rest of the scheduled drive through the town. It was only when Francis Ferdinand insisted that before going on to the museum, which was the next scheduled stop, he wanted to visit the military hospital . . . , that Potiorek proposed evasive action. . . .

AN AMATEUR ATTEMPT THAT SUCCEEDS

A new car was brought up. The Archduke and Sophie got in— she had insisted on accompanying him—while Count Harrach, shielding his royal master with his body, stood on the left-hand running board, nearest the embankment; that is the direction the bomb had come from earlier. The chief of police and the deputy mayor took their places in the lead car. The Archduke's again came second. Both lurched into gear and began to speed along the embankment, following the morning's route in reverse. . . .

The hunters of men who earlier had set up their firing line along the Miljacka embankment had given up in panic or despair by the time their intended victim left the city hall. . . . The assassination plot was one of those inept but nonetheless deadly conspiratorial operations combining professional planning with amateur execution. The executors were six untrained youths. It was virtually certain under the circumstances that some links in the murder chain would break down, but very likely that at least one would hold. This likelihood was nearly upset. . . .

As the lead car reached the Latin Bridge . . . it turned right off the embankment up what was then named Francis Joseph Street—the originally scheduled itinerary for the party. Nobody had thought to tell the chauffeur that it had been changed. The Archduke's chauffeur blindly followed. Even so, the royal couple might have escaped if Potiorek had not intervened to set things right.

"Not that way, you fool," he yelled at the chauffeur. "Keep straight on."

The rattled flunky stopped so he could shift into reverse—not two yards from a slight, hollowed-eyed boy of nineteen [Gavrilo Princip] who had just come out of a coffeehouse where he had gone to steady his nerves; his world had collapsed about him half an hour before when the grenade thrown by his friend Cabrinovic went wild and there seemed to be nothing left to live for. He had a loaded automatic pistol in his pocket that he had given up the hope of being able to use. Now, though dazed by the miraculous second chance that fate had offered him, he drew it out and remembered to aim. He could hardly have missed. The range was less than ten feet and as long as Sophie sat straight there was no obstacle between the Archduke and the killer's gun; he was at the curb on the right; Harrach was standing on the left side of the car, his useless sword dangling in his hand. . . .

The assassin fired twice. The first shot hit Francis Ferdinand, tearing through his chest and lodging against his spine. The second, aimed at Potiorek, hit Sophie in the abdomen. . . . For a few seconds both of them continued to sit straight; Potiorek thought that the assassin—grabbed by neighbors in the crowd just as he was raising the automatic to put a bullet in his own head—had missed. Then, as the chauffeur finally got the car turned in the right direction and it leaped forward, the Duchess collapsed against the Archduke. He remained upright, but a thin dark rivulet of blood stained the front of his tunic, and the corners of his mouth were red. . . .

At first glance the whole Sarajevo plot, despite its ultimate success, looks like a schoolboy escapade that somehow turned into tragedy. . . . Counting Princip, six persons took part in the actual killing: five Serbo-Croats from Bosnia and one Bosnian Moslem. None was more than nineteen and one was only seventeen. The genesis of the crime is steeped in adolescent romanticism. It goes back to the cafes of the Green Crown and the Golden Sturgeon in Belgrade where Bosnian exiles and . . . veterans of the Balkan War used to congregate to talk politics and murder. . . . Among the patrons of these two colorful establishments . . . were three youthful Bosnian ex-patriates—really refugees from the Austrian school system: Princip, Cabrinovic, who was then working at the Serbian state printing plant and who was to throw the bomb at the Archduke, and Trifko Grabez, the eighteen-year-old son of a Bosnian village pope. . . .

The decision to kill Francis Ferdinand was an afterthought— or so the boys believed—inspired by a newspaper clipping announcing his visit to Sarajevo. . . .

When the time came for action the schoolboy conspirators— with the exception of Princip—behaved as might have been expected. Cabrinovic at least acted, though wildly and ineffectually. Three simply panicked and ran when they heard his grenade explode. Grabez waited for a while, then rushed to his uncle's house where he hid his bomb under the toilet seat.

Only Princip kept his nerve. When he saw Cabrinovic being dragged away he toyed a moment with the idea of shooting him "so things would go no further," then killing himself. He dropped the scheme when he saw the Archduke's car speed by— too fast for a shot or a bomb—and realized that Cabrinovic had missed after all. For a while he walked around in a daze, not knowing what to do next, had his cup of coffee, and—as we have already seen—turned up by accident on the very spot where the royal car came to a halt. . . .

At the trial of the conspirators—most of whom were caught by the Austrians—Princip stood out both as the strongest personality and the clearest mind among them.

"I am a South Slav nationalist," he explained in court, concisely summarizing the objectives of the conspiracy. "My aim is the union of all Yugoslavs, under whatever political regime, and their liberation from Austria."

"By what means did you think to accomplish that?" the judge asked.

"By terrorism," was the unhesitating answer.

THE SINKING OF THE *LUSITANIA*

JOHN M. TAYLOR

War was waging in Europe in 1915 when the luxury liner *Lusitania* set sail from New York Harbor for Europe. Historical author and biographer John M. Taylor explains that, although the Central Powers were winning the war on land, the British Royal Navy ruled the seas and was successfully cutting off the Germans from overseas supplies of food and raw materials. To counter the blockade, Taylor writes, the Germans declared the waters surrounding Great Britain and Ireland a war zone and announced that they would destroy without warning any enemy merchant ship that entered the zone. Disregarding the warnings and knowing that the *Lusitania* was carrying contraband, the captain took the ship into the war zone. Taylor relates how the captain abandoned wartime procedures, putting the liner right in the path of German U-boat torpedoes. According to Taylor, the sinking of the *Lusitania* made Americans more sympathetic to the Allied cause and helped propel them into World War I.

S hortly after noon on a drizzly spring day in 1915, the Cunard liner *Lusitania* backed slowly away from Pier 54 on New York's Lower West Side. It was *Lusitania*'s 202nd Atlantic crossing, and as usual the luxury liner's sailing attracted a crowd, for the 32,500-ton vessel was one of the fastest and most glamorous ships afloat. In the words of the London *Times*, she was "a veritable greyhound of the seas."

Passengers, not yet settled in their accommodations, marveled at the ship's size and splendor. With a length of 745 feet, she was

From "Fateful Voyage of *Lusitania*," by John M. Taylor, *MHQ: The Quarterly Journal of Military History*, vol. 11, no. 3 (Spring 1999). Copyright © 1999 MHQ: The Quarterly Journal of Military History. Reprinted with the permission of PRIMEDIA Enthusiasts Publications (History Group).

one of the largest man-made objects in the world. First-class passengers could eat in a two-story Edwardian-style dining salon that featured a plasterwork dome arching some thirty feet above the floor. Those who traveled first class also occupied regal suites, consisting of twin bedrooms with a parlor, bathroom, and private dining area, for which they paid four thousand dollars one way. Second-class accommodations on *Lusitania* compared favorably with first-class staterooms on many other ships.

People strolling through nearby Battery Park watched as three tugs worked to point the liner's prow downriver toward the Narrows and the great ocean beyond. While well-wishers on the pier waved handkerchiefs and straw hats, ribbons of smoke began to stream from three of the liner's four tall funnels. Seagulls hovered astern as the liner slowly began to pick up speed. . . .

In 1908, on one of her first Atlantic crossings, *Lusitania* broke the existing transatlantic speed record, making the run from Liverpool to New York in four and one-half days, traveling at slightly more than twenty-five knots. Like her sister ship, *Mauritania*, she could generate sixty-eight thousand horsepower in her twenty-five boilers. *Lusitania* was also versatile, for the government subsidy that helped pay for her construction required her to have features that would facilitate her conversion to an armed cruiser if necessary. The liner's engine rooms were under the waterline, and she incorporated deck supports sufficient to permit the installation of six-inch guns.

It was May 1, 1915, and *Lusitania*, with 1,257 passengers and a crew of 702, was beginning a slightly nervous crossing. War was raging in Europe, and although no major passenger liner had ever been sunk by a submarine, some passengers were uneasy. The German embassy had inserted advertisements in a number of American newspapers warning of dangers in the waters around the British Isles.

Because this warning appeared only on the day of sailing, not all of those who boarded *Lusitania* saw it. . . .

GERMANY TAKES DRASTIC MEASURES

Despite the warning posted by the German embassy, *Lusitania*'s captain was not nervous. When Captain William Turner was asked about the U-boat threat he reportedly laughed, remarking that "by the look of the pier and the passenger list," the Germans had not scared away many people.

By the spring of 1915 the land war in Europe had settled into a bloody stalemate, but one in which the Central Powers held the advantage. . . .

The war at sea, however, was a different matter. The Royal

Navy's numerical superiority made it perilous for the German fleet to venture out of port and enabled the Allies to move troops and materiel by sea. Most important of all, Allied control of the sea had cut the Central Powers off from overseas supplies of food and raw materials. . . . British cruisers patrolled choke points well away from German ports, halting all vessels suspected of carrying supplies to Germany and enlarging the traditional definition of contraband to include even raw materials and food.

Not all contraband was headed for Germany. *Lusitania* carried some forty-two hundred cases of Remington rifle cartridges destined for the Western Front. Her cargo also included fuses and 1,250 cases of empty shrapnel shells. Although the Germans had no knowledge of this cargo, it is clear that British authorities were prepared to compromise *Lusitania's* nonbelligerent status as a passenger liner for a small amount of war materiel.

The growing effectiveness of the Allied blockade had forced Germany to take drastic measures. Germany's most promising offensive weapon at sea was the submarine, but international law of the time prohibited its most effective employment. If a submarine encountered a vessel that might belong to an enemy or might be carrying contraband, the U-boat had to surface, warn her intended victim, and "remove crew, ship papers, and, if possible, the cargo" before destroying her prey.

In response to Britain's unilateral redefinition of a naval blockade, Germany issued a proclamation of its own, declaring the waters surrounding Great Britain and Ireland to be a war zone. From February 18, 1915, on, Berlin had declared, enemy merchant vessels found within the zone would be subject to destruction without warning.

THE *LUSITANIA* PLOWS AHEAD

The day before *Lusitania* sailed from Pier 54, *U-20*, skippered by thirty-two-year-old *Kapitänleutnant* (Lt. Cmdr.) Walther Schwieger, left the German naval base at Emden on the North Sea. Schwieger's orders were to take *U-20* around Scotland and Ireland to the Irish Sea. There he was to operate in the approaches to Liverpool for as long as his supplies permitted. His orders allowed him to sink, with or without warning, all enemy ships and any other vessels whose appearance or behavior suggested that they might be disguised enemy vessels. The British were known to dispatch ships under neutral flags. . . .

Although *Lusitania* had left New York City with much of the pomp of a peacetime crossing, not all was well aboard the liner. To conserve coal, six of the ship's twenty-five boilers had been shut down, effectively reducing her top speed from twenty-five to twenty-one knots. Perhaps most important, there was a shortage of experienced seamen on *Lusitania*. The Royal Navy had called up most reservists, leaving Cunard to recruit crewmen as best it could.

Nevertheless, the ship was in the hands of one of the most experienced skippers on the Atlantic run. Captain Turner, sixty-three, had been assigned to *Lusitania* just before her previous crossing, but he was a veteran commander. . . .

Much would later be made of Turner's seeming lack of concern about the submarine menace. But the skipper knew that no ship the size and speed of *Lusitania* had ever fallen victim to a U-boat. Even steaming at a reduced speed, *Lusitania* could outrun any submarine, underwater or on the surface.

The liner plowed ahead on its northeasterly course, averaging about twenty knots. The normally festive atmosphere on board had been dampened somewhat by the war; indeed, Cunard had obtained a full passenger list only by reducing some fares. The only gilt-edged celebrity on board was multimillionaire Alfred Gwynne Vanderbilt, en route to Britain for a meeting of horse breeders. . . . Other first-class passengers included Broadway impresario Charles Frohman, scouting for new theatrical offerings, and Elbert Hubbard, the homespun writer of inspirational essays such as "A Message to Garcia."

THE *LUSITANIA* ENTERS DANGEROUS WATERS

On Sunday, May 2, the first day out, Captain Turner conducted church services in the main lounge. The following day found the liner off Newfoundland's Grand Banks. On May 4, *Lusitania* was halfway to her destination. The weather was fine, and Turner had reason to anticipate an easy crossing. Even so, the war was never entirely forgotten. On the morning of May 6, as the ship prepared to enter Berlin's proclaimed war zone, some passengers were startled by the creak of lifeboat davits. Early risers on B deck saw the Cunard liner's lifeboats being uncovered and swung out over the sides of the ship, where they would remain during the final, most dangerous portion of the voyage.

That evening Turner was called away from dinner to receive a radio message from the British Admiralty that warned of submarine activity off the southern coast of Ireland. . . . Forty minutes later, however, came an explicit order to all British ships: "Take Liverpool pilot at bar, and avoid headlands. Pass harbors at full speed. Steer midchannel course. Submarines off Fastnet."

Lusitania acknowledged the message and continued on course. She was now about 375 miles from Liverpool, making twenty-one knots. Turner ordered all watertight doors closed except those providing access to essential machinery, and he doubled the watch. Stewards were instructed to see that portholes were secured and blacked out.

May 7 began with a heavy fog, and *Lusitania*'s passengers awakened to the deep blasts of the liner's foghorn. Turner maintained a course of eighty-seven degrees east but because of the fog ordered a reduction in speed to eighteen knots. The skipper was timing his arrival at the Liverpool bar for high tide so that, if no pilot was immediately available, he could enter the Mersey River without stopping.

Some 130 miles east, in his surfaced boat, Schwieger was wondering whether, given the poor visibility, he should continue on station. He recalled:

> We had started back for Wilhelmshaven and were drawing near the Channel. There was a heavy sea and a thick fog, with small chance of sinking anything. At the same time, a destroyer steaming through the fog might stumble over us before we knew anything about it. So I submerged to twenty meters, below periscope depth.

> About an hour and a half later . . . I noticed that the fog was lifting. . . . I brought the boat to the surface, and we continued our course above water. A few minutes after we emerged I sighted on the horizon a forest of masts and stacks. At first I thought they must belong to several ships. Then I saw it was a great steamer coming over the horizon. It was coming our way. I dived at once, hoping to get a shot at it.

A German Torpedo Hits Its Mark

Until midday, Turner had taken most of the measures that a prudent captain would be expected to take during wartime. On the fateful afternoon of May 7, however, he reverted to peacetime procedures. The coast of Ireland was in clear view at 1 P.M., but Turner was uncertain of his exact position. Ignoring Admiralty orders to zigzag in dangerous waters, to maintain top speed, and to avoid headlands, Turner changed *Lusitania*'s course toward land to fix his position. At 1:40 P.M. he recognized the Old Head of Kinsale, one of the most familiar headlands of the Irish coast. With cottages on the coast clearly visible to her passengers, *Lusitania* swung back toward her earlier course of eighty-seven degrees east and headed toward her reckoning.

The change of course involved two turns. In Schwieger's recollection:

> When the steamer was two miles away it changed its

course. I had no hope now, even if we hurried at our best speed, of getting near enough to attack her. . . . [Then] I saw the steamer change her course again. She was coming directly at us. She could not have steered a more perfect course if she had deliberately tried to give us a dead shot. . . .

I had already shot away my best torpedoes and had left only two bronze ones—not so good. The steamer was four hundred yards away when I gave an order to fire. The torpedo hit, and there was a rather small detonation and instantly after a much heavier one. The pilot was beside me. I told him to have a look at close range. He put his eye to the periscope and after a brief scrutiny yelled: "My God, it's the *Lusitania.*"

U-20's torpedo, carrying three hundred pounds of explosives in its warhead, struck between the first and second funnels, throwing a huge cloud of debris into the air. Turner, who had been in his cabin when the torpedo wake was spotted, rushed to the bridge. Survivors later testified almost unanimously that a second, heavier explosion followed. Power was cut off throughout the ship, preventing Turner from communicating with the engine room and trapping some people belowdecks. . . .

THE *LUSITANIA* GOES DOWN

Above, confusion was rampant. Passengers rushed to the boat deck, only to be told that the ship was safe and that no boats need be launched. Most life rafts were still lashed to the decks. Passengers and crewmen alike milled about; although *Lusitania* carried ample lifeboats, passengers had never been informed to which boat they were assigned in case of an emergency. Charles Lauriat, a Boston bookseller, later noted that as many as half the passengers had put on their life jackets improperly.

The ship immediately took on a heavy list to starboard that made it impossible to lower boats from the port side. The inexperienced crew could not cope. When Third Officer Albert Bestic reached the No. 2 lifeboat on the port side, he found it filled with women—most in full-length skirts—but only one crewman was available to man the davits. When Bestic, the crewman, and a male passenger attempted to lower the boat, there was a sharp crack. One of the guys had snapped, dropping the bow of the lifeboat and spilling its passengers against the rail and into the sea. . . .

Although Turner never gave an order to abandon ship, individual officers began loading boats on their own initiative. But the fact that the liner was still underway made it difficult to launch even the starboard boats. Several capsized, spilling their occupants into the water. Only eighteen minutes after Schwieger's torpedo struck, *Lusitania* sank with a roar that reminded one passenger of the collapse of a great building during a fire. Hundreds of passengers went down with her, trapped in elevators or between decks. Hundreds of others were swept off the ship and drowned in the roiled waters. Because *Lusitania* was nearly eight hundred feet long, her black-painted stern and four great screws were still visible to horrified onlookers on shore at Kinsale when the liner's bow struck bottom at 360 feet.

Not a ship was in sight when the liner went down; other skippers appear to have taken the submarine warnings more seriously than had Turner. But a stream of fishing boats from nearby Queenstown collected the living and the dead during the afternoon and evening of May 7. More than 60 percent of the people on board died—a total of 1,198—of whom 128 were Americans. About 140 unidentified victims were buried at Queenstown, but the remains of nine hundred others were never found. Of the American celebrities, all three—Frohman, Hubbard, and Vanderbilt—went down with the ship. One survivor recalled, "Actuated by a less acute fear or by a higher degree of bravery which the well-bred man seems to feel in moments of danger, the men of wealth and position for the most part hung back while others rushed for the boats."

A Violent Aftermath

Whatever *Lusitania* may have been carrying as cargo, the death toll aboard the liner ensured that the sinking would become a public relations disaster for Germany. Instead of issuing an apology, however, or at least holding out the promise of an investigation, Berlin first sought to deflect responsibility. Adding insult to injury, thousands of Germans purchased postcards that portrayed Schwieger's torpedo striking *Lusitania*, with an inset of Admiral Alfred von Tirpitz. The newspaper of one of the centrist political parties, *Kolniche Volkszeilung*, editorialized:

> The sinking of the *Lusitania* is a success of our submarines which must be placed beside the greatest achievements of this naval war. . . . It will not be the last. The English wish to abandon the German people to death by starvation. We are more humane. We simply sank an English ship with passengers who, at their own risk and responsibility entered the zone of operations.

In Britain, reaction to the sinking was immediate and violent. British officials denied German suspicions that *Lusitania* was carrying contraband, and in London and Liverpool, mobs attacked German-owned shops. The reaction in the United States was less destructive but more ominous. Former President Theodore Roosevelt denounced the sinking as piracy. . . . The press reaction outside the German-American community was almost uniformly condemning. The *New York Tribune* warned that "the nation which remembered the *Maine* [U.S. battleship sunk in the Havana, Cuba, harbor in 1989] will not forget the civilians of the *Lusitania*.". . .

The United States was not yet ready for war, however, and amid the indignation there were calls for restraint. But the *Lusitania* tragedy caused thousands of Americans, heretofore indifferent to the war in Europe, to side with the Allies. On May 12 the British government released a report on German atrocities in Belgium. The report exaggerated the extent of German depredations, but in the aftermath of *Lusitania*'s sinking most Americans were a receptive audience. The German ambassador in Washington reported that the *Lusitania* affair had dealt a fatal blow to his efforts to enhance his country's image.

The foreign reaction was sufficiently disturbing to the German government that Schwieger, on his return to Germany, met with a cool reception. Then *U-20*'s log mysteriously disappeared. Typewritten versions of Schwieger's log, made available after *Lusitania* survivors had reported a second explosion, included this sentence: "It would have been impossible for me . . . to fire a second torpedo into this crowd of people struggling to save their lives.". . .

Turner, who survived the sinking of his ship, was roundly criticized for having failed to maintain top speed and for having ignored Admiralty orders to avoid headlands such as the Old Head of Kinsale. He never again took a Cunard liner to sea. As for Schwieger, he went on to become one of Germany's top U-boat aces, receiving his country's highest decoration for having destroyed 190,000 tons of Allied shipping. About five weeks after receiving his decoration, however, Schwieger took *U-88* on what proved to be his last cruise. The submarine never returned; she apparently struck a mine and went down with all hands.

AN ACT OF GENOCIDE

ARNOLD TOYNBEE

During World War I, Armenians from the Caucasus region formed volunteer battalions to help the Russians fight the Turks. When the volunteers began recruiting Turkish Armenians to help them in their fight, the Turkish government retaliated by ordering that more than 1.75 million Armenians—men, women, and children—be deported to Syria and Mesopotamia. The forced deportation resulted in the death of hundreds of thousands of Armenians of all ages. In documents prepared for Viscount Grey of Fallodon, the British secretary of state for foreign affairs from 1905 to 1916, British academician and renowned historian Arnold J. Toynbee describes the treatment the Armenians received at the hands of the Turks. In the following excerpt from those documents, Toynbee recounts the humiliations, abuse, and torture that the exiled Armenians not massacred at the outset were forced to endure.

O n the 8th of April, 1915, the final phase of the deportations of Armenians from Turkey began and the process carried out at Zeitoun was applied to one Armenian centre after another throughout the Ottoman Empire. On a certain date, in whatever town or village it might be . . . the public crier went through the streets announcing that every male Armenian must present himself forthwith at the Government Building. In some cases the warning was given by the soldiery or gendarmerie slaughtering every male Armenian they encountered in the streets . . . , but usually a summons to the Government Building was the preliminary stage. The men presented themselves in their working clothes, leaving their shops and work-rooms open, their ploughs in the field, their cattle on the mountain side. When they

From *The Treatment of Armenians in the Ottoman Empire*, by Arnold Toynbee (London: Hodder & Stoughton, 1916).

arrived, they were thrown without explanation into prison, kept there a day or two, and then marched out of the town in batches, roped man to man, along some southerly or south-easterly road. They were starting, they were told, on a long journey—to Mosul or perhaps to Baghdad. It was a dreadful prospect to men un-equipped for travel, who had neither scrip nor staff, food nor clothes nor bedding. They had bidden no farewell to their fami-lies, they had not wound up their affairs. But they had not long to ponder over their plight, for they were halted and massacred at the first lonely place on the road. The same process was applied to those other Armenian men (and they numbered hundreds or even thousands in the larger centres) who had been imprisoned during the winter months on the charge of conspiracy or concealment of arms, though in some instances these prisoners are said to have been overlooked—an involuntary form of reprieve. . . .

THE SENTENCE OF DEPORTATION

After the Armenian men had been summoned away to their death, there was usually a few days' interval in whatever town it might be, and then the crier was heard again in the streets, bid-ding all Armenians who remained to prepare themselves for de-portation, while placards to the same effect were posted on the walls. This applied, in actual fact, to the women and children, and to a poor remnant of the men who, through sickness, infirmity or age, had escaped the fate marked out for their sex. A period of grace was in most cases accorded for the settlement of their affairs and the preparation of their journey; but here, again, there were cases in which the victims were taken without warning from the loom, the fountain or even from their beds, and the respite, where granted, was in great measure illusory. The ordinary term given was a bare week, and it was never more than a fortnight—a time utterly insufficient for all that had to be done. There were in-stances, moreover, in which the Government broke its promise, and carried away its victims before the stated day arrived.

For the women there was an alternative to deportation. They might escape it by conversion to Islam; but conversion for an Ar-menian woman in 1915 meant something more physical than a change of theology. It could only be ratified by immediate mar-riage with a Moslem man, and if the woman were already a wife (or, rather, a widow, for by this time few Armenian husbands re-mained alive), she must part with any children she had, and sur-render them to be brought up as true Moslems in a "Government Orphanage"—a fate of uncertain meaning, for no such institu-tions were known to be in existence. If the convert could find no Turk to take her, or shrank from the embraces of the bridegroom who offered himself, then she and her children must be deported with the rest, however fervently she had professed the creed of Islam. Deportation was the alternative adopted by, or imposed upon, the great majority.

The sentence of deportation was a paralysing blow, yet those condemned to it had to spend their week of grace in feverish activity, procuring themselves clothing, provisions and ready money for the road. The local authorities placed every possible obstacle in their way. There was an official fiction that their banishment was only temporary, and they were therefore prohibited from selling their real property or their stock. The Government set its seal upon the vacated houses, lands and merchandise, "to keep them safe against their owners' return"; yet before these rightful owners started on their march they often saw these very possessions, which they had not been allowed to realise, made over by the authorities as a free gift to Moslem immigrants, who had been concentrated in the neighbourhood, in readiness to step into the Armenians' place. And even such household or personal chattels as they were permitted to dispose of were of little avail, for their Moslem neighbours took shameless advantage of their necessity, and beat them down to an almost nominal price, so that when the day of departure arrived they were often poorly equipped to meet it.

The Government charged itself with their transport, and indeed they were not in a position to arrange for it themselves, for their ultimate destination was seldom divulged. The exiles from each centre were broken up into several convoys, which varied in size from two or three hundred to three or four thousand members. A detachment of gendarmerie was assigned to every convoy, to guard them on the way, and the civil authorities hired or requisitioned a certain number of ox-carts (arabas), usually one to a family, which they placed at their disposal; and so the convoy started out. The mental misery of exile was sufficiently acute, but it was soon ousted by more material cares. A few days, or even a few hours, after the start, the carters would refuse to drive them further, and the gendarmes, as fellow-Moslems, would connive at their mutinousness. So the carts turned back, and the exiles had to go forward on foot. This was the beginning of their physical torments, for they were not travelling over soft country or graded roads, but by mule-tracks across some of the roughest country in the world. It was the hot season, the wells and springs were sometimes many hours' journey apart, and the gendarmes often amused themselves by forbidding their fainting victims to drink. It would have been an arduous march for soldiers on active service, but the members of these convoys were none of them fitted or trained for physical hardship. They were the women and children, the old and the sick. Some of the women had been delicately brought up and lived in comfort all their lives; some had to carry children in their arms too young to walk; others had been sent off with the convoy when they were far gone with child, and gave birth on the road. None of these latter survived, for they were forced to march on again after a few hours' respite; they died on the road, and the new-born babies perished with them. Many others died of hunger and thirst, sunstroke, apoplexy or sheer exhaustion. . . .

The Government which condemned them to exile knew what the journey would mean, and the servants of the Government who conducted them did everything to aggravate their inevitable physical sufferings. Yet this was the least part of their torture; far worse were the atrocities of violence wantonly inflicted upon them by fellow human beings.

No Place to Hide

From the moment they left the outskirts of the towns they were never safe from outrage. The Moslem peasants mobbed and plundered them as they passed through the cultivated lands, and the gendarmes connived at the peasants' brutality, as they had connived at the desertion of the drivers with their carts. When they arrived at a village they were exhibited like slaves in a public place, often before the windows of the Government Building itself, and every Moslem inhabitant was allowed to view them and take his choice of them for his harem; the gendarmes themselves began to make free with the rest, and compelled them to sleep with them at night. There were still more horrible outrages when they came to the mountains, for here they were met by bands of "chettis" and Kurds. The "chettis" were brigands, recruited from the public prisons; they had been deliberately released by the authorities on a consideration which may have been tacit but which both parties clearly understood. . . .

When these Kurds and chettis waylaid the convoys, the gendarmes always fraternised with them and followed their lead, and it would be hard to say which took the most active part in the ensuing massacre—for this was the work which the brigands came to do. The first to be butchered were the old men and boys—all the males that were to be found in the convoy except the infants in arms—but the women were massacred also. It depended on the whim of the moment whether a Kurd cut a woman down or carried her away into the hills. When they were carried away their babies were left on the ground or dashed against the stones. But while the convoy dwindled, the remnant had always to march on. The cruelty of the gendarmes towards the victims grew greater as their physical sufferings grew more intense; the gendarmes seemed impatient to make a hasty end of their task. Women who lagged behind were bayoneted on the road, or pushed over precipices, or over bridges. The passage of rivers, and especially of the Euphrates, was always an occasion of wholesale murder. Women and children were driven into the water, and were shot as they struggled, if they seemed likely to reach the further bank. The lust and covetousness of their tormentors had no limit. The last survivors often staggered into Aleppo naked; every shred of their clothing had been torn from them on the way. Witnesses who saw their arrival remark that there was not one young or pretty face to be seen among them, and there was assuredly none surviving that was truly old—except in so far as it had been aged by suffering. The only chance to survive was to be plain enough to escape their torturers' lust, and vigorous enough to bear the fatigues of the road.

Those were the exiles that arrived on foot, but there were others, from the metropolitan districts and the north-west, who were transported to Aleppo by rail. These escaped the violence of the Kurds, but the sum of their suffering can hardly have been less. They were packed in cattle-trucks, often filthy and always overcrowded, and their journey was infinitely slow, for the line was congested by their multitude and by the passage of troops. At every stopping-place they were simply turned out into the open, without food or shelter, to wait for days, or even weeks, till the line was clear and rolling-stock available to carry them a further stage. The gendarmes in charge of them seem to have been as brutal as those with the convoys on foot, and when they came to the two breaks in the Baghdad Railway, where the route crosses the ranges of the Taurus and Amanus Mountains, they too had to traverse these, the most arduous stages of all, on foot. At Bozanti, the rail-head west of Taurus, and again at Osmania, Mamouret, Islohia and Kotmo, stations on either slope of the Amanus chain, vast and incredibly foul concentration camps grew up, where the exiles were delayed for months, and died literally by thousands of hunger, exposure, and epidemics. The portion of them that finally reached Aleppo were in as deplorable a condition as those that had made the journey on foot from beginning to end.

Aleppo was the focus upon which all the convoys converged. In April, it is true, half the Zeitounlis had been sent northwestward to Sultania, . . . one of the most unhealthy spots in the Anatolian Desert. But the authorities changed their mind, and despatched the exiles at Sultania southeast again, to join their fellow-townsmen in the Desert of Syria. Thenceforward, the south-eastern desert was the destination of them all, and Aleppo, and in a secondary degree Ourfa and Rasul-Ain, were the natural centres of distribution.

Some of the exiles were planted in the immediate neighbour-hood of Aleppo itself—at places like Moumbidj, Bab, Ma'ara, Idlib—but these seem to have been comparatively few, and it is not certain whether their quarters there were intended to be per-manent. Many more were deported southward from Aleppo along the Syrian Railway, and allowed to find a resting-place in the districts of Hama, Homs and Damascus. A still larger num-ber were sent towards the east, and cantoned on the banks of the Euphrates, in the desert section of its course. There were some at Rakka; Der-el-Zor was the largest depôt of all. . . .

The dispersal of the exiles was thus extremely wide, as the au-thors of the scheme had intended that it should be, but certain features are common to all the places to which they were sent. They were all inhabited by Moslem populations alien to the Ar-menians in language and habits of life; they were all unhealthy—either malarious or sultry or in some other respect markedly un-suitable for the residence of people used to a temperate climate; and they were all remote from the exiles' original homes—the re-motest places, in fact, which the Government could find within the Ottoman frontiers, since Christians were debarred from set-ting foot on the sacred deserts of the Hidjaz, and a British expe-ditionary force was occupying the marshes of Irak. The Ottoman Government had to content itself with the worst districts at its disposal, and it did its utmost to heighten the climate's natural effect by marooning the exiles there, after an exhausting journey, with neither food, nor shelter, nor clothing, and with no able-bodied men among them to supply these deficiencies by their labour and resource.

THE WORLD GOES TO WAR

JOHN KEEGAN

When World War I began, young men from Britain, France, Germany, Austria, and Russia marched off in high spirits eager to fight for their respective countries. In the following excerpt from his work *The First World War*, John Keegan describes the gaiety and carefree attitude that characterized the scenes of mobilization as men embarked for the fields of war. He contends that feet—those of men and of horses—were the backbone of the fighting forces. Keegan writes, as soon as the men got off the trains that carried them to the concentration area, they began marching—and kept on marching. John Keegan, considered by many one of the foremost contemporary military historians, has authored many books about warfare. He is also a journalist who served as a political analyst for the U.S. Embassy in London and was a senior lecturer in history at the Royal Military Academy in Sandhurst, England, for more than twenty years.

Statesmen were filled with foreboding by the coming of war but its declaration was greeted with enormous popular enthusiasm in the capitals of all combatant countries. Crowds thronged the streets, shouting, cheering and singing patriotic songs. In St. Petersburg the French ambassador, Maurice Paléologue, found his way into the Winter Palace Square, "where an enormous crowd had congregated with flags, banners, icons and portraits of the Tsar. The Emperor appeared on the balcony. The entire crowd at once knelt and sang the Russian national anthem. To those thousands of men on their knees at that moment

From *The First World War*, by John Keegan. Copyright © 1998 by John Keegan. Used by permission of Alfred A. Knopf, a division of Random House, Inc., and by permission of The Random House Group Limited.

the Tsar was really the autocrat appointed of God, the military, political and religious leader of his people, the absolute master of their bodies and souls." The day was 2 August [1914]. On 1 August a similar crowd had gathered in the Odeonsplatz in Munich, capital of the German kingdom of Bavaria, to hear the proclamation of mobilisation. In it was Adolf Hitler who was "not ashamed to acknowledge that I was carried away by the enthusiasm of the moment and . . . sank down upon my knees and thanked Heaven out of the fullness of my heart for the favour of having been permitted to live in such times." In Berlin the Kaiser appeared on his palace balcony, dressed in field-grey uniform, to address a tumultuous crowd: "A fateful hour has fallen upon Germany. Envious people on all sides are compelling us to resort to a just defence. The sword is being forced into our hands. . . . And now I command you all to go to church, kneel before God and pray to him to help our gallant army." In the Berlin cathedral, the Kaiser's pastor led a huge congregation in the recitation of Psalm 130 and at the Oranienstrasse synagogue the rabbi conducted prayers for victory.

There were to be similar scenes in London on 5 August. In Paris it was the departure of the city's mobilised regiments to the Gare de l'Est and Gare du Nord which brought forth the crowds. "At six in the morning," an infantry officer reported,

> without any signal, the train slowly steamed out of the station. At that moment, quite spontaneously, like a smouldering fire suddenly erupting into roaring flames, an immense clamour arose as the *Marseillaise* burst from a thousand throats. All the men were standing at the train's windows, waving their képis. From the track, quais and the neighbouring trains, the crowds waved back. . . . Crowds gathered at every station, behind every barrier, and at every window along the road. Cries of "Vive la France! Vive l'armée" could be heard everywhere, while people waved handkerchiefs and hats. The women were throwing kisses and heaped flowers on our convoy. The young men were shouting: *"Au revoir! A bientôt!"*

All too soon, for most of the young men, the summons to follow would come. Reservists not yet called were already putting their affairs in order; in most armies the day before the stipulated date for reporting was a "free day" for farewells to family and employer. "Complete strangers," recorded Richard Cobb, the great historian of France, "could be heard addressing one another in bizarre fashion, as if Parisians had all at once become figures out of Alice [in Wonderland]: playing cards, days of the week, or dates in a new sort of calendar. 'What day are you?' And, before the other could get in an answer, 'I am on the first' (as if to suggest: 'beat that'). 'I am the ninth' ('Bad luck, you'll miss all the fun, it'll be over by then'). 'I am the third, so won't have to wait *too* long. 'I am the eleventh' ('You'll never make Berlin at that rate')." . . .

Horses, like men, were mustering in hundreds of thousands all over Europe in the first week of August. Even Britain's little army called up 165,000, mounts for the cavalry and draught animals for the artillery and regimental transport waggons. The Austrian army mobilised 600,000, the German 715,000, the Russian—with its twenty-four cavalry divisions—over a million. The armies of 1914 remained Napoleonic in their dependence on the horse; staff officers calculated the proportion between horses and men at 1:3. . . .

THE TROOPS MOBILISE

Trains were to fill the memories of all who went to war in 1914. The railway section of the German Great General Staff timetabled the movement of 11,000 trains in the mobilisation period. . . . The chief French railway companies, Nord, Est, Ouest, PLM, POM, had since May 1912 had a plan to concentrate 7,000 trains for mobilisation. Many had moved near the entraining centres before war began.

> Travellers coming in [to Paris] from Melun brought extraordinary accounts of empty, stationary trains, engineless and often of mixed provenance, the carriages from different companies strung up together, passenger ones mixed up with guard trucks, many with chalk marks on their sides . . . waiting on side-lines the whole way from the *chef-lieu* of the Seine-et-Marne to the approaches of the Gare de Lyon. Equally bizarre were the reports brought in by travellers to the Gare du Nord of the presence along the immense sidings of Creil of several hundred stationary locomotives, smokeless and passive.

They were not long stationary. Soon they would be moving, filled with hundreds of thousands of young men making their way, at ten or twenty miles an hour and often with lengthy, unexplained waits, to the detraining points just behind the frontiers. Long prepared, many of the frontier stations were sleepy village halts, where platforms three-quarters of a mile long had not justified the trickle of peacetime comings and goings. Images of those journeys are among the strongest to come down to us from the first two weeks of August 1914: the chalk scrawls on the waggon sides—*"Ausflug nach Paris,"* and *"à Berlin"*—the eager young faces above the open collars of unworn uniforms, khaki, field-grey, pike-grey, olive-green, dark blue, crowding the windows. The faces glow in the bright sun of the harvest month and there are smiles, uplifted hands, the grimace of unheard shouts, the intangible mood of holiday, release from routine. Departure had everywhere been holidaylike, with wives and sweethearts, hobble-skirted, high-waisted, marching down the road to the terminus arm-in-arm with the men in the outside ranks. The Germans marched to war with flowers in the muzzles of their rifles or stuck between the top buttons of their tunics; the French marched in close-pressed ranks, bowed under the weight of enormous packs, forcing a passage between crowds overspilling the pavements. One photograph of Paris that first week of August catches a sergeant marching backwards before his section a they lean towards him, he like a conductor orchestrating the rhythm of their footfalls on the cobbles, they urgent with the effort of departure and the call to arms. An unseen band seems to be playing "Sambre-et-Meuse" or "le chant du départ." Russian soldiers paraded before their regimental icons for a blessing by the chaplain, Austrians to shouts of loyalty to Franz Joseph, symbol of unity among the dozen nationalities of his creaking empire. In whichever country, mobilisation entailed enormous upheaval, the translation of civil society into the nation in arms. The British army, all-regular as it was, stood the readiest for war; once its reservists were recalled, it was prepared to deploy. "We found the barracks full of Reservists—many still in civilian dress—and more were flocking in by almost every train," wrote Bandsman H.V. Sawyer of the 1st Rifle Brigade at Colchester on 5 August. . . .

THE DISTINCTION OF UNIFORMS

Bandsman Shaw packed his peacetime kit and sent it home by rail. "As it turned out, I needn't have bothered. But I wasn't to know that I'd packed that lovely dark green review order tunic for the last time in my life." In Paris Lieutenant Edward Spears, 11th Hussars, on exchange from the British to the French army, changed into khaki. "'How funny you look, disguised as a dusty canary,' observed the female concierge who let me in at one of the more obscure entrances to the *Ministère de la guerre*. This was disappointing, but one became used to the fact that for a long time the French thought that to go to war in a collar and tie [British officers wore an open-necked tunic in service uniform] represented an attitude of levity quite out of keeping with the seriousness of the situation.". . .

The Austrian cavalry rode to war in uniforms as antiquated as the French; only the infantry had been re-equipped with service grey. The Russians were unexpectedly modern. Their service dress was a loose olive-green overshirt, the *gymnastirka* modelled on an athlete's tunic; but there were exotic exceptions, notably the Astrakhan caps of the light cavalry. Only the Germans had made as clean a sweep as the British. Their army was uniformly field-grey. . . .

THE INFANTRY AND THE CAVALRY

However clothed, the infantrymen of every army were afflicted by the enormous weight of their equipment: a rifle weighing ten pounds, bayonet, entrenching tool, ammunition pouches holding a hundred rounds or more, water bottle, large pack containing spare socks and shirt, haversack with iron rations and field dressing; that was a common outfit. . . . However arranged, no infantryman's marching load weighed less than sixty pounds; and it had to be plodded forward, mile after mile for an expected twenty miles a day, in stiff, clumsy, nailed boots—"dice-boxes," *brodequins, Bluchers,* to the British, French and Germans—which were agony until broken to the shape of the foot.

Feet were as important as trains in August 1914, horses' feet as well as men's feet for, after detrainment in the concentration area, cavalry and infantry deployed on to the line of march. That, for the Germans, presaged days of marching west and southwards, days in which human feet would bleed and horses throw shoes. The telltale clink of a loose nail warned a cavalryman that he must find the shoeing-smith if he were to keep up next day with the column; the same sound to the senior driver of a gun-team threatened the mobility of his six harnessed animals. There were 5,000 horses in an infantry division in 1914, more than 5,000 in a cavalry division. All had to be kept shod and healthy if the twenty miles of the day were to be covered to timetable, the infantry fed, reconnaissance reports returned, small-arms combat covered by artillery fire should the enemy be encountered. Fourteen miles of road was filled by an infantry division on the march and the endurance of horses—those pulling the wheeled field-kitchens, cooking on the march, quite as much as those drawing the ammunition waggons of the artillery brigades—counted with that of the infantry in the race to drive the advance forward.

The race was tripartite. For the French it was north-eastward from their detraining points at Sedan, Montmédy, Toul, Nancy and Belfort behind the 1870 frontier. For the British Expeditionary Force, which began to disembark at Boulogne on 14 August, it was south-eastward towards Le Cateau, just before the Belgian border. These were short marches. For the Germans the marches planned were long, westward first and then southward towards Châlons, Epernay, Compiègne, Abbeville and Paris. General von Kluck's First Army on the right faced a march of 200 miles from its detraining points at Aachen to the French capital.

WAR IN THE TRENCHES

PATRICK MACGILL

Irish writer Patrick MacGill fought in the British army during World War I. He wrote *The Great Push: An Episode of the Great War*, from which the following selection is taken, in part at the scene of a battle in which he participated and in part in a Versailles, France, hospital where he was taken when wounded in battle in Loos, Belgium, in 1915. In this selection, MacGill recalls one night when his battalion dug trenches close to enemy lines. As a stretcher-bearer who did not have to dig unless he wanted to, MacGill watched his companions and listened to the sounds not only of his own working party but of enemy German transports and German soldiers working nearby to strengthen their barbed-wire entanglements.

W e marched down the reserve slope of the hill in silence. At the end of the road was the village; our firing trench fringed the outer row of houses. Two months before an impudent red chimney stack stood high in air here; but humbled now, it had fallen upon itself, and its own bricks lay still as sandbags at its base, a forgotten ghost with blurred outlines, it brooded, a stricken giant.

The long road down the hill was a tedious, deceptive way; it took a deal of marching to make the village. Bill Teake growled. "One would think the place was tied to a string," he grumbled, "and some one pullin' it away!"

We were going to dig a sap out from the front trench towards the German line; we drew our spades and shovels for the work from the Engineers' store at the rear and made our way into the labyrinth of trenches. Men were at their posts on the fire positions, their Balaclava helmets resting on their cars, their bayonets

From *The Great Push: An Episode of the Great War*, by Patrick MacGill (New York: George H. Doran, 1916).

gleaming bright in the moonshine, their hands close to their rifle barrels. Sleepers lay stretched out on the banquette with their overcoats over their heads and bodies. Out on the front the Engineers had already taped out the night's work; our battalion had to dig some two hundred and fifty yards of trench 3 ft. wide and 6 ft. deep before dawn, and the work had to be performed with all possible dispatch. Rumour spoke of thrilling days ahead; and men spoke of a big push which was shortly to take place. Between the lines there are no slackers; the safety of a man so often depends upon the dexterous handling of his spade; the deeper a man digs, the better is his shelter from bullet and bomb; the spade is the key to safety.

The men set to work eagerly, one picked up the earth with a spade and a mate shovelled the loose stuff out over the meadow. The grass, very long now and tapering tall as the props that held the web of wire entanglements in air, shook gently backwards and forwards as the slight breezes caught it. The night was wonderfully calm and peaceful; it seemed as if heaven and earth held no threat for the men who delved in the alleys of war.

IN SIGHT OF THE ENEMY

Out ahead lay the German trenches. I could discern their line of sandbags winding over the meadows and losing itself for a moment when it disappeared behind the ruins of a farm-house—a favourite resort of the enemy snipers, until our artillery blew the place to atoms. Silent and full of mystery as it lay there in the moonlight, the place had a strange fascination for me. How interesting it would be to go out there beyond our most advanced outpost and have a peep at the place all by myself. Being a stretcher-bearer there was no necessity for me to dig; my work began when my mates ceased their labours and fell wounded.

Out in front of me lay a line of barbed wire entanglements.

"Our wire?" I asked the Engineer.

"No—the Germans'," he answered.

I noticed a path through it, and I took my way to the other side. Behind me I could hear the thud of picks and the sharp, rasping sound of shovels digging into the earth, and now and again the whispered words of command passing from lip to lip. The long grass impeded my movements, tripping me as I walked, and lurking shellholes caught me twice by the foot and flung me to the ground. Twenty yards out from the wire I noticed in front of me something moving on the ground, wiggling, as I thought, towards the enemy's line. I threw myself flat and watched.

There was no mistaking it now; it was a man, belly flat on the ground, moving off from our lines. Being a non-combatant I had no rifle, no weapon to defend myself with if attacked. I wriggled back a few yards, then got to my feet, recrossed the line of wires and found a company-sergeant-major speaking to an officer.

"There's somebody out there lying on the ground," I said. "A man moving off towards the German trenches."

The three of us went off together and approached the figure on the ground, which had hardly changed its position since I last saw it. It was dressed in khaki, the dark barrel of a rifle stretched out in front. I saw stripes on a khaki sleeve. . . .

JUST DOING A JOB

"One of a covering-party?" asked the sergeant-major.

"That's right," came the answer from the grass, and a white face looked up at us.

"Quiet?" asked the S.-M.

"Nothing doing," said the voice from the ground. "It's cold lying here, though. We've been out for four hours."

"I did not think that the covering-party was so far out," said the officer and the two men returned to their company.

I sat in the long grass with the watcher; he was the sergeant in command of the covering party.

"Are your party out digging?" he asked.

"Yes, out behind us," I answered. "Is the covering-party a large one?"

Trench warfare, where soldiers dig trenches to protect themselves from enemy fire, became a standard fighting strategy during WWI.

"About fifty of us," said the sergeant. "They've all got orders to shoot on sight when they see anything suspicious. Do you hear the Germans at work out there?"

I listened; from the right front came the sound of hammering.

"They're putting up barbed wire entanglements and digging a sap," said the sergeant. "Both sides are working and none are fighting. I must have another smoke," said the sergeant. . . .

It was so very quiet lying there. The grasses nodded together, whispering to one another. To speak of the grasses whispering during the day is merely a sweet idea; but God! they do whisper at night. . . .

OBSERVING THE ENEMY UP CLOSE

At the end of half an hour I ventured to go nearer the German lines. The sergeant told me to be careful and not to go too close to the enemy's trenches or working parties. "And mind your own covering-party when you're coming in," said the sergeant. "They may slip you a bullet or two if you're unlucky."

Absurd silvery shadows chased one another up and down the entanglement props. In front, behind the German lines, I could hear sounds of railway wagons being shunted, and the clank of rails being unloaded. The enemy's transports were busy; they clattered along the roads, and now and again the neighing of horses came to my ears. On my right a working party was out; the clank of hammers filled the air. The Germans were strengthening their wire entanglements; the barbs stuck out, I could see them in front of me, waiting to rip our men if ever we dared to charge. I had a feeling of horror for a moment. Then, having one more look round, I went back, got through the line of outposts, and came up to our working party, which was deep in the earth already. Shovels and picks were rising and falling, and long lines of black clay bulked up on either side of the trench.

I took off my coat, got hold of a mate's idle shovel, and began to work. . . .

It was quite easy to make headway; the clay was crisp and brittle, and the pick went in easily, making very little sound. M'Crone, one of our section, was working three paces ahead, shattering a square foot of earth at every blow of his instrument.

"It's very quiet here," he said. "I suppose they won't fire on us, having their own party out. By Jove, I'm sweating at this."

"When does the shift come to an end?" I asked.

"At dawn," came the reply. He rubbed the perspiration from his brow as he spoke. "The nights are growing longer," he said, "and it will soon be winter again. It *will* be cold then."

As he spoke we heard the sound of rifle firing out by the German wires. Half a dozen shots were fired, then followed a long moment of silent suspense. . . .

Five minutes afterwards a sergeant and two men came in from listening patrol and reported to our officer.

"We've just encountered a strong German patrol between the lines," said the sergeant. "We exchanged shots with them and then withdrew. We have no casualties, but the Germans have one man out of action, shot through the stomach."

"How do you know it went through his stomach?" asked the officer.

"In this way," said the sergeant. "When we fired one of the Germans (we were quite close to them) put his hands across his stomach and fell to the ground yellin' 'Mein Gutt! Mein Gutt!'". . .

"You fool!" exclaimed Pryor. "It was 'My God' that the German said.". . .

When dawn showed pale yellow in a cold sky, and stars were fading in the west, we packed up and took our way out and marched back to Nouex-les-Mines, there to rest for a day or two.

THE TRIUMPH OF
BOLSHEVISM IN RUSSIA

HARRISON E. SALISBURY

Harrison E. Salisbury, who has authored a number of nonfiction and fiction books with Russian themes, is considered one of the foremost authorities on Russia. He served as a correspondent in Russia during World War II and spent many years there as bureau chief of the *New York Times*. In this selection from his book *Russia in Revolution: 1900–1930*, he focuses on the Bolshevik takeover of Petrograd in 1917. Salisbury describes the final hours of Alexander Kerensky's Provisional Government and the Bolshevik uprising that finally brought it down. According to Salisbury, Lenin kept a relatively low profile during the last hours of the uprising, the final events of which were disorganized almost to the point of being laughable.

A ll through Tuesday Lenin waited alone in the Fofanova apartment [the home of a female Russian agronomist] on the Vyborg side where he had been living since returning to Petrograd. He was isolated from the Central Committee at the Smolny Institute. Bolshevik historians claim that he was in touch with the Committee by courier during the day, frequently exchanging notes, reports and instructions. This may be true but none of these communications have survived. What is positively known is that Fofanova got back to her flat around 5 P.M. and told Lenin that alarming rumors were circulating in Petrograd and that the Neva bridges had been raised. Lenin rushed to his room, dashed off a note and asked Fofanova to deliver it immediately to his wife, Nadezhda Krupskaya, to be passed on to his com-

From *Russia in Revolution, 1900–1930*, by Harrison E. Salisbury. Copyright © 1978 by André Deutsch Limited. Reprinted with permission.

rades. He told Fofanova that it was necessary to get on with the uprising this very evening—there could be no more temporizing, and he should be at Smolny.

In the letter he declared that "the situation is critical in the extreme" and that further delay in the uprising would be fatal. The Provisional Government was tottering and "it must be given the death blow at all costs." (Lenin himself underlined the phrase.) He didn't care how it was done—so long as it was done immediately. . . .

Lenin exchanged several notes with Krupskaya that evening. The texts of none of these notes have ever been published. Nor has anyone offered a logical explanation why Lenin did not simply join his colleagues at Smolny, nor why they did not urgently summon him. Whatever the explanation, Lenin finally scribbled a message to Fofanova saying: "I've gone where you didn't want me to go," and set off for Smolny with a man named Rahja, a Finn who had accompanied him during his days in hiding in Finland.

Lenin and Rahja made their way across Petrograd on foot and by streetcar and despite an encounter or two with patrols arrived safely at Smolny not long before 11 P.M. With Lenin's arrival the pace of events gradually began to quicken. But no timetable for the uprising was ever agreed upon.

KERENSKY FLEES THE CAPITAL

After addressing the Pre-Parliament [Provisional Government president] Alexander Kerensky went back to the Winter Palace and sat down with his colleagues in the famous Malachite Chamber with its green Urals stone columns and fireplaces, its malachite tables and vases. The Palace was something of a shambles. Many of its furnishings and the famous works of art from the Hermitage had been packed for shipment in Moscow because of fears that advancing German troops might capture Petrograd. A large portion of the Palace was occupied by a hospital as convalescent quarters for the wounded and another section was being used as barracks for the small defense force.

Kerensky met with his ministers until about 2 A.M. when they wearily made their ways home, leaving Kerensky nervous and distraught. He and his deputy Konovalev went across Palace Square to the General Staff building after the others had departed. They stayed there until about 7 A.M. issuing orders to troops to come to the defense of Petrograd (none of the units ever appeared). Then they returned to the Winter Palace. It was a dark cold morning and Kerensky lay down on his bed, which once had been used by Nicholas II, for a little rest. He rose at 9 A.M. to find his telephone dead. Pulling back the heavy curtains he saw the sun just rising and discovered that the Palace bridge over the Neva was now in the hands of the Bolsheviks.

Kerensky decided he could not remain a moment longer. He must leave the capital, round up some reliable troops from the front and return to save the situation. The decision was easier to make than to carry out because all of the cars in the Palace court-yard had been disabled by Bolshevik chauffeurs. Finally Kerensky managed to borrow a Renault belonging to the American embassy and a Pierce-Arrow from some other source, possibly the British. With the Renault in front, flying an American flag, Kerensky sat in the open Pierce-Arrow, raced through the heart of Petrograd and out of town to Gatchin and Pskov to try to rally troops to his side.

Lenin was now in charge at Smolny. He had been up most of the night exhorting his colleagues, consulting members of the Military Revolutionary Committee, making certain that *this time* the coup would really get going. About 10 A.M. he drafted a proclamation and Bolshevik trucks rushed through Petrograd, plastering it on the city walls. . . .

It said:

To the Citizens of Russia!

The Provisional Government has been deposed. State power has passed into the hands of the organ of the Petrograd Soviet of Workers and Soldiers Deputies—the Revolutionary Military Committee, which heads the Petrograd proletariat and the garrison.

The cause for which the people have fought, namely, the immediate offer of a democratic peace, the abolition of landed proprietorship, workers' control over production and the establishment of Soviet power—this cause has been secured.

Long live the revolution of workers, soldiers and peasants!

THE PROVISIONAL GOVERNMENT'S LAST STAND

Actually, the Provisional Government had not been deposed. Not at this hour. It still existed. The Bolsheviks had taken over a good part of the central section of Petrograd. But not the Mariinsky Palace where the Pre-Parliament was still meeting, not the City Duma (and City Administration), not the War Ministry across from St Isaac's Cathedral in the city's heart, not the Winter Palace and, of course, not the country nor its military and staff head-quarters still engaged in combat (rather listless to be sure) with the Germans along the 1,200-mile front.

The truth was that the streets of Petrograd were perfectly quiet. There was none of the rampaging about town by trucks loaded with grim and picturesque soldiers which had marked earlier crises. True, a few dozen Bolshevik troops did visit the Mariinsky Palace in the early afternoon and closed down the session of the Pre-Parliament. . . . A big Kronstadt sailor (the Bolsheviks had brought several thousand sailors from Kronstadt and the Baltic fleet into Petrograd) simply marched into the red-and-gold assembly hall and announced: "No more Council. Go along home!" The members docilely filed out and the Bolsheviks didn't even bother to arrest them.

A picket line of junkers, young cadets from training schools, had been strung out in front of the Winter Palace but neither they nor a similar picket line of Bolshevik soldiers and red guards which appeared in the Square a little later made much fuss about letting people through. By mid-afternoon a dozen or more newsmen . . . had got into the Winter Palace.

There in the Malachite Chamber, so symbolic of the old Russian order, Kerensky's Ministers had gathered for a last stand. They were only gradually becoming aware of the control the Bolsheviks now exercised in Petrograd. The Bolsheviks held the telephone exchange, the post office and telegraph station, the railroad stations and most of the public buildings. Except for the Winter Palace itself—a vast complex spreading for a half mile along the Neva river—and the facing General Staff building with its grandiose arch, the Bolsheviks had, in fact, taken over the city. But neither the Provisional Ministers nor the Bolsheviks quite realized this. Lenin's nerves were growing jagged. He kept insisting that the Winter Palace be taken. The Soviet was meeting that afternoon at Smolny and he wanted to announce the fall of the Palace. Without that his Proclamation seemed a bit wobbly. The Military Revolutionary Committee made promises but nothing happened. It was after 1 P.M. by the time they managed to close down the Pre-Parliament in the Mariinsky Palace (and they completely forgot about taking over the War Ministry; not until 6 P.M. did Bolsheviks appear there). Telephone service to the Winter Palace was supposedly cut off but actually a number of lines remained open and the Ministers used them, calling Staff Headquarters at Mogilev, telephoning to various Party headquarters in town, to the City Duma, to prominent citizens, trying to drum up support. They kept hoping some of the Cossack troops would come to their aid but only a handful turned up. None of the Petrograd troops wanted to get involved.

THE BOLSHEVIKS MOVE IN

The afternoon wore by. Petrograd's shops stayed open. Streetcars jangled past. Shoppers queued up at the butchers and bakers. Except for Lenin's proclamation there was no sign anything unusual was underway. Nowhere were there armed collisions. Nowhere did revolutionary combat break out.

Lenin finally made his speech to the Soviet at Smolny. He simply ignored the Winter Palace and repeated his proclamation of the morning. The Military Revolutionary Committee worked out a plan of action. The Winter Palace would be sent an ultimatum to surrender. If it refused a red lantern would be hoisted on the tower of the Peter and Paul Fortress. The cruiser *Aurora* would fire a blank round from its six-inch guns and the assault on the Winter Palace would be on. . . .

The young cadets who were defending the Winter Palace . . . were mostly teenagers. ("Children" was what the French correspondent Claude Anet called them.) They fiddled with their guns and one swore he was keeping the last bullet for himself. His comrades chimed in that they were doing the same. . . . Outside in the Square a busy little man with a box camera set up a tripod, put his head under a black cloth and began to take pictures of the junkers and the Women's Battalion lugging logs from the Kremlin's winter heating supply and hoisting them up into barricades before the main Palace entrance.

In the Malachite Chamber the Ministers got a promise from Mogilev Staff headquarters that if they could hold out 48 hours reinforcements would be sent. Some of the Palace defenders began to trickle away including a Cossack detachment that clattered out of the Palace courtyard on horseback, leaving behind its machine guns after a big argument. More and more Bolsheviks infiltrated the Winter Palace, coming in through undefended entrances (there were several hundred doors to the huge complex). Most of the infiltrators permitted themselves to be taken into custody without argument but their sheer numbers began to raise the question of whether the handful of defenders would not be swamped by their "prisoners."

Events resembled a theater of the absurd. The Military Revolutionary Committee couldn't find a red lantern to give the signal for the bombardment to start. The guns on the Fortress of Peter and Paul hadn't been cleaned and oiled and were not fit to open fire. The Committee heard that the Winter Palace had surrendered. Two members went to verify the report, were fired upon and almost captured. The rumor, it was obvious, was not true. Finally, an ultimatum was delivered to the Winter Palace warning that an attack would be opened in half an hour (it was delivered by bicycle and had only five minutes to run when it was turned in). The Ministers refused to surrender and nothing happened. No attack was launched. But a panicking Government General surrendered the General Staff building to the Bolsheviks because he got tired of waiting on the telephone for an answer from the Malachite Chamber. Now the Provisional Government's writ ran only in the 2,000 rooms of the Winter Palace. It was obvious that the end was near.

LENIN'S REVOLUTION PREVAILS

At Smolny Lenin and [fellow Bolshevik Leon] Trotsky lay down on a blanket in a closet-like room to get a little rest. Lenin could not understand why the Winter Palace hadn't been assaulted. Trotsky offered to investigate but Lenin said he'd send someone to find out what was going on.

At about 10:30 the red lantern was run up and shrapnel shells were lobbed over the Neva river by the Fortress and blanks fired by the cruiser *Aurora*. Small guns and armored cars in the Square in front of the Palace opened fire. After half an hour the firing petered out and a telegraph agency reported the Bolshevik attack was weak and had easily been beaten off. . . .

The Nevsky Prospekt, Petrograd's principal thoroughfare . . . was blacked out but . . . a procession [was] under way. It was made up of two hundred members of the City Duma which had voted to go to the Winter Palace and "die with the Government" if the Bolsheviks carried through their attack. The procession had been halted in the murk by a Bolshevik patrol of twenty Baltic sailors.

"Let us pass," a deputy shouted. "Let us sacrifice ourselves."

According to [reporter] Louise Bryant a sailor retorted: "Go home and take poison but don't expect to die here. We have orders not to allow it." After an argument the delegates gave up trying to force their way through, went back to the City Duma and set up a "Committee to Save the Revolution."

At Smolny the Soviet began its session with an angry debate. Non-Bolsheviks attacked Lenin and his associates for trying to seize power and for shelling the Winter Palace. Lenin did not speak but Trotsky angrily responded that the opposition "are just so much refuse which will be swept into the garbage-heap of history."

At the Winter Palace members of the Military Revolutionary Committee busied themselves persuading cadets and other defenders to leave. About midnight they realized that the Provisional Government had only a handful of defenders left and a direct assault was ordered.

The first to notice the attack was the Palace switchboard operator. At 1:20 A.M. she rang the phone in the Malachite Chamber
and reported "a delegation of three hundred to four hundred is
approaching." This was the assault force. . . . Actually the throng
of "attackers" simply crossed the Square and entered the auxiliary entrances to the palace. They swarmed up the broad stair-
cases (doing a good bit of looting on the way), and arrived at the
Malachite Chamber just before 2 A.M. A small guard of armed
junkers was prepared to defend Kerensky's ministers to the
death but the ministers decided to surrender. At 2:10, a protocol
of arrest having been signed, the Ministerial contingent was led
out under the guard of Antonov-Ovseenko, a chief of the Military Revolutionary Committee, and taken to the Fortress of Peter and Paul. Casualties in the assault were six men killed.

It was 3:10 A.M. October 27 when Lev Kamenev (one of the
most sturdy opponents of Lenin's plans for insurrection) rose in
the white-columned hall of Smolny Institute and announced officially the news which all had known for an hour or more—that
the Winter Palace had fallen, Kerensky's ministers had been arrested and the Provisional Government was no more.

There was wild cheering but in a few moments the Soviet was
plunged once more into a wrangle, this time touched off by peasant delegates violently objecting to the arrest and imprisonment
of revolutionary members of the Kerensky Cabinet. The debate
went on until 5:15 A.M. Lenin, who had not made a public appearance all evening, slipped away to a friend's apartment to
work on the speech he was going to give on the evening of November 8 and to get a little rest.

The radical revolution to which Lenin had devoted his adult
life had been achieved. How long it might last was the question
now. Lenin himself was not too sanguine. He had never really
believed that Russian radicalism could triumph on its own. It
had to have the support and assistance of the revolutionaries of
western Europe. His first objective would be to survive. If he and
his Bolsheviks could stay on top for longer than the seventy-day
life of the Paris Commune he would be pleased.

BRITAIN ISSUES THE BALFOUR DECLARATION

DONALD NEFF

The Balfour Declaration has been the subject of debate and controversy since it was first issued in 1917. According to Donald Neff, author, editor, and former foreign correspondent for the *Los Angeles Times* and *Time* magazine, Arabs and anti-Zionists opposed the British directive for many reasons, not the least of which was the declaration's overtly pro-Zionist bias and total disregard of British wartime promises of Arab independence. Neff argues that the British were led to believe that favoring the Zionists would gain them the favor of influential American Jews who, in turn, would help the British gain U.S. support for their postwar goals. Neff also recounts the roles played by the head of the Zionist movement in Britain, Chaim Weizmann, and by Supreme Court justice Louis Brandeis in seeking—and obtaining—U.S. president Woodrow Wilson's support for the Zionist dream of a Jewish state in Palestine.

O n Nov. 2, 1917, Britain issued the Balfour Declaration, a fateful statement that Zionists henceforth claimed gave Jews a legal right to a homeland in Palestine. The statement came in the form of a personal letter from Foreign Secretary Arthur James Balfour to a prominent British Jew, Lionel Walter, the second Lord Rothschild:

Foreign Office, November 2nd, 1917

Reprinted, with permission, from "Britain Issues the Balfour Declaration," by Donald Neff, *Washington Report on Middle East Affairs*, October/November 1995. Endnotes in the original have been omitted.

Dear Lord Rothschild,

I have much pleasure in conveying to you, on behalf of His Majesty's Government, the following declaration of sympathy with Jewish Zionist aspirations which has been submitted to, and approved by, the Cabinet:

"His Majesty's Government view with favour the establishment in Palestine of a national home for the Jewish people, and will use their best endeavours to facilitate the achievement of this object, it being clearly understood that nothing shall be done which may prejudice the civil and religious rights of existing non-Jewish communities in Palestine, or the rights and political status enjoyed by Jews in any other country."

I should be grateful if you would bring this declaration to the knowledge of the Zionist Federation.

Yours,

Arthur James Balfour

Arabs and anti-Zionists could not help noting the totally pro-Zionist content of the declaration. It failed to mention Christians or Muslims, Arabs or Palestinians, even though they remained by far the majority population in Palestine. At the time, there were about 55,000 Jews and 600,000 Palestinians in Palestine. The declaration spoke of a homeland, but that was widely understood to mean a Jewish state. And it pledged actively to help Jews while merely promising to protect the rights of "the non-Jewish communities."

VOICES OF OPPOSITION

Arabs far beyond Palestine were alarmed and disappointed. It was clear to them that British wartime promises of Arab independence were being ignored by London. The campaign to chase the Turks from Palestine was being concluded in late 1917 with Arab help. British forces stood at the gates of Jerusalem and soon they would clear the area and Palestine would pass from the Ottoman to the British Empire. But Arab aspirations for independence were being ignored.

Opposition came not only from Arabs and Muslims but within England as well. The only Jew in the Cabinet, Edwin Montague, the secretary of state for India, had opposed the original idea. He supported his position by enlisting the views of one of the greatest Arabists of the time, Gertrude Bell, a colleague of T.E. Lawrence and currently involved in British intelligence in Cairo.

She wrote the Cabinet that "two considerations rule out the conception of an independent Jewish Palestine from practical politics. The first is that the province as we know it is not Jewish, and that neither Mohammedan nor Arab would accept Jewish authority; the second that the capital, Jerusalem, is equally sacred to three faiths, Jewish, Christian and Muslim, and should never, if it can be avoided, be put under the exclusive control of any one location, no matter how carefully the rights of the other two may be safeguarded."

Another dissent came from the Middle East from A.P. Albina, a Levantine Catholic merchant from Jerusalem who enjoyed good relations with top British officials. He wrote that it was contradictory for the Western powers to grant freedom to small nationalities while at the same time planning to give Palestine to the Jews. He described the Zionists as:

> A foreign and hated race, a motley crowd of Poles, Russians, Romanians, Spaniards, Yemenites, etc., who can claim absolutely no right over the country, except that of sentiment and the fact that their forefathers inhabited it over two thousand years ago[.] The introduction into Palestine of Jewish rule, or even Jewish predominance, will mean the spoliation of the Arab inhabitants of their hereditary rights and the upsetting of the principles of nationalities. . . . Politically, a Jewish State in Palestine will mean a permanent danger to a lasting peace in the Near East.

BRITISH INTERESTS

Despite such concerns, and the opposition of the entire Arab and Islamic worlds, there were a number of reasons favoring the Zionist campaign to gain official British sanction. Foremost among these was the favorable attitude toward a Jewish homeland shared by both Foreign Secretary Balfour and Britain's prime minister, David Lloyd George. Welshman Lloyd George was a firm believer in the Old Testament's claim to the right of the Jews to Palestine. Balfour had been prime minister in the early 1900s at the time of the British offer of "Uganda" as a Jewish homeland and, although not Jewish, he considered himself a Zionist.

Beyond . . . sentimental and religious reasons, however, there were other motivations having to do with Britain's interests, among them a common concern for gaining U.S. support for Britain's post-war goals in dividing up the tottering Ottoman Empire, including Britain's ambition of taking over Palestine. In this, they were advised by the British embassy in Washington that Britain could be helped in achieving U.S. backing by finding favor with Jewish Americans. Reported the embassy: "They are far better organized than the Irish and far more formidable. We should be in a position to get into their good graces."

One obvious way to do this was to follow the natural inclinations of Lloyd George and Balfour and support Zionist ambitions in Palestine, if only London could be sure President Woodrow Wilson agreed with such a path. In this they were immeasurably helped, as well as goaded, by a persistent and persuasive Russian-born Jewish chemist by the name of Chaim Weizmann. In 1917 he was head of the Zionist movement in Britain and a tireless worker in that cause. . . .

WEIZMANN AND BRANDEIS LOBBY THE PRESIDENT

Aware of Lloyd George's and Balfour's desire for U.S. support, Weizmann sought a backdoor past the anti-Zionist State Department to the White House via America's foremost Zionist, Louis B. Brandeis, an intimate of President Wilson, who had appointed Brandeis in 1916 to the Supreme Court. On April 8, 1917, Weizmann cabled Brandeis, advising that "an expression of opinion coming from yourself and perhaps other gentlemen connected with the Government in favor of a Jewish Palestine under a British protectorate would greatly strengthen our hands." A month later, following America's entry into the war, Brandeis had a 45-minute meeting with Wilson. As a son of a Presbyterian clergyman and a daily reader of the Bible, Wilson shared with a number of Christians support for a Jewish homeland in Palestine. Indeed, Brandeis found the president's views of Palestine "entirely sympathetic to the aims of the Zionist Movement" and, moreover, was able to encourage the British by adding that Wilson favored a British protectorate in Palestine.

However, Wilson did not want to make a public declaration because of his concern with French ambitions toward the region and a futile hope that Turkey still could be persuaded to quit the war. Thus, when Britain sought Wilson's endorsement in September 1917 of a draft declaration, he responded that the time was "not opportune" for him to go public. In desperation, Weizmann cabled Brandeis that it "would greatly help if President Wilson and yourself would support the text. Matter most urgent. Please telegraph." Brandeis was able to use his access to the White House to meet with a Jewish adviser to Wilson, Colonel Edward Mandell House, and together they assured Weizmann that

> From talks I have had with President and from expressions of opinion given to closest advisers I feel I can an-

swer you in that he is [in] entire sympathy with declaration quoted in yours of nineteenth as approved by
the foreign office and the Prime Minister. I of course
heartily agree.

When the British sent a revised draft of the statement for Wilson's examination in early October, he turned it over to Brandeis for his comments. The Justice and his aides redrafted it in slightly stronger and cleaner language, substituting "the Jewish people" for "the Jewish race"—thereby muting the vexing question of who's-a-Jew—and making the final clause read that there would be no prejudice to the "rights and political status enjoyed by Jews in any other country."

Colonel House sent the revision on to Wilson. But, in the midst of world war, he felt no urgency about the matter. It was not until Oct. 13 that he sent a memo to House saying:

I find in my pocket the memorandum you gave me
about the Zionist Movement. I am afraid I did not say
to you that I concurred in the formula suggested by the
other side. I do, and would be obliged if you would let
them know it.

So casual was Wilson about this momentous decision that he never did inform his secretary of state, or publicly announce his decision. Nonetheless, his private assurance to Britain of his support was enough for Lloyd George's Cabinet to adopt the declaration. In the corridors of power, it was well known that the president of the United States quietly supported the Balfour Declaration.

Thus, in the most off-handed way possible, Wilson lent his enormous weight to supporting the Zionist dream of a Jewish state in Palestine. It was a decision that was to have a profound effect on Middle East history and U.S. foreign policy, and especially on the daily lives of Palestinians and the world Jewish community.

AFTER THE ARMISTICE

JAY WINTER

In this selection, author Jay Winter describes the overwhelming sense of loss and fatigue shared by the survivors of World War I in 1918. According to Winter, a reader in modern history and a fellow of Pembroke College in Cambridge, England, underneath the thin veneer of the celebrations of the November 11 armistice that ended the Great War was a sorrow and a relief too deep to deny. He concludes that the reflections and feelings of French poet Blaise Cendrars, British writer Virginia Woolf, and Austrian soldier Adolf Hitler were not that different from one another on Armistice Day. They and most of their compatriots had suffered an exhausting war that had cost 9 million lives. Winter believes that the only outcome of the war was the hatreds it generated and the determination it fostered in the Germans to avenge their dead.

O f the 70 million men who put on a uniform in the 1914–18 war, over nine million were dead by the Armistice of November 11th, 1918. Today, nearly all the veterans of the Great War have passed away, and with them has gone a sense of direct experience, an immediacy of retrieval of a unique moment in history. But how did contemporaries feel on that grey November day? If one word sums up a constellation of reactions in a myriad of towns, villages and cities at the end of the war, it is lassitude. Exhaustion was the prevailing feeling after four-and-a-half years of carnage. Fatigue marked the faces of the crowds in the celebrating Allied capitals, just as it did in the sombre streets of Berlin and Vienna. Exuberance in some urban crowds was real enough, but it was superficial. It was a passing mood, thinly veiling too many sacrifices, too many wounds, too many losses.

Reprinted, with permission, from "A Taste of Ashes," by Jay Winter, *History Today*, November 1998.

CELEBRATION AND SORROW IN PARIS

One—at least—of that army of the dead almost made it. He was the French poet Guillaume Apollinaire. The story of his November 1918, and its aftermath, tells us much about the gloomy mixture of celebration and sorrow that infused the moment the Armistice took effect.

Born Wilhelm de Kostrowitsky, of traditional Polish Catholic ancestry, Apollinaire (as he became known) was one of the great avant-garde poets of the pre-war years. . . . A volunteer in 1914—rewarded with French citizenship—he was wounded in the head two years later. After surviving a trepanning [ancient form of brain surgery] operation at the hands of military surgeons, Apollinaire was struck down in the last days of the war with the dreaded 'Spanish flu'.

The poet Blaise Cendrars, who had lost an arm in combat, bumped into his friend Apollinaire on Sunday, November 3rd, 1918. They lunched at Montparnasse and discussed 'the subject of the day', the flu epidemic, 'which had taken more victims than did the war'. Five days later, Cendrars passed the concierge of Apollinaire's apartment, who told him that his tenant had caught the flu. Cendrars bounded up the stairs, and was met by Apollinaire's wife Jacqueline. She, too, was ill, but not as badly as her husband who was 'all black' and still. Cendrars rushed to fetch a doctor, but it was too late to help the poet. Apollinaire died the following evening, Saturday, November 9th. The burial was held on Monday the 11th. Cendrars described the scene:

> . . . The final absolution having been given, the casket of Apollinaire left the church of St Thomas Aquinas, draped in a flag, Guillaume's lieutenant's helmet on the tricolor, among the flowers and wreaths. A guard of honour, a squad of soldiers, arms at their sides, led the slow convoy, the family behind the carriage, his mother, his wife, in their mourning veils, . . . all the other friends of Guillaume, . . . all of literary Paris, Paris of the arts, the press. But as it reached the corner of Saint-Germain, the cortege was besieged by a crowd of noisy celebrants of the Armistice, men and women with arms waving, singing, dancing, kissing, shouting deliriously the famous refrain of the end of the war: 'No, you don't have to go, Guillaume, No you don't have to go. . . .'

It was too much. Cendrars left the cortege with his lover and future wife, Raymone, and the soldier-artist Fernand Leger. They had a warm drink to protect themselves against the flu. Then they took a taxi to Pere Lachaise, the cemetery in north-east Paris, only to find that Apollinaire's cortege had proceeded faster than they thought. The ceremony was over, and the mourners were already leaving. The three friends asked directions to the grave and started searching among the headstones. They stumbled into two fresh graves, to the annoyance of the grave-diggers. . . . They asked the way, but though the gravediggers were decent men, they were of little help as Cendrars recounted:

> 'You understand, with the flu, with the war, they don't tell us the names of the dead we put in the ground. There are too many'. . . . But I said, he was a lieutenant, Lieutenant Guillaume Apollinaire or Kostrowitsky. We have to fire a salvo over his tomb!—'My dear sir', the head of the grave-digging team answered me, 'there were two salvoes. There were two lieutenants. We don't know which is the one you are looking for. Look for yourselves'.

They spied a grave with a bit of frozen earth nearby in exactly the shape of Apollinaire's head, with grass for hair around the scar where he had been trepanned. 'The psychisme was so intense, that one did not believe one's eyes':

> We were stunned. . . . We left the cemetery, where already a thick glacial mist was enveloping the tombs . . . and said: 'It was he. We saw him. Apollinaire isn't dead. Soon he will appear. Don't forget what I tell you'.

This surrealistic scene took place just across from the grave of Alain Kardec, the founder of French spiritualism. Cendrars and his friends noticed the inscription on Kardec's grave. It read: 'We live, we die, we return'. 'It was fantastic', Cendrars wrote, 'Paris celebrating. Apollinaire lost. I was full of melancholy. It was absurd'.

EXHAUSTION AND RELIEF IN BRITAIN

He was right. There was a sense of absurdity in the air of Paris at the Armistice. The same was also true of other cities, whose inhabitants marked the Allied victory, but in a half-hearted, subdued way that suggested the impropriety of acting in a jarring or jovial manner. They were, after all, making a noise in the shadow of the graveyards scattered throughout Europe and beyond.

[British writer] Virginia Woolf, thirty-six in 1918, observed and captured an element of this mood in London. Her husband Leonard was active in the Labour Party and its brand new international advisory committee. His early pamphlets contributed to the tide of opinion supporting the idea that it would be necessary to create a League of Nations to preserve the post-war stability of Europe. Despite her periodic bouts of mental illness, Virginia joined Leonard in their own corner of the dissenting community of Bloomsbury. They rubbed shoulders with pacifists and conscientious objectors, . . . and with government advisors like [economist] John Maynard Keynes. In 1916, Virginia had joined the Richmond branch of the Women's Cooperative Guild, chairing meetings in her own house. Her sensitivity to the effect of war on women and non-combatants can be traced from this period to her later writings about the traumatic consequences of combat in her novel *Mrs. Dalloway*.

But she had more direct experience of the costs of war. One brother-in-law, Cecil Woolf, was killed in 1917, and another, Philip Woolf, wounded by the same shell. The shadow of bereavement fell over her household as it did over millions of others. To Virginia Woolf, November 11th was a day of strange sounds and mixed images. In her diary she wrote:

> Twenty-five minutes ago the guns went off, announcing peace. A siren hooted on the river. They are hooting still. A few people ran to look out of windows. The rooks wheeled round and wore for a moment, the symbolic look of creatures performing some ceremony, partly of thanksgiving, partly of valediction over the grave. A very cloudy still day, the smoke toppling heavily towards the east; and that too wearing for a moment a look of something floating, waving, drooping. We looked out of the window; saw the housepainter give one look at the sky and go on with his job; the old man toddling along the street carrying a bag out of which a large loaf protruded, closely followed by his mongrel dog. So far neither bells nor flags, but the wailing of sirens and intermittent guns.

The wailing of sirens was hardly the sound of unambiguous celebration. Too many zeppelins had passed over the city for Londoners to hear sirens without thinking of the menace from above. Of course, there were crowds, parties and revelries, and the photographers captured them on film. But it is a mistake to take such photographs as a summary of reactions to the end of the war. Indeed, if you travelled a few miles away from the capital cities, into the towns and villages where most Europeans lived, where the photographers of *The War Illustrated* and other journals never reached, you would probably have encountered the same mood described by Virginia Woolf, the same tired faces, most etched with exhaustion and relief, rather than exuberance and jubilation.

THE ANGER OF DEFEAT IN GERMANY

How could it be otherwise in the defeated capitals? The Austrian and German empires had crumbled, their emperors toppled and displaced. After his forced abdication, Wilhelm II presented his sword to an astonished Dutch border guard and went into exile for the rest of his life. 'We are not shedding any tears after him', wrote the satirical Munich journal *Simplicissimus*, 'for he has not left us any to shed.'

One man with tears left to shed was Adolf Hitler. Despite having Austrian citizenship, he received permission via petition to the king of Bavaria to volunteer for a Bavarian regiment. With the 16th Reserve Infantry, known after its commander as the List Regiment, Hitler experienced his baptism of fire in the First Battle of Ypres in October 1914. He served as a courier between regimental headquarters and the front, a dangerous and solitary job. One superior remembered him as a 'quiet, rather unmilitary looking man'; others saw him as a loner and a dreamer. He was also brave, and received the honour—rare for an enlisted man—of the Iron Cross (First Class) in August 1918. By then he had gone through the worst of the final major German offensive and Allied counter-offensive. On October 13th, 1918, near Wervick in the Ypres salient, Hitler's unit was shelled with gas shells. He went blind. 'My eyes had turned to glowing coals', he wrote later. He was shipped out of the line to Pasewalk hospital in Pomerania. Hitler could barely see, and read the newspaper only with great difficulty. But the shock he felt when he learned that the Germans had lost the war was probably due more to his fanatical belief in German invincibility than to his temporary blindness.

A pastor visited the hospital and broke the news to Hitler and his fellow soldiers that the war had been lost, the emperor had abdicated and Germany was now a republic. The pastor sobbed, and suddenly, as Hitler recalled in [his book] *Mein Kampf*:

> I could stand it no longer. It became impossible for me to sit still one minute more. Again everything went black before my eyes; I tottered and groped my way back to the dormitory, threw myself on the bunk, and dug my burning head into my blanket and pillow. Since the day when I had stood at my mother's grave, I had not wept. When in my youth Fate seized me with merciless hardness, my defiance mounted. When in the long war years Death snatched so many a dear comrade and friend from out of the ranks, it would have seemed to me almost a sin to complain. And so it had all been in vain. In vain all the sacrifices and privations; in vain the hunger and thirst of months which were often endless;

in vain the hours in which, with mortal fear clutching at
our hearts, we nevertheless did our duty; and in vain
the deaths of the two million who died. Would not the
graves of all the hundreds of thousands open, the graves
of those who, with faith in the fatherland had marched
forth never to return? Would they not open and send the
silent mud- and blood-covered heroes back as spirits of
vengeance to the homeland which had cheated them
with such mockery of the highest sacrifice which a man
can make to his people in this world? Had they died for
this? . . . Was this the meaning of the sacrifice which the
German mother made to the fatherland when, with sore
heart, she let her best-loved boys march off, never to see
them again?

Hitler described how, there and then, he resolved to dedicate
his life to reversing this terrible debacle, to speaking for the men
who had died at the front, and avenging their suffering and
their deaths:

The shame of indignation and the disgrace of defeat
burned my brow. . . . In these nights, hatred grew in me,
hatred for those responsible for this deed. . . .

'I, for my part,' he concluded, 'decided to go into politics'.

A Lost Generation of Nine Million Men

Whether or not his vocation to punish the November criminals
arose, Luther-like, in this fit in the hospital, it is clear that Hitler's
November 11th, like that of so many others, was saturated with
the stench of the dead and the carnage of the war. At this moment, when the guns were silenced, the major conundrum of the
inter-war years appeared. It was formulated in many ways and
with many delays, but its central theme was clear: The Lost Generation was everywhere. Virtually every household had lost
someone in the war. What could possibly justify the slaughter?

One justification was the creation of a lasting peace, based on
the idea of the League of Nations that Leonard Woolf had helped
to promulgate. But by the time Woodrow Wilson had crossed the
Atlantic to join [British prime minister] Lloyd George, [French
prime minister] Clemenceau and Orlando in hammering out the
peace treaty, the League of Nations was already obscured by
older notions of imperial aggrandisement and national interest.
If the Lost Generation had died for a new world order, then it
was clear soon enough that they had died in vain. Another justification, the Allies maintained, was that aggression had been
punished and militarism, humbled. But, it was hard to see the

eclipse of militarism with Winston Churchill pressing a reluctant Woodrow Wilson and others to sponsor armed intervention in Russia to stem the tide of Bolshevism. Meanwhile there was little sign of aggression being suppressed in India, where, only a few months after Indians had joined their British comrades in celebrating the Armistice, General Dyer presided over a massacre of protestors in Amritsar.

Finally, there was the claim that Germany would no longer menace the peace of the world. The peace treaty reduced the maximum manpower of the German army by 80 per cent, curtailed the navy and the air force, and put a heavy toll on German economic recovery through reparations. True enough; this was the aim, but it was hopelessly misconceived. It could never work, for the same reason that intervention in Russia failed, and that the celebrations of the armistice were so sombre. The men and women who had gone through the war had simply had enough. They had been through one crusade and would be damned before going through another. The victors were too tired to enforce their peace on Germany. Germany was too tired to radically transform her institutions and to contribute, therefore, to a true rebuilding of Europe. And so the old ways returned. National interest and imperial defence on one side of the Rhine; half-hearted republican reconstruction on the other.

When viewed from a distance of eighty years, it is apparent that November 11th, 1918, changed very little. The war had been fought for many reasons, but at its core was a struggle between Britain and Germany for domination of north-west Europe. The Allied victory seemed to decide that contest in Britain's favour. But Britain's triumph was an illusion, a pyrrhic victory, if ever there was one. Impoverished by the effort to win, Britain could not fashion a stable peace. The 'German problem' was not solved. The Great War had simply produced great hatreds and determination on the German side to see the dead avenged. . . .

This is why the images of loss, depression and gloom tied to Apollinaire's surrealistic funeral in Paris and Virginia Woolf's musings in London are not so remote from Hitler's reflections on the day the war ended. They all reflect a very different November 11th to that evoked in newsreels, photographs and in the various political myths that still prevail today. To those who lived through those years, the day the war ended was a day with a bitter taste, a taste as of ashes, the ashes of a Lost Generation of nine million men.

1919–1929: From Boom to Bust

─────┤ CHAPTER 2 ├─────

THE WORST INFLUENZA EPIDEMIC IN HISTORY

BARBARA YOST

In 1918 millions of people died not as a result of the world war that had enveloped the world but as a result of the flu. In the selection that follows, *Arizona Republic* feature writer Barbara Yost describes what happened in the state of Arizona when the flu arrived there. According to Yost, public health officials were not too concerned at first because they did not expect Arizona to be hard hit. She explains that there were two waves of flu, the first much more deadly and of longer duration than the second. Official concern grew, writes Yost, as an increasing number of Arizona residents fell victim to influenza. She describes how one Arizona city after another shut down. People, writes Yost, were warned to stay away from crowds, not to encourage visits from out-of-towners, to avoid all intimate contact, and to wear face masks or risk a fine.

F lu now strikes the world every winter, and this year's strain seems especially brutal. But while today's victims cough, sneeze, ache, run fevers and are generally miserable, few die of the illness. This wasn't true in 1918, when the worst influenza epidemic in history killed 20 million people. The first victims were reported in San Sebastian, Spain, and so the epidemic was dubbed the Spanish Flu, much to the dismay of the people of Spain. In 1918, while American soldiers battled Germany's Kaiser Wilhelm II overseas, Americans at home were battling an even deadlier enemy.

Reprinted, with permission, from "1918–1919 Flu: Scrapbook of a Deadly Plague," by Barbara Yost, *Arizona Republic*, January 30, 2000.

In 19 months, World War I took the lives of 116,500 GIs. In one year, the influenza pandemic killed 500,000 Americans and at least 20 million people worldwide—more than any other plague, war or famine in so short a time.

In the close quarters of military camps, flu hit soldiers especially hard, and they brought it home. The disease felled rich and poor, young and old, killing 2.5 percent of its victims, more than twice the proportion in an ordinary flu season.

By the time the scourge had passed early in 1919, America had lost not only half a million of its citizens but also much of the optimism brought by turn-of-the-century prosperity. On Nov. 11, victory over the "Huns" was celebrated, but it was tarnished by the tragedy on the home front.

HIGHER HOPES FOR PHOENIX

As the summer of 1918 waned and state after state fell victim to influenza, Phoenix hoped to escape the coming plague.

With the Valley's temperate climate and the custom of sleeping in fresh air with windows open, public health officials predicted the state could expect only a light case.

Instead, Phoenix was one of the few large urban centers to suffer two waves of influenza.

Between September 1918 and February 1919, Arizona's capital lost 10 percent of its 28,000 population. Despite vaccinations, the closing of public venues and ordinances requiring citizens to wear flu masks in public, influenza struck the Valley hard.

Fearful residents snorted carbolic acid, popped laxatives, refrained from kissing and shied from crowds in the name of prevention. Traffic heading into the Valley was halted at highway checkpoints. Only locals or commuters with legitimate business were admitted.

Contraband whiskey was distributed by the Maricopa County Sheriff's Office in the belief it would ease flu symptoms. Begging exceptions to local prohibition laws, health officials prescribed "intoxicating beverages" for the afflicted.

Sporting events at Phoenix Union High school were suspended. The proposed Phoenix Symphony delayed formation.

Less hard hit, Tucson smugly suggested the state Legislature convene there instead of Phoenix and taunted its northern neighbor with the notion of moving the capital south.

Phoenix was not amused.

VALLEY RESIDENT REMEMBERS

Ignacio Soto was 7 years old when the flu epidemic struck the Valley. His Tempe pioneer family lived near what is now

Guadalupe and Alma School roads.

Soto, now 89, remembers "a lot of people dying," though his own family was spared. He remembers hearing talk of friends falling ill and his parents attending wake after wake. Sometimes, the little boy would go along as visitors said the rosary, prayed for the dead and came home to wait for the next death.

With no mortuary in the area and no hearses in service, families in Soto's community had to care for their own dead, he says, and transport them to a cemetery near the buttes.

His best friend then was Marcelo Urbano, whose family lived in a nearby adobe house with 300 chickens and four pigs.

Urbano was 5 in 1918, but he, too, has vivid memories of the epidemic. The public was told not to share belongings, to wash hands frequently or wear gloves and to perform deep breathing exercises.

"It was supposed to open up your lungs," says Urbano, 87, who moved to California in 1932 and now lives in a Saratoga retirement community.

"All the hospitals were full," he recalls. "It started with local hospitals, and then they had to build."

At first, St. Joseph's Hospital and the Arizona Deaconesses Hospital, precursor to Good Samaritan, handled most of the flu cases. When their rooms and hallways were full, the Phoenix Women's Club converted its facility into accommodations for 50 patients. Mesa turned Franklin School into an emergency hospital.

In Tucson, the University of Arizona's gymnasium became a makeshift clinic for flu-stricken students. UA suspended classes, and San Xavier del Bac mission closed to tourists.

Miners in Bisbee fell ill. Mexicans and Indians living in crowded, impoverished conditions were decimated. Victims in Flagstaff were transported to lower elevations in hopes of recovery.

Arizona prepared for a siege.

THE FIRST WAVE

The first wave arrived with a September 25 report in *The Arizona Republican*: SPANISH INFLUENZA SYMPTOMS FOUND IN PHOENIX BY DOCTOR.

Those symptoms, according to state Superintendent of Public Health Orville Henry Brown, included fever, chills and a "running" nose.

His advice:

- Drink 12 glasses of water a day.
- Do not allow business cares, war work or family responsibilities to "weigh too tiresomely upon the mind."

- Eat wisely. The underweight should add more fats and carbohydrates to their diet.
- Bathe regularly.
- Evacuate the bowels every 24 hours.
- At first sign of disease, go to bed and "get to the best physician you can afford."

Brown feared visitors from back East would bring the flu into Arizona.

He suggested that when eastern friends arrived, residents "have them send their clothing to be sunned and pressed, and that they pay particular attention to the cleansing of the noses and throats, as it is quite possible that they might be carriers."

One of the first victims in the Valley was Miss Gladys Buyers, "an attractive Chicago girl who was a great social favorite here." Miss Byers, frequent guest of Mr. and Mrs. Donald Dunbar, died October 4.

Bisbee reported seven cases of la grippe, three showing flu symptoms.

In Douglas, soldiers were forbidden to enter theaters, pool halls and other public meeting places.

Jerome announced the closing of schools, theaters, churches and "general suppression of public meetings."

In Flagstaff, the Red Cross closed its sewing room and canceled a flag-raising. Northern Arizona Normal School, now Northern Arizona University, was placed under quarantine.

On October 6, the Maricopa County Medical Society recommended the closing of all public and private schools, churches, theaters and pool halls, and that public gatherings be discontinued during "the present epidemic of influenza."

Two days later, the Glendale Board of Health followed suit.

The Rainbow Theater enjoyed a final performance by entertainer George Cox as the curtain came down on frivolity.

On October 9, Tucson closed its public facilities.

City by city, the state was shutting down.

THE PEOPLE RESPOND

People did their best to ward off influenza, as new principles of contagion were applied. The germ theory of infection was just a few decades old.

In 1918, flu remedies included vaccinations, gargling with hot saltwater and the wearing of "pneumonia jackets."

The Sun Drug Company in Phoenix recommended a flu-prevention spray "75 times as effective as Carbolic Acid; 100 times as effective as Formaldehyde; 3,300 times as effective as Hydrogen Peroxide."

Central Pharmacy of Phoenix touted a laxative called NR with the motto, "NR TO-NIGHT, Tomorrow alright." The tablets were said to keep "your organs of digestion and elimination active and your system free from poisonous accumulations."

The homes of flu victims were "placarded" to warn away visitors. City streets, public venues and drinking fountains were ordered scrubbed clean.

In Glendale, public eating houses were advised to sterilize knives, forks, spoons and other utensils.

Stay away from crowds, U.S. Surgeon General Rupert Blue warned, surmising that influenza "probably spreads mostly by inhaling some of the tiny droplets of germ-laden mucus sprayed into the air when ignorant or careless persons sneeze or cough without using a handkerchief" and through the "filthy habit of spitting on sidewalks, street cars and other public places."

In November came the most disturbing warning of all. "KISSING IS BARRED," a Phoenix headline screamed, and even married couples were told to avoid intimate contact. . . .

1918 MILESTONES

The year 1918 was historically significant for America in many respects.

In February, women's suffrage was again beaten in the U.S. Senate, and the 19th Amendment would struggle for ratification until 1920. Arizona, however, had granted women the right to vote when it became a state in 1912.

U.S. President Woodrow Wilson was working out a charter for the League of Nations, an international body created to prevent future wars.

"Champion of the World" boxer Jess Willard was set to fight Jack Dempsey.

Automobiles were selling like hot cakes—the Pierce-Arrow, the Hupmobile, the Kissel Kar.

In Arizona, Governor George W.P. Hunt knitted a sweater for a G.I. serving in the war.

A Southern Pacific railroad porter was arrested in Phoenix for selling a pint of whiskey to a passenger said to be suffering from the flu. The husband and father of two was fine $200 and spent a day in jail.

Ralph Walton, a 12-year-old Phoenix boy whose father was dead and whose mother was crippled with rheumatism, became bored when flu closed his school. Seeking adventure, young Walton burglarized a home and lumber yard.

He told arresting officers that "cheap, wild and woolly novers" had proved his undoing.

MASKS FOR EVERYONE

In late November, health officials around the state took another step to stem the tide of influenza. When morning dawned November 27, residents of Phoenix were walking the streets with faces covered in homemade flu masks.

Thanksgiving was only a day away.

Hoping to curb the spread of germs, city fathers across the Valley ordered their people to wear masks in public or risk fines up to $100. Health officials suggested making them from layers of gauze or folding a handkerchief diagonally "to be worn like a highwayman's mask."

Most residents complied, though some rigged bizarre contraptions, from muzzlelike baling wire to dangling jelly jars.

San Diego came up with a poem:

Obey the laws
And wear the gauze.
Protect your jaws—
From Septic Paws.

In Phoenix, the ditty went like this:

Owing to the cussed "flu,"
If you want to know who's who,
You will have to ask
"What is that behind the mask?"

Red Cross volunteers in Tucson worked tirelessly to keep up with demand for masks, but the city rankled at the ordinance. Plainclothes police officers walked the streets to spot the noncompliant before violators could spot them and quickly cover up.

A fruit stand operator was cited for covering his mouth but not his nose.

A window washer was arrested after removing his mask to blow on window panes for drying purposes.

Smokers were stymied as to how they could puff while wearing a mask.

Only days before Christmas, most cities rescinded the edict, though masks were still required in sick rooms.

The plague seemed to be waning. And then the second wave struck.

THE SECOND WAVE

On January 1, 1919, a second bout of influenza hit Phoenix with 101 new cases. Once again, health officials banned public and private gatherings, closed schools and quarantined the homes of flu victims.

When the owners of the Strand and Columbia theaters defied the order and tried to reopen their doors, they were arrested, convicted and fined.

But though the city relapsed, probably because of the too-hasty lifting of quarantines, the second incursion was less severe and of shorter duration. By February, reports of new cases had tapered off, and life in the Valley and in America began to return to normal.

The war was over and a new year had begun. Post-war optimism spread across the nation. As the decde ended, the Twenties were ready to roar. Women would win the right to vote. The League of Nations promised world peace.

Nothing could stop the United States of America—until 1929, when the stock market crashed and the country faced a new crisis.

Now it was the Great Depression infecting America, and it seemed every bit as deadly as the plague of influenza.

But there was no immunization against poverty. And this plague would last until the next world war.

THE WORLD IN 1920

MARK SULLIVAN

In the mid-1930s, American journalist Mark Sullivan published a six-volume history of the United States, *Our Times: The United States 1900–1925*. In this selection from volume 6 of his work, Sullivan describes a shell-shocked post-World War I world. According to Sullivan, a return to prewar normalcy, which was what most people craved, did not happen. He argues that the largest single cause of the world's confusion was a lack of equilibrium. The war cost Britain its status as the most powerful nation in the world, and the United States, which had emerged from the war as the richest and most powerful nation, had not stepped in and taken Britain's place. According to Sullivan, other factors also contributed to the postwar state of chaos, including a rupture in the trade routes that had bound the world together and some nations' inability to repay the huge amounts of money they had borrowed to finance the war.

O f all the nostalgic longing for the past that man has experienced since theology first taught him to look back toward Eden, hardly any was greater than the homesickness with which much of the world of 1920 looked back toward the world of 1914, in vain. . . .

A DISJOINTED WORLD

Hardly even was Shakespeare's phrase enough, "the time is out of joint." The world was, if we must use this kind of analogy, half-blind, half-deaf, and chronically dazed. . . .

To say, as cartoonists did, that the world walked on crutches, with its arm in a sling, and that it had besides several dislocated ribs and a fractured skull—all that would be a mild portrayal of

From *Our Times: The United States, 1900–1925*, vol. 6, by Mark Sullivan (New York: Scribner, 1935). Reprinted by permission of The Gale Group.

the degree of temporary decrepitude in which the war left the world. We should add, that it was shell-shocked besides; that term, as an item in a description of the post-war world, would be no figure of speech, it would be literal, the condition was patent.

Even that was not the whole of it. "Wounds" may be a convenient expedient with which to describe what had happened to the world. But to imply that the world was merely suffering from injuries, which could be restored, would be to mislead, seriously. Some were wounds, curable by the beneficent processes of nature or by the intelligence of man. . . . But some of what had occurred was fundamental alteration, from which we would never go back. . . .

Lack of equilibrium was the largest single cause of the world's confusion. . . .

It is not enough to say merely that the world had endured the greatest war of all time. . . . We must identify the respects in which the world had changed, at least the more important of them.

A WORLD OUT OF BALANCE

Of all the changes there was one that went deepest, and included many of the others. Preceding the Great War, the world had had a status, an equilibrium. Fundamental in that status—and fundamental in the status of the world during almost every period—was the existence of one nation more powerful than any of the others. For more than a century this position had been occupied by Britain, latest in a long and colorful line of dominating nations. . . .

The rôle of a dominating nation includes giving stability to the status quo; the status quo may be desirable or not, relative to past periods or succeeding ones; whatever the status quo is, the mere fact of the existence of one dominating nation tends to give it balance, and preserve it.

Britain had filled the rôle in a larger variety of ways than most of its predecessors. For upward of a hundred years Britain, to an increasing degree, had provided the world with most of its fabric of international trade; had supplied the unit of currency, the pound or the gold sovereign, in which most international transactions were carried on; had been the richest nation and the greatest lending nation, source and storehouse of most of the accumulated capital with which development of the world was carried on; had possessed the largest number of mercantile ships, and accompanying them, the most powerful navy; had kept order in many parts of the world; had been the source of international law, and the final authority under it—at all times, international law, in practice, consists of such concessions of power to enlightenment as the nation having the most powerful navy is willing to make. Britain had been the source of most of the ideas that the rest of the world was increasingly accepting—the English language and the Anglo-Saxon conception of jurisprudence were constantly spreading; spreading also was the British conception of government, maximum of liberty for the individual, minimum of power of government over the individual. In sum, Britain, measured by power of arms, power of wealth and power of ideas, was the center about which the world, in most respects, revolved.

This position, Germany envied. Germany called it the "place in the sun," coveted it and tried to take it. She had not succeeded, but she had weakened Britain seriously. In 1920 . . . it was uncertain whether there was any one leading nation. To that lack was due much of the chaos that the world suffered. . . .

In the course of nature, America should have stepped into Britain's vacated dominance. We emerged from the war by far the world's richest and most powerful nation. By analogy to what had happened in past eras, we should have become the most important mercantile nation, become the greatest lender, put the dollar in the place of the pound in international trade, built the largest navy, and accepted the rôle that fate thrust toward us. But America did not care for the power, or did not know how to use it; she did not take the responsibility.

For a time, the world considered a proposal that no longer should there be any dominant nation, no longer should the world be organized on a basis of, so to speak, national individualism; that instead we should have a federated world, a League of Nations. That, too, America rejected.

The result was two fundamental, world-embracing uncertainties. We did not know whether the world was to go forward on the basis of federation, or on the old basis of national individualism. And if the latter, we did not know which was the dominating nation, did not indeed know if there was to be a dominating nation. . . .

Out of this condition, more than any other, arose the confusion, and the apprehensions of worse, that bedeviled the world in 1920 and for at least fifteen years following.

NEW CONCEPTS OF GOVERNMENT

Associated with this cause of insecurity was another. There had come into the world a new conception of society and government. In Russia, some aggressive exponents of new thought about society, taking advantage of chaos arising out of collapse of the old régime, imposed on that country a conception of government that not only was novel but ran counter to every pattern

of society the world had ever experienced. The new ideal of society denied most of the things which governments are founded to secure. . . .

Additional causes, or details, of the confusion that beset the world in 1920 included:

Every great trade-route in the world had been interrupted; many completely paralyzed. Some would never recover, at least not within any foreseeable future. . . . It was as if the whole web of international trade, patiently woven through centuries, composed of sea-lanes intricately criss-crossing, had sunk beneath the water, and must be re-woven. By another figure of speech, these trade-routes were the links which bound the world together, and now many of them had been broken.

The currencies of the principal nations of the world were either in process of devaluation or were destined to be devalued. . . . Among other effects, these changes in the values of currencies, taking place in differing ratios in different countries, made international commerce difficult, accentuated the disruption of trade-routes.

The wealth of the world had been destroyed to a degree almost immeasurable. . . . Much tangible wealth had been ruined, and that part of wealth which consisted of goods in motion, goods in transit and in process—civilization as a "going concern"—had been ruined to an even greater extent.

Every great nation had borrowed enormous amounts. . . . The borrowings were beyond any possible capacity of the borrowers to repay.

ALTERED CONDITIONS PREVAIL

Three great nations [Russia, Germany, Austria], and some smaller ones, had passed through revolutions in their forms of government.

One great nation, Austria-Hungary, had been disrupted. Parts of it had been set up as political entities which did not have the economic basis to make their political autonomy possible.

Elsewhere throughout Europe, new nations, and new autonomies and hegemonies, had been set up, with new economic structures which, in many cases, had not the basis to endure. The number of separate nations in Europe when the World War began was 17; at the end the number was 26.

A wholly new conception of government had secured a foothold in the world, Communism in Russia. And the condition was such that yet another new conception, Fascism, was destined to emerge in Italy, to be followed, after ten years, by Nazism in Germany.

In all the leading nations, ancient moral concepts had been shattered. . . . Everywhere the tendency was for the state standards of morals to supplant the individual ones.

By the years of war-strain, the peoples of every great nation (especially the European ones) had been made spiritually and intellectually abnormal. (I use the word "abnormal" as meaning different from what had been, under previous conditions, normal.) The effect of the strain was greatest on growing children; consequently it would affect the peoples for many years to come. . . .

The altered conditions came not only as a direct consequence of the war. After the war had come the peace treaty, as after death comes judgment. The peace treaty had sought to put a strait jacket on the changed world, had sought to "freeze" it as it was, and had thereby made impossible whatever might have been the healing courses that nature would have taken. The peace treaty had fixed national boundaries that did not conform to nature; had imposed on the principal loser in the war, Germany, reparations she could not possibly pay, and had forbidden the exchanges of goods with which any large degree of payment could be made.

Using the hypothetical reparations as a base, the victorious nations fixed, among themselves, intergovernment obligations which must be defaulted so soon as Germany should default.

A Different America

Some of the changes were peculiar to America. We were affected, of course, by the universal changes, more affected than we were intelligent enough to see, or flexible enough to admit. But some of the changes had greater application to us than others, and some were local to us. . . .

Our economic structure had been seriously warped (though for the time being made seemingly more powerful). . . .

America had ceased to be a debtor nation and become a creditor one, had paid off some three billions which before the war it had owed to Europe, and assumed a creditor relation in which Europe owed America some ten billions. That reversal of position rendered it necessary that other changes, far-reaching ones, should be made in our relations with the world, and in our domestic economy, changes which required reversals in many of our ways of thinking about trade. The reversals of thought, it turned out, were difficult to make, and were not made soon enough.

Every male in America between 18 and 45 had been registered for the army; some four millions had actually been taken into military camps and nearly half sent abroad. The psychological effect of this experience varied, of course, with the temperaments of the

men. Large numbers who previously had accepted and practised
. . . the American ideal of self-help and reliance upon individual
initiative, had learned, through their army experience, to prefer a
status in which decision is made for them, their routine prescribed
for them, their needs provided for; they had learned to like im-
munity from responsibility, to prefer regimentation.

The war had accelerated the economic and social ferment that
is always at work in America; had wrought a change in the status
of large numbers of persons, whole groups and classes of them.
There was a "new rich" side by side with a "new poor.". . .

I have been speaking of changes that had accompanied the
Great War, changes that had occurred during some seven years
preceding 1921. These were accentuated and made more difficult
to meet by another group of changes. The latter group were the
advanced stages of developments that had been under way, with
cumulative force, for decades preceding. . . .

These innovations in the material world had many effects. The
one appropriate to point out here is the increased rapidity of
communication as respects both goods and ideas. The world had
been made smaller, peoples and nations brought closer together.
A result, one of the many important ones, was that dislocation at
any point would more quickly and more surely bring repercus-
sions elsewhere. . . . The area of what could be called purely domestic affairs was narrowed; domestic affairs and foreign relations tended almost to merge with each other.

THE NEW FEMINISM

BRUCE BLIVEN

The 1920s was the era of the flapper, "modern" young women who rebelled by refusing to conform to the accepted female behavior of the time. They cut their hair short, used makeup, and raised their hemlines to expose their knees. In the following selection that appeared in 1925 in the *New Republic,* journalist, author, and editor Bruce Bliven introduces a nineteen-year-old who epitomizes the flapper—and is proud of it. Bliven describes her appearance and her clothes, which he contends are "the style" that summer for women of all ages. Bliven argues that she and other youths like her are not really as wild as their elders think they are. In his view, the flapper is a symbol of the new feminism; she symbolizes the new assertive woman who considers herself as good as any man and is no longer content to play a subservient role.

J ane's a flapper. That is a quaint, old-fashioned term, but I hope you remember its meaning. . . . This Jane, being 19, is a flapper, though she urgently denies that she is a member of the younger generation. The younger generation, she will tell you, is aged 15 to 17; and she professes to be decidedly shocked at the things they do and say. That is a fact which would interest her minister, if he knew it—poor man, he knows so little! For he regards Jane as a perfectly horrible example of wild youth—paint, cigarettes, cocktails, petting parties—oooh! Yet if the younger generation shocks her as she says, query: how wild is Jane?

CLOTHES—AND MAKEUP—MAKE THE WOMAN

Before we come to this exciting question, let us take a look at the young person as she strolls across the lawn of her parents' sub-

From "Flapper Jane," by Bruce Bliven, *The New Republic*, September 9, 1925.

urban home, having just put the car away after driving sixty miles in two hours. She is, for one thing, a very pretty girl. Beauty is the fashion in 1925. She is frankly, heavily made up, not to imitate nature, but for an altogether artificial effect—pallor mortis, poisonously scarlet lips, richly ringed eyes—the latter looking not so much debauched (which is the intention) as diabetic. Her walk duplicates the swagger supposed by innocent America to go with the female half of a Paris Apache dance. And there are, finally, her clothes.

These were estimated the other day by some statistician to weigh two pounds. Probably a libel; I doubt they come within half a pound of such bulk. Jane isn't wearing much, this summer. If you'd like to know exactly, it is: one dress, one step-in, two stockings, two shoes.

A step-in . . . is underwear—one piece, light, exceedingly brief but roomy. Her dress, as you can't possibly help knowing if you have even one good eye, and get around at all outside the Old People's Home, is also brief. It is cut low where it might be high, and vice versa. The skirt comes just an inch below her knees, overlapping by a faint fraction her rolled and twisted stockings. The idea is that when she walks in a bit of a breeze, you shall now and then observe the knee (which is not rouged—that's just newspaper talk) but always in an accidental, Venus-surprised-at-the-bath sort of way. This is a bit of coyness which hardly fits in with Jane's general character.

Jane's haircut is also abbreviated. She wears of course the very newest thing in bobs, even closer than last year's shingle. It leaves her just about no hair at all in the back, and 20 percent more than that in the front—about as much as is being worn this season by a cellist (male); less than a pianist; and much, much less than a violinist. Because of this new style, one can confirm a rumor heard last year: Jane has ears.

The corset is as dead as the dodo's grandfather; no feeble publicity pipings by the manufacturers, or calling it a "clasp around" will enable it, as Jane says, to "do a Lazarus." The petticoat is even more defunct. Not even a snicker can be raised by telling Jane that once the nation was shattered to its foundations by the shadow-skirt. The brassiere has been abandoned, since 1924. While stockings are usually worn, they are not a sine-qua-nothing-doing. In hot weather Jane reserves the right to discard them, just as all the chorus girls did in 1923. As stockings are only a frantic, successful attempt to duplicate the color and texture of Jane's own sunburned slim legs, few but expert boulevardiers can tell the difference.

These which I have described are Jane's clothes, but they are not merely a flapper uniform. They are The Style, Summer of 1925 Eastern Seaboard. These things and none other are being worn by all of Jane's sisters and her cousins and her aunts. They are being worn by ladies who are three times Jane's age, and look ten years older; by those twice her age who look a hundred years older. Their use is so universal that in our larger cities the baggage transfer companies one and all declare they are being forced into bankruptcy. Ladies who used to go away for the summer with six trunks can now pack twenty dainty costumes in a bag.

Not since 1820 has feminine apparel been so frankly abbreviated as at present; and never, on this side of the Atlantic, until you go back to the little summer frocks of Pocahontas. This year's styles have gone quite a long step toward genuine nudity. Nor is this merely the sensible half of the population dressing as everyone ought to, in hot weather. Last winter's styles weren't so dissimilar, except that they were covered up by fur coats and you got the full effect only indoors. And improper costumes never have their full force unless worn on the street. Next year's styles, from all one hears, will be, as they already are on the continent [Europe], even More So.

Our great mentor has failed us: you will see none of the really up-to-date styles in the movies. . . . Under vigilant father Hays the ensilvered screen daren't reveal a costume equal to scores on Fifth Avenue, Broadway—or Wall Street.

Wall Street, by the way, is the one spot in which the New Nakedness seems most appropriate.

Where men's simple passions have the lowest boiling point; where the lust for possession is most frankly, brazenly revealed and indeed dominates the whole diurnal round—in such a place there is a high appropriateness in the fact that the priestesses in the temple of Mammon, though their service be no more than file clerk or stenographer, should be thus Dionysiac in apparelling themselves for their daily tasks.

Where will it all end? do you ask, thumbing the page ahead in an effort to know the worst. Apologetically I reply that no one can say where it will end. . . .

FASHIONS AND MORALS: MIRROR IMAGES?

Few any more are so naive as not to realize that there are fashions in morals and that these have a limitless capacity for modification. Costume, of course, is A Moral. . . .

At this point Billy Sunday, discussing this theme, would certainly drop into anecdotage. Were we to do the same, we might see Jane on the sun porch talking to a mixed group of her mother's week-end guests. "Jane," says one, "I hear you cut yourself in bathing."

"I'll say I did," comes crisply back. "Look!" She lifts her skirt three or four inches, revealing both brown knees, and above one of them a half-healed deep scratch. Proper murmurs of sympathy. From one quarter a chilly silence which draws our attention to the enpurpled countenance of a lady guest in the throes of what Eddie Cantor calls "the sex complex." Jane's knees have thrown her all a-twitter; and mistaking the character of her emotion she thinks it is justified indignation. She is glad to display it openly for the reproof thereby administered.

"Well, damn it," says Jane, in a subsequent private moment, "anybody who can't stand a knee or two, nowadays, might as well quit. And besides, she goes to the beaches and never turns a hair."

Here is a real point. The recent history of the Great Disrobing Movement can be checked up in another way by looking at the bathing costumes which have been accepted without question at successive intervals. There are still a few beaches near New York City which insist on more clothes than anyone can safely swim in, and thereby help to drown several young women each year. But in most places—universally in the West—a girl is now compelled to wear no more than is a man. The enpurpled one, to be consistent, ought to have apoplexy every time she goes to the shore. But as Jane observes, she doesn't.

"Jane," say I, "I am a reporter representing American inquisitiveness. Why do all of you dress the way you do?"

"I don't know," says Jane. This reply means nothing: it is just the device by which the younger generation gains time to think. Almost at once she adds:

"The old girls are doing it because youth is. Everybody wants to be young, now—though they want all us young people to be something else. Funny, isn't it?

"In a way," says Jane, "it's just honesty. Women have come down off the pedestal lately. They are tired of this mysterious-feminine-charm stuff. Maybe it goes with independence, earning your own living and voting and all that. There was always a bit of the harem in that cover-up-your-arms-and-legs business, don't you think?

"Women still want to be loved," goes on Jane, warming to her theme, "but they want it on a 50-50 basis, which includes being admired for the qualities they really possess. Dragging in this strange-allurement stuff doesn't seem sporting. It's like cheating in games, or lying."

"Ask me, did the War start all this?" says Jane helpfully.

"The answer is, how do I know ? How does anybody know?

"I read this book whaddaya-call-it by Rose Macaulay, and she showed where they'd been excited about wild youth for three generations anyhow—since 1870. I have a hunch maybe they've always been excited.

"Somebody wrote in a magazine how the War had upset the balance of the sexes in Europe and the girls over there were wearing the new styles as part of the competition for husbands. Sounds like the bunk to me. If you wanted to nail a man for life I think you'd do better to go in for the old-fashioned line: 'March' me to the altar, esteemed sir, before you learn whether I have limbs or not.'

"Of course, not so many girls are looking for a life mealticket nowadays. Lots of them prefer to earn their own living and omit the home-and-baby act. Well, anyhow, postpone it years and years. They think a bachelor girl can and should do everything a bachelor man does."

"It's funny," says Jane, "that just when women's clothes are getting scanty, men's should be going the other way. Look at the Oxford trousers!—as though a man had been caught by the ankles in a flannel quicksand."

Do the morals go with the clothes? Or the clothes with the morals? Or are they independent? These are questions I have not ventured to put to Jane, knowing that her answer would be "so's your old man." Generally speaking, however, it is safe to say that as regards the wildness of youth there is a good deal more smoke than fire. Anyhow, the new Era of Undressing, as already suggested, has spread far beyond the boundaries of Jane's group. The fashion is followed by hordes of unquestionably monogamous matrons, including many who join heartily in the general ululations as to what young people are coming to. Attempts to link the new freedom with prohibition, with the automobile, the decline of Fundamentalism, are certainly without foundation. These may be accessory, and indeed almost certainly are, but only after the fact.

THE NEW FEMINISM

That fact is, as Jane says, that women to-day are shaking off the shreds and patches of their age-old servitude. "Feminism" has won a victory so nearly complete that we have even forgotten the fierce challenge which once inhered in the very word. Women have highly resolved that they are just as good as men, and intend to be treated so. They don't mean to have any more unwanted children. They don't intend to be debarred from any profession or occupation which they choose to enter. They clearly mean (even though not all of them yet realize it) that in the great game of sexual selection they shall no longer be forced to play the role, simulated or real, of helpless quarry. If they want to wear their heads shaven, as a symbol of defiance against the former fate which for three millenia forced them to dress their heavy locks according to male decrees, they will have their way. If they should elect to go naked nothing is more certain than that naked they will go, while from the sidelines to which he has been relegated mere man is vouchsafed permission only to pipe a feeble Hurrah!

Hurrah!

THE DISCOVERY OF THE TOMB OF TUTANKHAMEN

HOWARD CARTER AND A.C. MACE

In 1922, after years of searching in Egypt's Valley of Kings, British archaeologist Howard Carter found the tomb of the Egyptian boy-king Tutankhamen. Considered by many the archaeological find of the century, the tomb yielded a treasure trove of precious artifacts. The excerpt that follows is from volume 1 of *The Tomb of Tut•Ankh•Amen Discovered by the Late Earl of Carnarvon and Howard Carter*, written in 1923 by Carter and his fellow excavator, professor Arthur Cruttenden Mace. In this selection, Carter describes his feelings as he and Mace make their way into the inner chamber where Tutankhamen had lain since his death three thousand years earlier. He recounts the painstaking steps he and his team members took to penetrate the sealed door that barred their entry to the inner chamber, and the feelings of reverence and awe that overcame them when they first viewed the treasures inside.

B y the middle of February our work in the Antechamber was finished. With the exception of the two sentinel statues, left for a special reason, all its contents had been removed to the laboratory, every inch of its floor had been swept and sifted for the last bead or fallen piece of inlay, and it now stood bare and empty. We were ready at last to penetrate the mystery of the sealed door.

Friday, the 17th, was the day appointed, and at two o'clock

From *The Tomb of Tut•Ankh•Amen Discovered by the Late Earl of Carnarvon and Howard Carter*, vol. 1, by Howard Carter and A.C. Mace (London: Cassell, 1923).

those who were to be privileged to witness the ceremony met by appointment above the tomb. . . . By a quarter past two the whole company had assembled, so we removed our coats and filed down the sloping passage into the tomb.

THE MYSTERY OF THE GOLDEN WALL REVEALED

In the Antechamber everything was prepared and ready. . . . We had screened the statues with boarding to protect them from possible damage, and between them we had erected a small platform, just high enough to enable us to reach the upper part of the doorway, having determined, as the safest plan, to work from the top downwards. A short distance back from the platform there was a barrier, and beyond, knowing that there might be hours of work ahead of us, we had provided chairs for the visitors. On either side standards had been set up for our lamps, their light shining full upon the doorway. Looking back, we realize what a strange, incongruous picture the chamber must have presented, but at the time I question whether such an idea even crossed our minds. One thought and one only was possible. There before us lay the sealed door, and with its opening we were to blot out the centuries and stand in the presence of a king who reigned three thousand years ago. My own feelings as I mounted the platform were a strange mixture, and it was with a trembling hand that I struck the first blow.

My first care was to locate the wooden lintel above the door: then very carefully I chipped away the plaster and picked out the small stones which formed the uppermost layer of the filling. The temptation to stop and peer inside at every moment was irresistible, and when, after about ten minutes' work, I had made a hole large enough to enable me to do so, I inserted an electric torch. An astonishing sight its light revealed, for there, within a yard of the doorway, stretching as far as one could see and blocking the entrance to the chamber, stood what to all appearance was a solid wall of gold. For the moment there was no clue as to its meaning, so as quickly as I dared I set to work to widen the hole. This had now become an operation of considerable difficulty, for the stones of the masonry were not accurately squared blocks built regularly upon one another, but rough slabs of varying size, some so heavy that it took all one's strength to lift them: many of them, too, as the weight above was removed, were left so precariously balanced that the least false movement would have sent them sliding inwards to crash upon the contents of the chamber below. We were also endeavouring to preserve the seal-impressions upon the thick mortar of the outer face, and this added considerably to the difficulty of handling the stones. Mace and Callender were helping me by this time, and each stone was cleared on a regular system. With a crowbar I gently eased it up, Mace holding it to prevent it falling forwards; then he and I lifted it out and passed it back to Callender, who transferred it on to one of the foremen, and so, by a chain of workmen, up the passage and out of the tomb altogether.

With the removal of a very few stones the mystery of the golden wall was solved. We were at the entrance of the actual burial-chamber of the king, and that which barred our way was the side of an immense gilt shrine built to cover and protect the sarcophagus. It was visible now from the Antechamber by the light of the standard lamps, and as stone after stone was removed, and its gilded surface came gradually into view, we could, as though by electric current, feel the tingle of excitement which thrilled the spectators behind the barrier. . . .

We who were doing the work were probably less excited, for our whole energies were taken up with the task in hand—that of removing the blocking without an accident. The fall of a single stone might have done irreparable damage to the delicate surface of the shrine, so, directly the hole was large enough, we made an additional protection for it by inserting a mattress on the inner side of the door-blocking, suspending it from the wooden lintel of the doorway. Two hours of hard work it took us to clear away the blocking, or at least as much of it as was necessary for the moment; and at one point, when near the bottom, we had to delay operations for a space while we collected the scattered beads from a necklace brought by the plunderers from the chamber within and dropped upon the threshold. This last was a terrible trial to our patience, for it was a slow business, and we were all of us excited to see what might be within; but finally it was done, the last stones were removed, and the way to the innermost chamber lay open before us.

THE SEPULCHRAL CHAMBER AT LAST

In clearing away the blocking of the doorway we had discovered that the level of the inner chamber was about four feet lower than that of the Antechamber, and this, combined with the fact that there was but a narrow space between door and shrine, made an entrance by no means easy to effect. Fortunately, there were no smaller antiquities at this end of the chamber, so I lowered myself down, and then, taking one of the portable lights, I edged cautiously to the corner of the shrine and looked beyond it. At the corner two beautiful alabaster vases blocked the way, but I could see that if these were removed we should have a clear path to the other end of the chamber; so, carefully marking the spot

on which they stood, I picked them up . . . and passed them back
to the Antechamber. Lord Carnarvon and M. Lacau now joined
me, and, picking our way along the narrow passage between
shrine and wall, paying out the wire of our light behind us, we
investigated further.

It was, beyond any question, the sepulchral chamber in which
we stood, for there, towering above us, was one of the great gilt
shrines beneath which kings were laid. So enormous was this
structure (17 feet by 11 feet, and 9 feet high, we found afterwards)
that it filled within a little the entire area of the chamber, a space
of some two feet only separating it from the walls on all four
sides, while its roof, with cornice top and torus moulding,
reached almost to the ceiling. From top to bottom it was overlaid
with gold, and upon its sides there were inlaid panels of brilliant
blue faience, in which were represented, repeated over and over,
the magic symbols which would ensure its strength and safety.
Around the shrine, resting upon the ground, there were a number of funerary emblems, and, at the north end, the seven magic
oars the king would need to ferry himself across the waters of the
underworld. The walls of the chamber, unlike those of the Antechamber, were decorated with brightly painted scenes and in-
scriptions, brilliant in their colours, but evidently somewhat
hastily executed.

These last details we must have noticed subsequently, for at
the time our one thought was of the shrine and of its safety. Had
the thieves penetrated within it and disturbed the royal burial?
Here, on the eastern end, were the great folding doors, closed
and bolted, but not sealed, that would answer the question for
us. Eagerly we drew the bolts, swung back the doors, and there
within was a second shrine with similar bolted doors, and upon
the bolts a seal, intact. This seal we determined not to break, for
our doubts were resolved, and we could not penetrate further
without risk of serious damage to the monument. I think at the
moment we did not even want to break the seal, for a feeling of
intrusion had descended heavily upon us with the opening of the
doors, heightened, probably, by the almost painful impressive-
ness of a linen pall, decorated with golden rosettes, which
drooped above the inner shrine. We felt that we were in the presence of the dead King and must do him reverence, and in imagination could see the doors of the successive shrines open one after the other till the innermost disclosed the King himself.
Carefully, and as silently as possible, we re-closed the great swing
doors, and passed on to the farther end of the chamber.

Here a surprise awaited us, for a low door, eastwards from
the sepulchral chamber, gave entrance to yet another chamber,

smaller than the outer ones and not so lofty. This doorway, unlike the others, had not been closed and sealed. We were able, from where we stood, to get a clear view of the whole of the contents, and a single glance sufficed to tell us that here, within this little chamber, lay the greatest treasures of the tomb. Facing the doorway, on the farther side, stood the most beautiful monument that I have ever seen—so lovely that it made one gasp with wonder and admiration. The central portion of it consisted of a large shrine-shaped chest, completely overlaid with gold, and surmounted by a cornice of sacred cobras. Surrounding this, freestanding, were statues of the four tutelary goddesses of the dead—gracious figures with outstretched protective arms, so natural and lifelike in their pose, so pitiful and compassionate the expression upon their faces, that one felt it almost sacrilege to look at them. One guarded the shrine on each of its four sides, but whereas the figures at front and back kept their gaze firmly fixed upon their charge, an additional note of touching realism was imparted by the other two, for their heads were turned sideways, looking over their shoulders towards the entrance, as though to watch against surprise. There is a simple grandeur about this monument that made an irresistible appeal to the imagination, and I am not ashamed to confess that it brought a lump to my throat. It is undoubtedly the Canopic chest and contains the jars which play such an important part in the ritual of mummification.

There were a number of other wonderful things in the chamber, but we found it hard to take them in at the time, so inevitably were one's eyes drawn back again and again to the lovely little goddess figures. Immediately in front of the entrance lay the figure of the jackal god Anubis, upon his shrine, swathed in linen cloth, and resting upon a portable sled, and behind this the head of a bull upon a stand—emblems, these, of the underworld. In the south side of the chamber lay an endless number of black shrines and chests, all closed and sealed save one, whose open doors revealed statues of Tut-ankh-Amen standing upon black leopards. On the farther wall were more shrine-shaped boxes and miniature coffins of gilded wood, these last undoubtedly containing funerary statuettes of the king. In the centre of the room, left of the Anubis and the bull, there was a row of magnificent caskets of ivory and wood, decorated and inlaid with gold and blue faience, one, whose lid we raised, containing a gorgeous ostrich-feather fan with ivory handle, fresh and strong to all appearance as when it left the maker's hand. There were also, distributed in different quarters of the chamber, a number of model boats with sails and rigging all complete, and, at the north side, yet another chariot.

Such, from a hurried survey, were the contents of this innermost chamber. We looked anxiously for evidence of plundering, but on the surface there was none. Unquestionably the thieves must have entered, but they cannot have done more than open two or three of the caskets. Most of the boxes, as has been said, have still their seals intact, and the whole contents of the chamber, in fortunate contrast to those of the Antechamber and the Annexe, still remain in position exactly as they were placed at the time of burial.

How much time we occupied in this first survey of the wonders of the tomb I cannot say, but it must have seemed endless to those anxiously waiting in the Antechamber. Not more than three at a time could be admitted with safety. . . . It was curious, as we stood in the Antechamber, to watch their faces as, one by one, they emerged from the door. Each had a dazed, bewildered look in his eyes, and each in turn, as he came out, threw up his hands before him, an unconscious gesture of impotence to describe in words the wonders that he had seen. They were indeed indescribable, and the emotions they had aroused in our minds were of too intimate a nature to communicate, even though we had the words at our command. It was an experience which, I am sure, none of us who were present is ever likely to forget, for in imagination—and not wholly in imagination either—we had been present at the funeral ceremonies of a king long dead and almost forgotten. At a quarter past two we had filed down into the tomb, and when, three hours later, hot, dusty, and dishevelled, we came out once more into the light of day, the very Valley seemed to have changed for us and taken on a more personal aspect. We had been given the Freedom.

THE TRIUMPH OF MUSSOLINI AND THE FASCISTS

BENITO MUSSOLINI

In 1922, Fascist leader Benito Mussolini sent his black-shirted troops to march on Rome to take over the government and create a new Fascist Italy. The action was a prelude to the end of Italy's parliamentary government in 1928 and its reorganization as a Fascist corporative state. In this selection from his 1928 autobiography, Mussolini describes his role in preparing for the march on Rome and affirms his intention to bring order—and fascism—to Italy and restore the nation's former strength and glory. He explains how he reacted to requests to compromise and to Italian king Victor Emmanuel III's request that he take charge of forming a new Italian ministry. In Mussolini's opinion, he was respected, even revered, for his actions, for his leadership, and for bringing through fascism "the dawn of new history for Italy and perhaps dawn on a new path of civilization."

I have always had a vision of life which was altruistic. I have groped in the dark of theories, but I groped not to relieve myself, but to bring something to others. I have fought, but not for my advantage, indirect or immediate. I have aimed for the supreme advantages of my nation. I desired finally that Fascism should rule Italy for her glory and her good fortune. . . .

The *Popolo d'Italia*, my paper, without attracting too much attention from outsiders and from my enemies, had become the

From *My Autobiography*, by Benito Mussolini (New York: Scribner, 1928).

headquarters of the spiritual and material preparation for the March on Rome. . . .

I assembled the Central Committee of the Fasci Italiani di Combattimento—the Bundles of Fight—and we came to an accord on the outlines of the movement, which was to lead the black shirts triumphantly along the sacred roads to Rome. . . .

MUSSOLINI PREPARES

And now we were on the eve of the historic march on the Eternal City.

Having completed my survey and estimate of conditions in the provinces, having listened to the reports of the various chiefs of the black-shirts, having selected the plans of action and having determined in a general way upon the most favorable moment, I called together in Florence the chiefs of the Fascist movement and of the squads of action. . . .

It was necessary to give our movement the full advantage of opportunity and to make it spark and detonate. It was necessary to weigh, besides the military aspects, the political effects and values. We had to consider, finally, the painful possibility of a violent suppression, or a failure spreading from some slip to all of our plans. We were obliged to determine beforehand all the hows and whens, the details of the means, with what men and with what aims the Fascist assault could most wisely be launched.

The Fascist meeting in Naples . . . served to hide the beginnings of the real mobilization. At a fixed moment the squads of action of all Italy were to be in arms. They would have to occupy the vital nerve centres—the cities, and the post offices, the prefectures, police headquarters, railroad stations, and military barracks. . . .

We selected as general concentration headquarters the town of Perugia, capital of Umbria, where many roads flow to a centre and from which it is easy to reach Rome. . . . We selected the watchword; we fixed the details of the action. Everything had to be reported to me. . . . Trusted Fascist messengers wove webs like scurrying spiders. . . .

A PROCLAMATION OF REVOLUTION

When I knew that everything was ready, I issued from Milan . . . my proclamation of revolution. It had been signed by the quadrumvirate. Here is the text of the memorable document:

"Fascisti! Italians!

"The time for determined battle has come! Four years ago at this season the national army loosed the final offensive which brought it to Victory. To-day the army of the black shirts again takes possession of that Victory, which has been mutilated, and, going directly to Rome, brings Victory again to the glory of that Capitol. From now on 'principi' and 'triari' are mobilized. The martial law of Fascism now becomes a fact. By order of the Duce [Mussolini] all the military, political and administrative functions of the party management are taken over by a secret Quadrumvirate of Action with dictatorial powers.

"The army, the reserve and safeguard of the Nation, must not take part in this struggle. . . . Fascism . . . does not march against the police, but against a political class both cowardly and imbecile, which in four long years has not been able to give a Government to the Nation. Those who form the productive class must know that Fascism wants to impose nothing more than order and discipline upon the Nation and to help to raise the strength which will renew progress and prosperity. The people who work in the fields and in the factories, those who work in the railroads or in offices, have nothing to fear from the Fascist Government. Their just rights will be protected. We will even be generous with unarmed adversaries.

"Fascism draws its sword to cut the multiple Gordian knots which tie and burden Italian life. . . . Only one impulse sends us on, . . . only one passion burns within us—the impulse and the passion to contribute to the safety and greatness of our Country. . . .

I had composed my proclamation in a very short and resounding form; it had impressed the whole of the Italian people. . . .

MUSSOLINI REMAINS FIRM

I put on the black shirt. I barricaded the *Popolo d'Italia*. In the livid and gray morning Milan had a new and fantastic appearance. . . .

Frowning battalions of Royal Guards scouted the city and the monotonous rhythm of their feet sounded ominous echoes in the almost deserted streets.

The public services functioned on a reduced and meagre scale. The assaults of the Fascisti against the barracks and on the post offices were cause for fusillades of shots, which gave to the city a sinister echo of civil war.

I had provided the offices of my newspaper with everything needful for defense against attack. I knew that if the government authorities desired to give a proof of their strength they would have directed their first violent assault at the *Popolo d'Italia*. In fact, in the early hours of the morning, I saw trained upon the offices and upon me the ugly muzzles of the mitrailleuses. There was a rapid exchange of shots. . . .

A major of the Royal Guard finally asked for a truce in order to talk with me. After a brief initial conversation, we agreed that the Royal Guard should withdraw. . . .

At night a group of deputies, senators, and political men . . . came to the offices of the *Popolo d'Italia* to ask me to desist from a struggle which they asserted would be the beginning of a violent, grave and reprehensible civil war. They proposed to me a sort of armistice and a truce with the central government. Perhaps a ministerial crisis might save, they said, the situation and the country.

I smiled back at the parliamentarians because of their innocence. I answered them in words like these:

"Dear sirs, there is not the slightest question of any partial or total crisis or of substitution of one ministry for another. The game I have undertaken has a wider and more serious character. For three years we have lived in a caldron boiling with small battles and devastations. This time I will not lay down weapons until a full victory is concluded. It is time to change the direction not only of the government, but also of the whole of Italian life." . . .

Adolf Hitler (left) and Benito Mussolini stand together on a balcony in Venice, Italy. Mussolini took over Italy's parliamentary government to create a Fascist regime.

A SUMMONS FROM THE KING

The struggle continued with the objectives I had mapped out. . . . The Fascisti in compact files were already near the gates of Rome and were expecting me to go to the head of their military formations to march with them into the Capital.

On the afternoon of the 29th I received a very urgent telephone call from Rome on behalf of the Quirinal. General Cittadini, first aide-de-camp of His Majesty the King, asked me very kindly to go to Rome because the King, having examined the situation, wanted to charge me with forming a ministry. . . .

This was not yet victory, but the progress made was considerable. . . .

I was in a terrible state of nervous tension. Night after night I had been kept awake, giving orders, following the compact columns of the Fascisti, restricting the battle to the knightly practices of Fascism.

A period of greater responsibilities was about to begin for me; I must not fail in my duty or in my aims. I gathered all my strength to my aid, I invoked the memory of the dead, I asked the assistance of God, I called upon the faithful living to assist me in the great task that confronted me. . . .

When I had entrusted the newspaper to my brother I was off for Rome. . . .

The news of my departure sped all over Italy. In every station where the train stopped I found a gathering of the Fascisti and of the masses who wanted to bring me, even through the pouring rain, their cheers and their good-will. . . .

The train brought me into the midst of the Fascisti; I was in view of Rome at Santa Marinella. I reviewed the columns. I established the formalities for the entrance into Rome. I established connections between the quadrumvirate and the authorities. . . .

In Rome an indescribable welcome awaited me. I did not want any delay. Even before making contacts with my political friends I motored to the Quirinal. I wore a black shirt. I was introduced without formalities into the presence of His Majesty the King. . . . I obtained the Sovereign's approbation. I took up lodgings at the Savoy Hotel and began to work. First I made arrangements with the general command of the army to bring militia into Rome and to have them defile in proper formation in a review before the King. I gave detailed and precise orders. One hundred thousand black shirts paraded in perfect order before the Sovereign. They brought to him the homage of Fascist Italy!

I was then triumphant and in Rome! I killed at once all unnecessary demonstrations in my honor. I gave orders that not a single parade should take place without the permission of the General Fascist Command. It was necessary to give to everybody from the first moment a stern and rigid sense of discipline in line with the régime that I had conceived.

I discouraged every manifestation on the part of army officers who wanted to bring me their plaudits. I have always considered the army outside and above every kind of politics. The army must, in my opinion, be inspired by absolute and conscientious discipline; it must devote itself, with the deepest will, only to the defense of frontiers and of historical rights. The army is an institution which must be preserved inviolate. It must not suffer the slightest loss in its integrity and in its high dedication. . . .

A Different Kind of Revolution

Rome welcomed me as leader of national legions, as a representative, not of a party or a group, but of a great faith and of an entire people. . . .

The atmosphere was pregnant with the possibility of tragedy. I had mobilized three hundred thousand black shirts. They were waiting for my signal to move. They could be used for one purpose or another. I had in the Capital sixty thousand armed men ready for action. The March on Rome could have set tragic fires. It might have spilled much blood if it had followed the example of ancient and modern revolutions. . . .

I could have proclaimed a dictatorship, I could have formed a dictatorial ministry composed solely of Fascisti. . . . The Fascist revolution, however, had its unique characteristics; it had no antecedent in history. It was different from any other revolution also in its capacity to re-enter, with deliberate intent, legal, established traditions and forms. . . .

Mussolini Triumphant

First of all in the pressure of events, I desired to assure regularity to the country and to constitute a new government. Order came quickly. . . .

I forbade reprisals against the leaders of the oppositions. It was only by my great authority that I averted the destruction, not only rhetorical but also actual, of my most rabid enemies. I saved their skins for them. At the same time, in the space of a few hours, I constituted a new ministry. I discarded, as I said, the idea of a Fascist dictatorship, because I wanted to give to the country the impression of a normal life free from the selfish exclusiveness of a party. . . . I decided then, after having weighed everything, to compose a ministry of a nationalist character.

I have had the feeling, as I had then, that later there would become inevitable a process of clarification; but I preferred that it should come forth spontaneously from the succeeding political events. . . .

Finally I announced for November the 16th a meeting of the chamber of deputies. . . .

It was an exceptional meeting. The hall was filled to overflowing. Every deputy was present. My declarations were brief, clear, energetic. I left no misunderstanding. I stated sharply the rights of revolution. I called the attention of the audience to the fact that only the will of Fascism had the revolution remained within the boundaries of legality and tolerance. . . .

THE DAWN OF A NEW ITALY

On every subject I made weighty declarations that showed how Fascism had already been able to assay and analyze and solve varying and urgent problems, and to fix the future outlines of government. Finally I concluded:

Gentlemen:

From further communications you will know the Fascist programme in its details. I do not want, so long as I can avoid it, to rule against the Chamber; but the Chamber must feel its own position. That position opens the possibility that it may be dissolved in two days or in two years. We ask full powers because we want to assume full responsibility. . . . Every one of us has a religious sense of our difficult task. The Country cheers us and waits. We will give it not words but facts. We formally and solemnly promise to restore the budget to health. And we will restore it. We want to make a foreign policy of peace, but at the same time one of dignity and steadiness. We will do it. We intend to give the Nation a discipline. We will give it. Let none of our enemies of yesterday, of to-day, of to-morrow cherish illusions in regard to our permanence in power. . . .

The Fatherland has again found itself bound together from north to south, from the continent to the generous islands, which will never be forgotten, from the metropolis of the active colonies of the Mediterranean and the Atlantic Ocean. . . .

My political instinct told me that from that moment there would rise, with increasing truth and with increasing expansion of Fascist activity, the dawn of new history for Italy.

And perhaps dawn on a new path of civilization. . . .

ATATÜRK BRINGS WESTERN CIVILIZATION TO TURKEY

LORD KINROSS

In 1923, after six hundred years as the Ottoman Empire, Turkey became the Turkish Republic and Mustafa Kemal Atatürk, the first Republican president. Atatürk was convinced that Turkey would survive only by adapting Western ideas to Eastern needs and becoming a civilized state. In the following selection, journalist, author, broadcaster, and Scottish baron Lord Kinross, John Patrick Douglas Balfour, focuses on a major step in Atatürk's campaign to Westernize the Turks—replacing the fez, the national headgear, with the Western hat. Kinross explains that costume was of symbolic importance to Muslims, and the fez was the traditional symbol of Ottoman and Islamic orthodoxy. Thus, Kinross writes, Atatürk was taking a revolutionary step by trying to replace the fez with a hat. In Kinross's opinion, Atatürk equated civilization with costume and believed that the rest of the world would not consider Turkey a civilized nation until the people exchanged their traditional dress for Western dress.

T he Caliphate, the religious schools, the holy law had been swept away. Now . . . it was a good moment to sweep away all the dervish orders, regardless of complexion. These brotherhoods had played an important part in the reli-

Excerpted from pp. 66–73 of *Ataturk*, by Lord Kinross. Copyright © 1964 by Lord Kinross. Reprinted by permission of HarperCollins Publishers, Inc.

gious life of the Turks and had, with some exceptions, prevented them from becoming as fanatical as some of their Moslem neighbours. They represented a breakaway, still within the framework of Islam, from the aloof orthodox hierarchy. It was in the brotherhoods that the ordinary people of the country found the warm human outlet they sought for their intuitive faith.

END TO THE BROTHERHOODS

In so far as they were political the brotherhoods were traditionally opposed to the central authority. . . . No Moslem himself, [Kemal] saw the brotherhoods less as a help than as a danger. Independent in spirit and used to opposition, they could as likely oppose his own government as that of the Sultan—doubly so since it was a secular regime. Moreover they had power over the masses, and it was the masses that Kemal, having disarmed the formal religious hierarchy, now feared. To him the brotherhoods were "secret societies," such as he had learnt to mistrust since his early days. . . . Thus they must go.

In August 1925 he pronounced their doom in a speech at Kastamonu. The Turkish Republic was to be "a state of society entirely modern and completely civilized in spirit and form." Hence all superstitions must be crushed:

"To seek help from the dead is a disgrace to a civilized community. . . . I flatly refuse to believe that today, in the luminous presence of science, knowledge, and civilization in all its aspects, there exist, in the civilized community of Turkey, men so primitive as to seek their material and moral well-being from the guidance of one or another sheikh. Gentlemen, you and the whole nation must know, and know well, that the Republic of Turkey cannot be the land of sheikhs, dervishes, disciples, and lay brothers. . . . The heads of the brotherhoods will . . . at once close their monasteries and accept the fact that their disciples have at last come of age."

A series of decrees clinched the decision. Henceforth Turkey, at least in theory, was to be free not only from sheikhs and dervishes but from "fortunetellers, magicians, witch doctors, writers of amulets for the recovery of lost property or the fulfilment of wishes, as well as the services, dues, and costumes pertaining to these titles and qualities."

At the same time all sacred tombs were closed as places of worship and religious resort. When this closure aroused opposition in the Assembly—for some of whose members they involved vested interests in the form of their own defunct ancestors—a friend of Kemal who had been speaking against it was taken aside by him and enjoined in an undertone, "Don't oppose the motion. In ten years' time you'll be able to open them all up again." For all his agnosticism it was not Kemal's policy to attempt the eradication of religion. What he sought, as he once put it, was "to disengage it from the condition of being a political instrument, which it has been for centuries of habit.". . .

ATATÜRK AND THE FEZ

On his journey through the region of Kastamonu Kemal struck at another such outward and visible symbol. Its disappearance was to uproot a habit deeply ingrained in every male individual in Turkey. For it involved what he wore each day of his life on his head. This was the fez.

Costume, in the Islamic religion, had a deep symbolic significance. . . .

Kemal's plan to replace this symbol with that of the hat was thus a daring revolutionary gesture. It was one which had been quietly simmering in his mind since the days of his youth, when he had been humiliated abroad by the stigma of inferiority conferred by his national headgear. At Chankaya in the evenings he had been discussing the change with his friends, consulting those who had travelled abroad as to which form of hat was most suitable.

In his own costume he had been making experiments. He was photographed on a tractor on his model farm wearing a panama—without a black ribbon. An old friend came upon him one day in a train wearing a cloth cap with his brown tweed suit. "Does this become me?" Kemal asked, as though seeking assurance. He revealed that in recent months he had three times dreamed of the fez. "And whenever I did so Ismet knocked at my door in the morning to report a reactionary movement somewhere in the country." The idea of a reform was unobtrusively canvassed in the press, but still no newspaper dared use the ugly word *shapka*, or hat. The press preferred such euphemisms as "civilized headgear," "Protector from sunshine," or "head cover with a brim."

Kemal deliberately chose, for the disclosure of these various religious reforms, a province known for its reactionary sentiments. Boldly he was striking at the enemy at a strong point where, if his shock tactics succeeded, their impact would be twice as effective as elsewhere. . . .

EQUATING CIVILIZATION WITH COSTUME

Kemal, in that distaste for the darker forces of religion which had haunted him since youth, approached his tour with unusual nervousness, asking for water when he first spoke and finding that his hands, as he raised it to his lips, were trembling. He had left Ankara bareheaded, in an open car. The people, swarming down to the main road from their mountain villages, hardly knew what to expect from this first sight of their national hero. . . . One villager, a young student, recalled the scene years later: "When the President walked slowly down the street, greeting the crowds, there was not a sound. The clean-shaven Gazi was wearing a white, European-style summer suit, a sports shirt open at the neck, and a panama hat. The few officials applauded frantically, urging on those near them, but a flutter of hand-clapping was all they would muster, so great had been the shock." For the conqueror was wearing the costume of the infidel.

But the shock was slowly absorbed. Outside Kastamonu itself the Gazi got out of his car and walked into the town ahead of his entourage, first carrying the hat in his hand, then putting it on his head. His aides did the same. Had they done so a generation earlier, they might well have been stoned or manhandled by the crowd. But now they were greeted merely with silent curiosity. Throughout his tour Kemal's interest in costume and especially in headgear was made evident to all. Sometimes he remained hatless, in which case a few people out of politeness removed their own fezes. Inspecting a military detachment, he took off the cap of each soldier and examined it with attention. A few months earlier a narrow peak had been added to it, ostensibly for the protection of the soldier's eyes against the sun. For had not the Prophet enjoined his followers always to fight with their faces towards it?

His approach to the sartorial question was practical. At one meeting he turned to a tailor in the audience and asked him, pointing to a man in baggy Turkish trousers and a robe, which was the cheaper—this outfit or the modern, international type of suit. The tailor replied, "The international kind." Pointing the moral, Kemal said to the audience, "There, you see? Out of every costume such as this man is wearing you could make an extra suit."

All this was a mere foretaste of what was to come—an open declaration of national policy in which civilization was equated with costume. For this he chose the port of Inebolu itself. To symbolize their part in the War of Independence, its townspeople had decorated and placed in the square a boat and an oxcart of the type that had carried the munitions. Kemal was pelted with flowers as he drove into the town, which was bedecked with flags and branches. Later, wearing his panama, he walked through the streets while the people crowded around to kiss his hands and his garments. He conversed with all sections of the population, questioning them personally on their problems and enlightening them on his plans for their future.

For two days he took part in organized festivities. Sheep were sacrificed in his honour in barbarous fashion, but out of his sight at his request—a scruple which they ascribed to his deep devotion to animals. . . .

The climax was reached on the third day, when he delivered a long oration to a dazed and respectful audience, variously clad, in the clubroom of the Turkish Hearth.

"Gentlemen," he said, "the Turkish people, who founded the Turkish Republic, are civilized; they are civilized in history and reality. But I tell you . . . that the people of the Turkish Republic, who claim to be civilized, must prove that they are civilized, by their ideas and their mentality, by their family life and their way of living. . . . They must prove in fact that they are civilized and advanced persons in their outward aspect also. . . . I shall put my explanation to you in the form of a question.

"Is our dress national?" Cries of "No!"

"Is it civilized and international?" Cries of "No, no!"

"I agree with you. This grotesque mixture of styles is neither national nor international. . . . A civilized, international dress is worthy and appropriate for our nation, and we will wear it. Boots or shoes on our feet, trousers on our legs, shirt and tie, jacket and waistcoat—and of course, to complete these, a cover with a brim on our heads. I want to make this clear. This head covering is called 'hat.'"

The word was out. There was to be an end to all euphemisms. This and his other pronouncements were relayed by the news agencies to all parts of Turkey. . . .

A STEP CLOSER TO WESTERNIZATION

Towards the end of November 1925, when Kemal judged that public opinion was ripe, a new bill was passed by the Assembly which obliged all men to wear hats and made the wearing of the fez a criminal offence. For the present there were not enough hats to go round, and thousands went hatless or crowned with an odd diversity of headgear dumped on the market by the hatters of Europe. It was not until local hat factories came into full production that all were appropriately hatted. For the masses there were produced cloth caps with a peak designed to prevent the wearers from touching the ground with their heads as they prayed, but easily reversible and often reversed.

The hat law, however, caused widespread riots in the East. They were inflamed by placards in the name of religion on the walls of public buildings, which led to mass demonstrations beneath the green flag of Islam. The riots had been anticipated by the government, who sent Tribunals of Independence in advance to the danger spots. They were suppressed by ruthless means.

Of the abolition of the fez Kemal remarked later:

"We did it while the Law for the Maintenance of Order was still in force. Had it not been, we could have done it all the same, but it certainly is true that the existence of the law made it much easier for us. Indeed the existence of the Law for the Maintenance of Order prevented the large-scale poisoning of the nation by certain reactionaries."

By these various reforms the Gazi translated into action those plans which, in the days of the Young Turk intellectuals, had been confined to the realm of ideas. Abdullah Jevdet, an early influence on Kemal and his friends, had written in 1912 that there could be no civilization but Western civilization. His periodical *Ichtihad* published at that time a vision of the future Westernization of Turkey entitled "A Very Wakeful Sleep." It envisaged, among other changes, the replacement of the fez by a new form of headgear; the limitation of the turban and cloak to professional men of religion; the closing of the religious schools and brotherhoods and the use of their funds to assist a modern educational programme; the suppression of vows and offerings to the saints and of the activities of witch doctors and exorcists; and a reform of the whole legal system.

The dream, then considered a fantasy, had now become a reality.

CRASH!

FREDERICK LEWIS ALLEN

On October 29, 1929, the stock market crashed, and $30 billion seemingly disappeared. In the following selection from his classic work *Only Yesterday: An Informal History of the Nineteen-Twenties,* social historian Frederick Lewis Allen recounts the ups and downs during the days immediately preceding the crash. Allen describes the confusion, panic, and madness that characterized the scene on the trading floor of the Stock Exchange that "Black Tuesday" as a record more than 16 million shares changed hands. He goes on to explain how critical the day was for the banks, that had to decide whether to take over huge loans that corporations had made to brokers through the banks. According to Allen, the crash of the stock market shattered the hope of the American people and marked an abrupt end to the era of postwar prosperity.

I t [Thursday, October 24,] had been a frightful day. At seven o'clock that night the tickers in a thousand brokers' offices were still chattering; not till after 7:08 did they finally record the last sale made on the floor at three o'clock. The volume of trading had set a new record—12,894,650 shares. ("The time may come when we shall see a five-million-share day," the wise men of the Street had been saying twenty months before!) Incredible rumors had spread wildly during the early afternoon—that eleven speculators had committed suicide, that the Buffalo and Chicago exchanges had been closed, that troops were guarding the New York Stock Exchange against an angry mob. The country had known the bitter taste of panic. . . .

Things looked somewhat better on Friday and Saturday. Trading was still on an enormous scale, but prices for the most part

Excerpted from *Only Yesterday: An Informal History of the Nineteen-Twenties,* by Frederick L. Allen. Copyright © 1931 by Frederick Lewis Allen. Copyright renewed 1959 by Agnes Rogers Allen. Reprinted by permission of HarperCollins Publishers, Inc.

held. At the very moment when the bankers' pool was cautiously disposing of as much as possible of the stock which it had accumulated on Thursday and was thus preparing for future emergencies, traders who had sold out higher up were coming back into the market again with new purchases, in the hope that the bottom had been reached. (Hadn't they often been told that "the time to buy is when things look blackest"?) The newspapers carried a very pretty series of reassuring statements from the occupants of the seats of the mighty; President Herbert Hoover himself, in a White House statement, pointed out that "the fundamental business of the country, that is, production and distribution of commodities, is on a sound and prosperous basis." But toward the close of Saturday's session prices began to slip again. And on Monday the rout was under way once more.

BLACK TUESDAY DESCENDS

The losses registered on Monday were terrific—17½ points for Steel, 47½ for General Electric, 36 for Allied Chemical, 34½ for Westinghouse, and so on down a long and dismal list. All Saturday afternoon and Saturday night and Sunday the brokers had been struggling to post their records and go over their customers' accounts and sent out calls for further margin, and another avalanche of forced selling resulted. . . .

Once more the ticker dropped ridiculously far behind, the lights in the brokers' offices and the banks burned till dawn, and the telegraph companies distributed thousands of margin calls and requests for more collateral to back up loans at the banks. Bankers, brokers, clerks, messengers were almost at the end of their strength; for days and nights they had been driving themselves to keep pace with the most terrific volume of business that had ever descended upon them. It did not seem as if they could stand it much longer. But the worst was still ahead. It came the next day, Tuesday, October 29th.

The big gong had hardly sounded in the great hall of the Exchange at ten o'clock Tuesday morning before the storm broke in full force. Huge blocks of stock were thrown upon the market for what they would bring. Five thousand shares, ten thousand shares appeared at a time on the laboring ticker at fearful recessions in price. Not only were innumerable small traders being sold out, but big ones, too, protagonists of the new economic era who a few weeks before had counted themselves millionaires. Again and again the specialist in a stock would find himself surrounded by brokers fighting to sell—and nobody at all even thinking of buying. To give one single example: during the bull market the common stock of the White Sewing Machine Company had gone as high as 48; on Monday, October 28th, it had closed at 11 ⅛. On that black Tuesday, somebody—a clever messenger boy for the Exchange, it was rumored—had the bright idea of putting in an order to buy at 1—and in the temporarily complete absence of other bids he actually got his stock for a dollar a share! The scene on the floor was chaotic. Despite the jamming of the communication system, orders to buy and sell— mostly to sell—came in faster than human beings could possibly handle them; it was on that day that an exhausted broker, at the close of the session, found a large waste-basket which he had stuffed with orders to be executed and had carefully set aside for safekeeping—and then had completely forgotten. Within half an hour of the opening the volume of trading had passed three million shares, by twelve o'clock it had passed eight million, by half-past one it had passed twelve million, and when the closing gong brought the day's madness to an end the gigantic record of 16,410,030 shares had been set. Toward the close there was a rally, but by that time the average prices of fifty leading stocks, as compiled by the *New York Times,* had fallen nearly forty points. Meanwhile there was a near-panic in other markets—the foreign stock exchanges, the lesser American exchanges, the grain market.

So complete was the demoralization of the stock market and so exhausted were the brokers and their staffs and the Stock Exchange employees, that at noon that day, when the panic was at its worst, the Governing Committee met quietly to decide whether or not to close the Exchange. To quote from an address made some months later by Stock Exchange Vice President Richard Whitney: "In order not to give occasion for alarming rumors, this meeting was not held in the Governing Committee Room, but in the office of the president of the Stock Clearing Corporation directly beneath the Stock Exchange floor. . . . The forty governors came to the meeting in groups of two and three as unobtrusively as possible. The office they met in was never designed for large meetings of this sort, with the result that most of the governors were compelled to stand, or to sit on tables. As the meeting progressed, panic was raging overhead on the floor. . . . The feeling of those present was revealed by their habit of continually lighting cigarettes, taking a puff or two, putting them out and lighting new ones—a practice which soon made the narrow room blue with smoke." . . . After some deliberation, the governors finally decided not to close the Exchange.

It was a critical day for the banks, that Tuesday the 29th. Many of the corporations which had so cheerfully loaned money to brokers through the banks in order to obtain interest at 8 or 9 per cent were now clamoring to have these loans called—and the banks were faced with a choice between taking over the loans themselves and running the risk of precipitating further ruin. It was no laughing matter to assume the responsibility of millions of dollars' worth of loans secured by collateral which by the end of the day might prove to have dropped to a fraction of its former value. That the call money rate never rose above 6 per cent that day, that a money panic was not added to the stock panic, and that several Wall Street institutions did not go down into immediate bankruptcy, was due largely to the nerve shown by a few bankers in stepping into the breach. The story is told of one banker who went grimly on authorizing the taking over of loan after loan until one of his subordinate officers came in with a white face and told him that the bank was insolvent. "I dare say," said the banker, and went ahead unmoved. He knew that if he did not, more than one concern would face insolvency.

Recovery—and Collapse

The next day—Wednesday, October 30th—the outlook suddenly and providentially brightened. The directors of the Steel Corporation had declared an extra dividend; the directors of the American Can Company had not only declared an extra dividend, but had raised the regular dividend. There was another flood of reassuring statements—though by this time a cheerful statement from a financier fell upon somewhat skeptical ears. Julius Klein, Mr. Hoover's Assistant Secretary of Commerce, composed a rhapsody on continued prosperity. John J. Raskob declared that stocks were at bargain prices and that he and his friends were buying. John D. Rockefeller poured Standard Oil upon the waters: "Believing that fundamental conditions of the country are sound and that there is nothing in the business situation to warrant the destruction of values that has taken place on the exchanges during the past week, my son and I have for some days been purchasing sound common stocks." Better still, prices rose—steadily and buoyantly. Now at last the time had come when the strain on the Exchange could be relieved without causing undue alarm. At 1:40 o'clock Vice-President Whitney announced from the rostrum that the Exchange would not open until noon the following day and would remain closed all day Friday and Saturday—and to his immense relief the announcement was greeted, not with renewed panic, but with a cheer.

Throughout Thursday's short session the recovery continued. Prices gyrated wildly—for who could arrive at a reasonable idea of what a given stock was worth, now that all settled standards of value had been upset?—but the worst of the storm seemed to have blown over. The financial community breathed more easily; now they could have a chance to set their houses in order.

It was true that the worst of the panic was past. But not the worst prices. There was too much forced liquidation still to come as brokers' accounts were gradually straightened out, as banks called for more collateral, and terror was renewed. The next week, in a series of short sessions, the tide of prices receded once more—until at last on November 13th the bottom prices for the year 1929 were reached. Beside the figures hung up in the sunny days of September they made a tragic showing. . . .

The *New York Times* averages for fifty leading stocks had been almost cut in half, falling from a high of 311.90 in September to a low of 164.43 on November 13th; and the *Times* averages for twenty-five leading industrials had fared still worse, diving from 469.49 to 220.95.

END OF AN ERA

The Big Bull Market was dead. Billions of dollars' worth of profits—and paper profits—had disappeared. The grocer, the window-cleaner, and the seamstress had lost their capital. In every town there were families which had suddenly dropped from showy affluence into debt. Investors who had dreamed of retiring to live on their fortunes now found themselves back once more at the very beginning of the long road to riches. Day by day the newspapers printed the grim reports of suicides.

Coolidge-Hoover Prosperity was not yet dead, but it was dying. Under the impact of the shock of panic, a multitude of ills which hitherto had passed unnoticed, or had been offset by stock-market optimism began to beset the body economic. . . . Although the liquidation of nearly three billion dollars of brokers' loans contracted credit, and the Reserve Banks lowered the rediscount rate, and the way in which the larger banks and corporations of the country had survived the emergency without a single failure of large proportions offered real encouragement, nevertheless the poisons were there: overproduction of capital; overambitious expansion of business concerns; overproduction of commodities under the stimulus of installment buying and buying with stock-market profits; the maintenance of an artificial price level for many commodities; the depressed condition of European trade. No matter how many soothsayers of high finance proclaimed that all was well, no matter how earnestly the President set to work to repair the damage with soft words and White House conferences, a major depression was inevitably under way.

Nor was that all. Prosperity is more than an economic condition; it is a state of mind. The Big Bull Market had been more than the climax of a business cycle; it had been the climax of a cycle in

American mass thinking and mass emotion. There was hardly a man or woman in the country whose attitude toward life had not been affected by it in some degree and was not now affected by the sudden and brutal shattering of hope. With the Big Bull Market gone and prosperity going, Americans were soon to find themselves living in an altered world which called for new adjustments, new ideas, new habits of thought, and a new order of values. The psychological climate was changing; the ever-shifting currents of American life were turning into new channels.

The Post-war Decade had come to its close. An era had ended.

WORLD HISTORY BY ERA

1930–1939: A Time of Trial and Change

CHAPTER 3

HOW THE DEPRESSION STARTED

JOHN A. GARRATY

Beginning in the late 1920s, the economic stability experienced by some countries took a turn, giving way to a slowing down of the economy that turned into a worldwide depression. As academician and historian John A. Garraty explains in the following selection, opinions differed as to who was responsible for the events that caused the depression. He writes that many people blamed the United States, citing the 1929 stock market crash as the event that started it all. According to Garraty, the one thing on which there was general agreement at the time was that the depression was the downward phase of a business cycle. Garraty points out that no modern economist considers the United States solely responsible for the Great Depression. He contends that the depression was unavoidable given the structural imbalance that existed.

T he Great Depression of the 1930s was a worldwide phenomenon composed of an infinite number of separate but related events. The relationships were often obscure; even today some of the most important of them remain baffling. But it is indisputable that there was a pattern to the trend of events nearly everywhere. After the Great War of 1914–18, both belligerents and neutrals experienced a period of adjustment and reconstruction that lasted until about 1925. By that date, the economies of most countries had gotten back at least to the levels of 1913. There followed a few years of rapid growth, but in 1929 and 1930 the prosperity ended. Then came a precipitous plunge, which lasted until early 1933. This dark period was fol-

Excerpted from *The Great Depression*, by John A. Garraty. Copyright © 1986 by John A. Garraty. Reprinted by permission of Harcourt, Inc.

lowed by a gradual, if spotty, recovery. The revival was aborted, however, by the sudden, steep recession of 1937–38. Finally, a still more cataclysmic event, the outbreak of World War II in the summer of 1939, put an end to the depression.

DISAGREEMENT ON WHO WAS TO BLAME

At the time, this developing pattern was not immediately clear. The people of every country were, however, aware that the same forces were at work everywhere and that these forces had caused an economic catastrophe of unprecedented proportions.

Surely if the Great Depression was basically the same everywhere, international cooperation was essential for ending it. That much was recognized almost from the start. But despite the urgings of economists and statesmen, the nations were singularly unsuccessful in coordinating their attempts to overcome the depression. . . .

In retrospect it seems likely that if the nations had cooperated with one another better in dealing with their economic problems, they could have avoided or at least ameliorated the terrible economic losses that all of them suffered during that decade of depression. Certainly the actions that many nations took (as well as some that they could have taken but did not) influenced the course of the depression in observable ways.

Knowledgeable people at the time had a good grasp of the causes of the depression, and modern experts have not added a great deal to what these observers understood. . . .

During the depression, politicians and businessmen and even supposedly disinterested scholars tended to blame the collapse on events that took place outside their own countries. Many still do. Since the depression was worldwide, and since what happened in one region affected conditions in many others, all such statements, whether well or ill informed, contain at least a germ of truth. But in a sense, the depression was like syphilis, which before its nature was fully understood was referred to in England as the French pox, as the Spanish disease in France, the Italian sickness in Spain, and so on. As the British civil servant Sir Arthur Salter noted in a 1932 speech about the depression, "There is a natural human tendency after any great disaster to search for a single scapegoat, to whom the responsibility that should be shared by others may be diverted."

SOMEBODY ELSE'S FAULT

Many years after it ended, former President Herbert Hoover offered an elaborate explanation of the Great Depression. . . . "THE DEPRESSION WAS NOT STARTED IN THE UNITED STATES," he insisted. The "primary cause" was the war of 1914–18. . . .

Hoover blamed America's troubles on an "orgy of specula-tion" in the late 1920s that resulted from the cheap-money poli-cies that the "mediocrities" who made up the majority of the Fed-eral Reserve Board had adopted in a futile effort to support the value of the British pound and other European currencies. . . .

Hoover could not use this argument to explain the further de-cline that occurred in the United States in 1930, 1931, and 1932, when he was running the country. He blamed that on foreign de-velopments. European statesmen "did not have the courage to meet the real issues," he claimed. Their rivalries and their heavy spending on arms and "frantic public works programs to meet unemployment" led to unbalanced budgets and inflation that "tore their systems asunder." The ultimate result of these unsound policies was the collapse of the German banking system in 1931; that turned what would have been no more than a minor eco-nomic downturn into the Great Depression. "The hurricane that swept our shores," wrote Hoover, "was of European origin."

The Prime Minister of Great Britain during the depression was Ramsay MacDonald, a socialist. He blamed capitalism for the debacle. "We are not on trial," he said in 1930; "it is the sys-tem under which we live. It has broken down, not only in this little island . . . it has broken down everywhere, as it was bound to break down." The Germans argued that the depression was political in origin. The harsh terms imposed on them by the Ver-sailles Treaty and especially the reparations payments that, they claimed, sapped the economic vitality of their country, had caused it. One conservative German economist, Hero Moeller, blamed the World War naval blockade for his country's eco-nomic troubles in the 1930s. "The English merchant fleet helped to build up the world economy," he said; "the British Navy helped to destroy it."

France escaped the initial impact of the depression. During its early stages, French leaders attributed this happy circumstance to the particular qualities of their country. "France is a garden," they explained. But when the slump became serious in France in 1932, they accused Great Britain of causing it by adopting irresponsible monetary policies and the United States of "exporting unem-ployment" by substituting machines for workers. "Mechaniza-tion," a writer in the *Revue d'Economie Politique* explained in 1932, "is an essential element in the worsening of the depression."

A DOWNWARD PHASE OF THE BUSINESS CYCLE

At the time, a substantial majority of Americans and nearly all foreigners who expressed opinions on the subject believed that the Wall Street stock market crash of October 1929 had triggered the depression, thereby suggesting that the United States was the birthplace of the disaster. . . .

But there have always been students of the subject who have disagreed—among them, not surprisingly, the president of the New York Stock Exchange in 1929, E.H.H. Simmons. He insisted that the September 1929 failure of the financial empire of the English entrepreneur Clarence Hatry had precipitated the collapse. Nowadays, most historians play down the importance of the crash. . . .

One thing that experts at the time did agree on—without regard for their nationality—was that the depression was the downward phase of a business cycle. . . .

In the beginning, the Great Depression appeared to be a typical cyclical downswing, the precipitating crisis being the Wall Street stock market crash of October 1929. By September 1930, however, it was severe enough to cause the League of Nations to commission the economist Gottfried Haberler to make a study of the theories that had been advanced to explain "the recurrence of periods of economic depression." . . .

Meanwhile, as month after month passed without signs of recovery, the terms *crisis* and *cycle* seemed less and less adequate as an explanation of what was going on. . . .

"We may no longer be in a 'cycle', but in a 'chute'," an English economist said in 1932. German authorities of varying schools spoke of a "permanent depression"; the "automatic" corrections were not occurring. "What we are now experiencing," said the German banker Dr. Karl Melchior as early as 1931, "is the destruction of the rules of the game of the capitalist system." . . .

THE UNITED STATES NOT THE CAUSE

American economist and academician Charles P. Kindleberger [argued] effectively in *The World in Depression* (1973). Since Great Britain could no longer supply the international leadership it had provided before the Great War, probably the United States should have stepped into the breach. What was needed was not merely American cooperation but American financial leadership. If the United States had been willing to act as a lender of last resort to economically distressed nations in 1931, when the Austrian, German, and British banks were threatened with collapse, and if it had agreed to keep its own market open to cheap foreign goods even at some cost to American producers, the depression would have been less disastrous for all nations, including the United States. The United States did not lend generously because it feared it would be throwing good money after bad. . . .

Kindleberger does not blame the length of the depression entirely on the United States. He concedes that "intense international interaction produced both the boom and the collapse." And he admits that American public opinion, "bemused by domestic concerns," was unwilling to support the kind of leadership that was needed. He also points out that the necessary financial actions were "perhaps beyond the power of policy . . . in the existing state of knowledge," which comes close to saying that the depression was unavoidable.

More important, neither Kindleberger nor any other leading student of the subject claims that the United States alone was responsible for the depression. American financial policy had little to do with the underlying imbalances in the world economy of the 1920s, principally the persistent, pervasive slump in the prices of agricultural commodities and of nearly all raw materials. This structural imbalance hampered economic growth in nonindustrial countries and deprived the industrial countries of potential markets. Because of it, the boom of the late twenties was sure to come to an unhappy end, no matter what any government did or did not do. The war debt and reparations tangle, for which the United States was only partially responsible, also had much to do with the severity of the depression. In any case, the Great Depression occurred and ran its course.

HARD TIMES IN AMERICA

FREDERICK LEWIS ALLEN

The worldwide depression of the 1930s hit America especially hard, creating what social historian Frederick Lewis Allen labeled the "economic paralysis of 1932." As Allen explains in the following selection, statistics alone do not tell the whole story of the deprivations imposed on the American people. He points to signs of the effects of the depression found almost universally in cities and towns—the breadlines, the Hoovervilles, the homeless sleeping on park benches, and the growing numbers of transients. Allen also describes how the depression cut across all classes to varying degrees, from the well-to-do to those at the very bottom of the economic scale. According to Allen, the worst thing about the depression was that it dragged on year after year and tended to bring out the worst in many people.

S tatistics are bloodless things.

To say that during the year 1932, the cruelest year of the Depression, the average number of unemployed people in the United States was 12½ million by the estimates of the National Industrial Conference Board, a little over 13 million by the estimates of the American Federation of Labor, and by other estimates (differently arrived at, and defining unemployment in various ways) anywhere from 8½ to 17 million—to say this is to give no living impression of the jobless men going from office to office or from factory gate to factory gate; of the disheartening inevitability of the phrase, "We'll let you know if anything shows up"; of men thumbing the want ads in cold tenements, spending

Excerpted from *Since Yesterday: The 1930s in America, September 3, 1929–September 3, 1939*, by Frederick Lewis Allen. Copyright © 1939, 1940 by Frederick Lewis Allen; renewed 1968 by Agnes Rogers Allen. Reprinted by permission of HarperCollins Publishers, Inc.

fruitless hours, day after day and week after week, in the sidewalk crowds before the employment offices; using up the money
in the savings bank, borrowing on their life insurance, selling
whatever possessions could be sold, borrowing from relatives
less and less able to lend, tasting the bitterness of inadequacy,
and at last swallowing their pride and going to apply for relief—
if there was any to be got. . . .

HIDDEN SIGNS OF THE DEPRESSION

But cold statistics gave us little sense of the human realities of the
economic paralysis of 1932. Let us try another approach.

Walking through an American city, you might find few signs
of the Depression visible—or at least conspicuous—to the casual
eye. You might notice that a great many shops were untenanted,
with dusty plate-glass windows and signs indicating that they
were ready to lease; that few factory chimneys were smoking;
that the streets were not so crowded with trucks as in earlier
years, that there was no uproar of riveters to assail the ear, that
beggars and panhandlers were on the sidewalks in unprecedented numbers (in the Park Avenue district of New York a man
might be asked for money four or five times in a ten-block walk).
Traveling by railroad, you might notice that the trains were
shorter, the Pullman cars fewer—and that fewer freight trains
were on the line. Traveling overnight, you might find only two
or three other passengers in your sleeping car. (By contrast, there
were more filling stations by the motor highways than ever before, and of all the retail businesses in "Middletown" only the filling stations showed no large drop in business during the black
years; for although few new automobiles were being bought,
those which would still stand up were being used more than
ever—to the dismay of the railroads.)

Otherwise things might seem to you to be going on much as
usual. The major phenomena of the Depression were mostly neg-
ative and did not assail the eye.

But if you knew where to look, some of them would begin to
appear. First, the breadlines in the poorer districts. Second, those
bleak settlements ironically known as "Hoovervilles" in the outskirts of the cities and on vacant lots—groups of makeshift
shacks constructed out of packing boxes, scrap iron, anything
that could be picked up free in a diligent combing of the city
dumps: shacks in which men and sometimes whole families of
evicted people were sleeping on automobile seats carried from
auto-graveyards, warming themselves before fires of rubbish in
grease drums. Third, the homeless people sleeping in doorways
or on park benches, and going the rounds of the restaurants for

left-over half-eaten biscuits, piecrusts, anything to keep the fires of life burning. Fourth, the vastly increased number of thumbers on the highways, and particularly of freight-car transients on the railroads: a huge army of drifters ever on the move, searching half-aimlessly for a place where there might be a job. . . .

Among them were large numbers of young boys, and girls disguised as boys. According to the Children's Bureau, there were 200,000 children thus drifting about the United States. So huge was the number of freight-car hoppers in the Southwest that in a number of places the railroad police simply had to give up trying to remove them from the trains: there were far too many of them.

THE EFFECT ON THE "WELL-TO-DO"

Among the comparatively well-to-do people of the country (those, let us say, whose pre-Depression incomes had been over $5,000 a year) the great majority were living on a reduced scale, for salary cuts had been extensive, especially since 1931, and dividends were dwindling. These people were discharging servants, or cutting servants' wages to a minimum, or in some cases "letting" a servant stay on without other compensation than board and lodging. In many pretty houses, wives who had never before . . . "done their own work" were cooking and scrubbing. Husbands were wearing the old suit longer, resigning from the golf club, deciding, perhaps, that this year the family couldn't afford to go to the beach for the summer, paying seventy-five cents for lunch instead of a dollar at the restaurant or thirty-five instead of fifty at the lunch counter. When those who had flown high with the stock market in 1929 looked at the stockmarket page of the newspapers nowadays their only consoling thought (if they still had any stock left) was that a judicious sale or two would result in such a capital loss that they need pay no income tax at all this year.

Alongside these men and women of the well-to-do classes whose fortunes had been merely reduced by the Depression were others whose fortunes had been shattered. The crowd of men waiting for the 8:14 train at the prosperous suburb included many who had lost their jobs, and were going to town as usual not merely to look stubbornly and almost hopelessly for other work but also to keep up a bold front of activity. (In this latter effort they usually succeeded: one would never have guessed, seeing them chatting with their friends as train-time approached, how close to desperation some of them had come.) There were architects and engineers bound for offices to which no clients had come in weeks. There were doctors who thought themselves lucky when a patient paid a bill. Mrs. Jones, who went daily to her stenographic job, was now the economic mainstay of her family, for Mr. Jones was jobless and was doing the cooking and looking after the children (with singular distaste and inefficiency). Next door to the Joneses lived Mrs. Smith, the widow of a successful lawyer: she had always had a comfortable income, she prided herself on her "nice things," she was pathetically unfitted to earn a dollar even if jobs were to be had; her capital had been invested in South American bonds and United Founders stock and other similarly misnamed "securities," and now she was completely dependent upon handouts from her relatives, and didn't even have carfare in her imported pocketbook.

The Browns had retreated to their "farmhouse" in the country and were trying to raise crops on its stony acres; they talked warmly about primal simplicities but couldn't help longing sometimes for electric light and running hot water, and couldn't cope with the potato bugs. (Large numbers of city dwellers thus moved to the country, but not enough of them engaged in real farming to do more than partially check the long-term movement from the farms of America to the cities and towns.) It was being whispered about the community that the Robinson family, though they lived in a $40,000 house and had always spent money freely, were in desperate straits: Mr. Robinson had lost his job, the house could not be sold, they had realized on every asset at their command, and now they were actually going hungry—though their house still looked like the abode of affluence.

CONDITIONS WORSEN WITH TIME

Further down in the economic scale, particularly in those industrial communities in which the factories were running at twenty per cent of capacity or had closed down altogether, conditions were infinitely worse. . . . In every American city, quantities of families were being evicted from their inadequate apartments; moving in with other families till ten or twelve people would be sharing three or four rooms; or shivering through the winter in heatless houses because they could afford no coal, eating meat once a week or not at all. If employers sometimes found that former employees who had been discharged did not seem eager for re-employment ("They won't take a job if you offer them one!"), often the reason was panic: a dreadful fear of inadequacy which was one of the Depression's commonest psycho-pathological results. A woman clerk, offered piecework after being jobless for a year, confessed that she almost had not dared to come to the office, she had been in such terror lest she wouldn't know where to hang her coat, wouldn't know how to find the washroom, wouldn't understand the boss's directions for her job.

For perhaps the worst thing about this Depression was its inexorable continuance year after year. Men who have been sturdy and self-respecting workers can take unemployment without flinching for a few weeks, a few months, even if they have to see their families suffer; but it is different after a year . . . two years . . . three years. . . . Among the miserable creatures curled up on park benches or standing in dreary lines before the soup kitchens in 1932 were men who had been jobless since the end of 1929.

At the very bottom of the economic scale the conditions may perhaps best be suggested by two brief quotations. The first, from Jonathan Norton Leonard's *Three Years Down*, describes the plight of Pennsylvania miners who had been put out of company villages after a blind and hopeless strike in 1931: "Reporters from the more liberal metropolitan papers found thousands of them huddled on the mountainsides, crowded three or four families together in one-room shacks, living on dandelions and wild weed-roots. Half of them were sick, but no local doctor would care for the evicted strikers. All of them were hungry and many were dying of those providential diseases which enable welfare authorities to claim that no one has starved." The other quotation is from Louise V. Armstrong's *We Too Are the People*, and the scene is Chicago in the late spring of 1932:

"One vivid, gruesome moment of those dark days we shall never forget. We saw a crowd of some fifty men fighting over a barrel of garbage which had been set outside the back door of a restaurant. American citizens fighting for scraps of food like animals!"

THE ADVERSE EFFECT ON HUMAN NATURE

Human behavior under unaccustomed conditions is always various. One thinks of the corporation executive to whom was delegated the job of discharging several hundred men: he insisted on seeing every one of them personally and taking an interest in each man's predicament, and at the end of a few months his hair had turned prematurely gray. . . . The Junior League girl who reported with pride a Depression economy: she had cut a piece out of an old fur coat in the attic and bound it to serve as a bathmat. . . . The banker who had been plunged deeply into debt by the collapse of his bank: he got a $30,000 job with another bank, lived on $3,000 a year, and honorably paid $27,000 a year to his creditors. . . . The wealthy family who lost most of their money but announced bravely that they had "solved their Depression problem" by discharging fifteen of their twenty servants, and showed no signs of curiosity as to what would happen to these fifteen. . . . The little knot of corporation officials in a magnificent skyscraper office doctoring the books of the company to dodge bankruptcy. . . . The crowd of Chicago Negroes standing tight-packed before a tenement-house door to prevent the landlord's agents from evicting a neighbor family: as they stood there, hour by hour, they sang hymns. . . . The one-time clerk carefully cutting out pieces of cardboard to put inside his shoes before setting out on his endless job-hunting round, and telling his wife the shoes were now better than ever. . . . The man in the little apartment next door who had given up hunting for jobs, given up all interest, all activity, and sat hour by hour in staring apathy. . . .

It was a strange time in which to graduate from school or college. High schools had a larger attendance than ever before, especially in the upper grades, because there were few jobs to tempt any one away. Likewise college graduates who could afford to go on to graduate school were continuing their studies—after a hopeless hunt for jobs—rather than be idle. . . .

The effects of the economic dislocation were ubiquitous. Not business alone was disturbed, but churches, museums, theatres, schools, colleges, charitable organizations, clubs, lodges, sports organizations, and so on clear through the list of human enterprises; one and all they felt the effects of dwindling gifts, declining memberships, decreasing box-office returns, uncollectible bills, revenue insufficient to pay the interest on the mortgage.

Furthermore, as the tide of business receded, it laid bare the evidence of many an unsavory incident of the past. . . .

As banks went under, as corporations got into difficulties, the accountants learned what otherwise might never have been discovered: that the respected family in the big house on the hill had been hand-in-hand with gangsters; that the benevolent company president had been living in such style only because he placed company orders at fat prices with an associated company which he personally controlled; that the corporation lawyer who passed the plate at the Presbyterian church had been falsifying his income-tax returns. And with every such disclosure came a new disillusionment.

F.D.R. Bolsters American Confidence

Franklin Delano Roosevelt

Franklin Delano Roosevelt was elected to his first term as president of the United States in 1932, at the very height of the Great Depression. On Saturday, March 4, 1933, Roosevelt made his first inaugural address. The intent of the address was to bolster the confidence of the American people and assure them that the government was going to take action to pull the nation out of the depression. In the speech, he warns the American people that they must face the fact of the depression and its devastating effect on the nation. Proclaiming that "the only thing we have to fear is fear itself," Roosevelt reminds Americans that the current depression is not the first crisis the nation has endured and avers that the nation will survive this crisis as it did previous ones.

I am certain that my fellow Americans expect that on my induction into the Presidency I will address them with a candor and a decision which the present situation of our Nation impels. This is preeminently the time to speak the truth, the whole truth, frankly and boldly. Nor need we shrink from honestly facing conditions in our country today. This great Nation will endure as it has endured, will revive and will prosper. So, first of all, let me assert my firm belief that the only thing we have to fear is fear itself—nameless, unreasoning, unjustified terror which paralyzes needed efforts to convert retreat into advance. In every dark hour of our national life a leadership of

From Franklin Delano Roosevelt's First Inaugural Address, March 4, 1933.

frankness and vigor has met with that understanding and support of the people themselves which is essential to victory. I am convinced that you will again give that support to leadership in these critical days.

In such a spirit on my part and on yours we face our common difficulties. They concern, thank God, only material things. Values have shrunken to fantastic levels; taxes have risen; our ability to pay has fallen; government of all kinds is faced by serious curtailment of income; the means of exchange are frozen in the currents of trade; the withered leaves of industrial enterprise lie on every side; farmers find no markets for their produce; the savings of many years in thousands of families are gone.

More important, a host of unemployed citizens face the grim problem of existence, and an equally great number toil with little return. Only a foolish optimist can deny the dark realities of the moment.

MONEY IS NOT THE ANSWER

Yet our distress comes from no failure of substance. We are stricken by no plague of locusts. Compared with the perils which our forefathers conquered because they believed and were not afraid, we have still much to be thankful for. Nature still offers her bounty and human efforts have multiplied it. Plenty is at our doorstep, but a generous use of it languishes in the very sight of the supply. Primarily this is because the rulers of the exchange of mankind's goods have failed, through their own stubbornness and their own incompetence, have admitted their failure, and abdicated. Practices of the unscrupulous money changers stand indicted in the court of public opinion, rejected by the hearts and minds of men.

True they have tried, but their efforts have been cast in the pattern of an outworn tradition. Faced by failure of credit they have proposed only the lending of more money. Stripped of the lure of profit by which to induce our people to follow their false leadership, they have resorted to exhortations, pleading tearfully for restored confidence. They know only the rules of a generation of self-seekers. They have no vision, and when there is no vision the people perish.

The money changers have fled from their high seats in the temple of our civilization. We may now restore that temple to the ancient truths. The measure of the restoration lies in the extent to which we apply social values more noble than mere monetary profit.

Happiness lies not in the mere possession of money; it lies in the joy of achievement, in the thrill of creative effort. The joy and moral stimulation of work no longer must be forgotten in the mad chase of evanescent profits. These dark days will be worth all they cost us if they teach us that our true destiny is not to be ministered unto but to minister to ourselves and to our fellow men.

Recognition of the falsity of material wealth as the standard of success goes hand in hand with the abandonment of the false belief that public office and high political position are to be valued only by the standards of pride of place and personal profit; and there must be an end to a conduct in banking and in business which too often has given to a sacred trust the likeness of callous and selfish wrongdoing. Small wonder that confidence languishes, for it thrives only on honesty, on honor, on the sacredness of obligations, on faithful protection, on unselfish performance; without them it cannot live.

ROOSEVELT CALLS FOR ACTION

Restoration calls, however, not for changes in ethics alone. This Nation asks for action, and action now.

Our greatest primary task is to put people to work. This is no unsolvable problem if we face it wisely and courageously. It can be accomplished in part by direct recruiting by the Government itself, treating the task as we would treat the emergency of a war, but at the same time, through this employment, accomplishing greatly needed projects to stimulate and reorganize the use of our natural resources.

Hand in hand with this we must frankly recognize the overbalance of population in our industrial centers and, by engaging on a national scale in a redistribution, endeavor to provide a better use of the land for those best fitted for the land. The task can be helped by definite efforts to raise the values of agricultural products and with this the power to purchase the output of our cities. It can be helped by preventing realistically the tragedy of the growing loss through foreclosure of our small homes and our farms. It can be helped by insistence that the Federal, State, and local governments act forthwith on the demand that their cost be drastically reduced. It can be helped by the unifying of relief activities which today are often scattered, uneconomical, and unequal. It can be helped by national planning for and supervision of all forms of transportation and of communications and other utilities which have a definitely public character. There are many ways in which it can be helped, but it can never be helped merely by talking about it. We must act and act quickly.

Finally, in our progress toward a resumption of work we require two safeguards against a return of the evils of the old order; there must be a strict supervision of all banking and credits and investments; there must be an end to speculation with other people's money, and there must be provision for an adequate but sound currency.

There are the lines of attack. I shall presently urge upon a new Congress in special session detailed measures for their fulfillment, and I shall seek the immediate assistance of the several States.

Through this program of action we address ourselves to putting our own national house in order and making income balance outgo. Our international trade relations, though vastly important, are in point of time and necessity secondary to the establishment of a sound national economy. I favor as a practical policy the putting of first things first. I shall spare no effort to restore world trade by international economic readjustment, but the emergency at home cannot wait on that accomplishment.

AMERICA AS THE GOOD NEIGHBOR

The basic thought that guides these specific means of national recovery is not narrowly nationalistic. It is the insistence, as a first consideration, upon the interdependence of the various elements in all parts of the United States—a recognition of the old and permanently important manifestation of the American spirit of the pioneer. It is the way to recovery. It is the immediate way. It is the strongest assurance that the recovery will endure.

In the field of world policy I would dedicate this Nation to the policy of the good neighbor—the neighbor who resolutely respects himself and, because he does so, respects the rights of others—the neighbor who respects his obligations and respects the sanctity of his agreements in and with a world of neighbors.

If I read the temper of our people correctly, we now realize as we have never realized before our interdependence on each other; that we can not merely take but we must give as well; that if we are to go forward, we must move as a trained and loyal army willing to sacrifice for the good of a common discipline, because without such discipline no progress is made, no leadership becomes effective. We are, I know, ready and willing to submit our lives and property to such discipline, because it makes possible a leadership which aims at a larger good. This I propose to offer, pledging that the larger purposes will bind upon us all as a sacred obligation with a unity of duty hitherto evoked only in time of armed strife.

With this pledge taken, I assume unhesitatingly the leadership of this great army of our people dedicated to a disciplined attack upon our common problems.

GANDHI, SALT, AND SATYAGRAHA

RAJENDRA PRASAD

As a leader of India's drive for *purna swaraj*, complete independence from British rule in India, Mohandas K. Gandhi—often
called *Mohatma*, or "great soul"—advocated the practice of satyagraha, passive resistance and nonviolent civil disobedience.
Among Gandhi's many followers was Rajendra Prasad, who
served four terms as president of the Indian National Congress.
In the following selection, Prasad writes of Gandhi's determination to use a program of satyagraha to break the British Salt
Laws, which imposed a tax on salt and made it illegal to make,
manufacture, or sell it without government authorization. Prasad
describes the Indian people's reactions to Gandhi's Salt March in
1930, when Gandhi and eighty of his followers marched 240
miles to the small village of Dandi on the shores of the Arabian
Sea to illegally make salt, thus launching a nationwide campaign
of mass civil disobedience in protest of British law.

A meeting of the Working Committee [of the Lahore, India,
Congress] was held at Sabarmati. I attended it. Mahatmaji [Mohandas K. Gandhi] laid down the programme
of Satyagraha and decided that Civil Disobedience should be offered by breaking the Salt Laws. There was a tax on salt which
brought to the Government of India an annual revenue of crores
of rupees. No one could either make or manufacture salt or sell
it without Government authorisation. It was a tax which no one
could escape. The poorest among the poor, who got a bit of food
even after starving for two days, had to pay his share of the tax

From *At the Feet of Mahatma Gandhi*, by Rajendra Prasad (Bombay: Hind Kitabs, n.d.).

on every morsel that he ate because nobody could take food without salt.

THE SALT LAWS

India is surrounded by sea on three sides. On the seacoast, one can get salt simply by collecting it, without having to do anything else. But even the poorest among the poor cannot collect the salt which nature has provided in plenty, and he cannot eat it without paying the tax. The result was that the consumption of salt in India per capita was lower than in other countries of the world. It had its effect on the health of the population, for salt is an essential article of food. Mahatmaji had thought that by breaking the Salt Laws he would be able to demonstrate even to the poorest that civil disobedience had been started with a view to helping them. At the same time, non-payment of this tax would not injure any third party, for it would only be the Government which stood to lose their revenue. When Mahatmaji placed this proposal before the Working Committee, many of us felt that it could not arouse the enthusiasm and the spirit of the people, particularly in places which were far from the sea-coast, where people get their salt only by purchasing it from traders. They would not even know the amount of the tax which they were paying when they were purchasing it, any more than they would realize that the tax was larger than the cost of producing it. Moreover, they would be at a loss to know how to break the Salt Laws because they were not on the sea-coast where they could collect it without Government authorisation, nor could they get salt water from which they could manufacture salt illegally by boiling the water. Considerable practical difficulty would thus be encountered in the actual breaking of the law. But Mahatmaji was firm in his opinion, and it was decided that it should be defied.

In several districts of Bihar, salt-peter and salt used to be manufactured out of earth. I had seen this being done in my own village. . . . There are many places like this where salt can be manufactured from earth. Moreover, there are many lakes which have salt-water from which salt can be easily manufactured. It was thought that the people living in sea-coast towns and villages would be able to break the law simply by collecting the salt. In other places, they would do so by making salt out of earth, while others would sell and purchase the salt so manufactured and thus set the law at naught. The method and process of making salt from earth were publicised in newspapers and in leaflets, which were distributed in large numbers. I had serious doubts about our ability to enthuse the people in Bihar to break the salt law. I said this much to Mahatmaji. . . .

A MARCH TO DANDI

I made up my mind to do whatever was possible by way of civil disobedience in my Province in connection with the breaking of Salt Laws. Nevertheless, I was afraid that we would not be successful, even though I knew that there would be no difficulty in breaking the Salt Laws in many districts because of the fact that in most villages there were people who knew how to make salt out of earth, and they could easily instruct others in the process. On my return to Bihar, I started the work in this connection and achieved splendid success there as well as in other places.

Mahatmaji had decided that he would be the first to break the Salt Laws. For this purpose, he would start on a march from the Sabarmati Ashram near Ahmedabad to a place near Dandi on the sea-coast. A date was fixed. He was to break the Salt Laws by collecting salt at Dandi on the 6th of April. Dandi is at considerable distance from Sabarmati; and it took him a little longer than three weeks to cover the distance on foot. The places where he was to halt on the way were decided upon beforehand. Mahatmaji started for Dandi with eighty followers. At the time he set out, he announced that he would return to the Ashram after winning Swaraj; if he did not, people would find his body floating in the sea. He also announced that they should get ready for civil disobedience; but as long as he did not actually break the laws and authorise others to do so, none should launch upon Satyagraha.

A tremendous wave of enthusiasm swept over the country following the commencement of Gandhiji's march. Behind his eighty followers marched large crowds of people, who would accompany them some distance and return home after people from other villages had joined them. Thus there was always a big crowd with them during the march. Enthusiasm mounted; but it was not confined only to the route of the march: it was noticeable all over the country. Everywhere people began to prepare for Satyagraha and look forward eagerly to the day when Mahatmaji would tell them to go ahead. . . .

It is not possible to give here the history of the Satyagraha movement; some incidents, however, which have special significance, may be mentioned. It has already been stated that Mahatma Gandhi had declared at the time he started on the Dandi March that he would return to the Ashram after the attainment of Swaraj, or not at all. He kept this promise, for he never returned to the Sabarmati Ashram. After the civil disobedience movement of 1930 he went to Wardha, where he spent some time before moving on to a village nearby, which came to be known as Sevagram. He never uttered a word without endowing it with its full significance; and he was always prepared to act on it. It was in order to keep his word that he left the Ashram for good—an *ashram* . . . in the building up of which he had spent fifteen years of his precious life. . . .

Mahatmaji always used to carry in his mind a couplet of Shri Tulsidas, and would unfailingly act on it: "It has always been the tradition in the house of Raghu to sacrifice one's life itself rather than prove false to one's word."

GANDHI AND THE HARIJANS

We had another shining example of this some time later, when, in 1932, he opposed, from inside the Yeravda Jail, the establishment of separate electorates for Harijans [Untouchables]. When he attended the Round Table Conference in 1931, he was unable to settle the Hindu-Muslim problem. He came to know there that a demand had been pressed forward, on behalf of the Harijans, for separate electorates. He, therefore, declared in one of his speeches that he would resist with his life any move for separate electorates for the Harijans, which would divide them from the other Hindus for good. Yet Prime Minister Ramsay Macdonald, in his Communal Award, accepted the demand for separate electorates for the Harijans. Mahatmaji was in jail when this decision was made public. He started correspondence with Government from inside the jail. . . . He told them that unless they altered their decision, he would have to . . . stake his life to get it reversed. When Government did not pay heed to him, he undertook a fast, and proclaimed that as long as the former did not change the award, he would not take any food. Fortunately, one of the clauses of the Award was that if all the parties concerned with any particular part of it agreed and unanimously wanted it to be changed, it would be changed in that respect. The result was that there was an agreement between the Harijans and other Hindus that there should be no separate electorates for the former, but that the latter would have reserved seats in the Legislative Assemblies in proportion to their number in the population. As a consequence, the Harijans got many more seats than had been given to them by Mr Macdonald's award. But the method of election was changed: separate electorates were done away with. As soon as this agreement was reached, the British Government accepted it, and modified the Award in accordance with the compromise. When Mahatmaji had made that statement about staking his life, nobody had thought that he would literally act on it. When Government published his letter in which he had expressed his intention to carry out what he had said by resorting to a fast, there was consternation in the country, which resulted in the aforementioned compromise and a modification of the Communal Award.

THE SUCCESS OF SATYAGRAHA

When Mahatmaji was preparing for the Dandi March, it was the desire of some friends that he should, before its commencement, record a message for the country, so that it could be played in every village. It was hoped that this historic message would thus be carried to every village, not only in his own words, but in his own voice as well. It was also hoped—for it was not known how long Mahatmaji would be left free by Government—that if the message could be heard by the people in his own voice even after he had gone to jail, it would be of immense help to the Satyagraha Movement. I was at Sabarmati at that time, and I was asked by friends to make this proposal to Mahatmaji. The reply which he gave shows his indomitable faith in truth and its ultimate success. He said: "If there is truth in my message, then whether I am inside or outside the jail, people are bound to pay heed to it. But if there is no truth in it, then in spite of all your efforts, and even with the help of the gramophone, you would not be able to carry it to the people. If the Satyagraha we are going to start is really Satyagraha, that is to say, if it means an insistence on truth and if we are prepared to go ahead on the basis of truth and non-violence, it is bound to succeed, whether people hear my words or not, and whether my voice reaches their ears or not. Therefore, a record like this is neither necessary nor likely to be of any help." After this no one had the courage to press for it.

When Satyagraha commenced and respectable people began to court imprisonment, it was not only the public at large that was affected, but also Government servants, particularly those on whom devolved the duty of suppressing the movement. This could be seen in every part of the country. . . .

I was constantly receiving news from all places where salt was being manufactured that the police would arrive on the scene, break the pots and pans which had been collected for making salt, and in some places even assault and beat up the assembled people. They, however, did not generally make arrests; when they did, they took into custody only a very small number of people. I do not know how it happened, but I was not arrested for some time. I was making a hurricane tour of the districts. When I arrived in a district, I would take a car and run through it from one corner to another in a day or two, or at the most in three days. On my way, I would visit the places where salt was being made; inspect what was being done and encourage the people; and, in this way, address some ten or twelve small and big meetings in a day. Enthusiasm ran high. People were anxious to take me to every village, so that I might see for myself that villagers were not lagging behind in defiance of the Salt Laws. I would also sell by auction at public meetings such quantities of salt as had been made, and thus collect some money for the movement; for every little packet of salt containing half an ounce or so would be sold for Rs. 20 or more. Inspite of all this enthusiasm and excitement, there was not, as far as I know, a single case in the whole Province, of people becoming violent or riotous.

Adolf Hitler and Germany's Return to Power

In 1939, *Time* magazine named German Führer Adolf Hitler "1938's Man of the Year." In the excerpt from the 1939 "Man of the Year" article, *Time* explains that by 1938 Hitler had taken over much of Europe and had become "the greatest threatening force" facing the "democratic, freedom-loving world." According to *Time*, Hitler brought barbarism to a new height and was responsible for resurrecting the issue of barbaric authoritarianism versus civilized liberty, which has been the root cause of past wars. Hitler, writes *Time*, was of little or no importance until 1919 when he joined a fledgling political party and embarked on a political career. *Time* describes how in less than six years Hitler and the Nazis won over the German people, united the nation under the swastika, and turned Germany once again into a military power to be reckoned with—methodically eradicating individual rights and freedoms in the process.

[T he] greatest single news event of 1938 took place on September 29, when four statesmen met at the Fuhrerhaus, in Munich, to redraw the map of Europe. The three visiting statesmen at that historic conference were Prime Minister Neville Chamberlain of Great Britain, Premier Edouard Daladier of France, and Dictator Benito Mussolini of Italy. But by all odds the dominating figure at Munich was the German host, Adolf Hitler.

Excerpted from "Man of the Year: Adolf Hitler," by *Time*, January 2, 1939. Copyright © 1939 Time Inc. Reprinted with permission.

Fuhrer of the German people, Commander-in-Chief of the German Army, Navy & Air Force, Chancellor of the Third Reich, Herr Hitler reaped on that day at Munich the harvest of an audacious, defiant, ruthless foreign policy he had pursued for five and a half years. He had torn the Treaty of Versailles to shreds. He had rearmed Germany to the teeth—or as close to the tooth as he was able. He had stolen Austria before the eyes of a horrified and apparently impotent world.

All these events were shocking to nations which had defeated Germany on the battlefield only 20 years before, but nothing so terrified the world as the ruthless, methodical, Nazi-directed events which during late summer and early autumn threatened a world war over Czechoslovakia. When without loss of blood he reduced Czechoslovakia to a German puppet state, forced a drastic revision of Europe's defensive alliances, and won a free hand for himself in Eastern Europe by getting a "hands-off" promise from powerful Britain (and later France), Adolf Hitler without doubt became 1938's Man of the Year. . . .

LIBERTY VERSUS AUTHORITARIANISM

The figure of Adolf Hitler strode over a cringing Europe with all the swagger of a conqueror. Not the mere fact that the Fuhrer brought 10,500,000 more people (7,000,000 Austrians, 3,500,000 Sudetens) under his absolute rule made him the Man of 1938. Japan during the same time added tens of millions of Chinese to her empire. More significant was the fact Hitler became in 1938 the greatest threatening force that the democratic, freedom-loving world faces today.

His shadow fell far beyond Germany's frontier. Small, neighboring States (Denmark, Norway, Czechoslovakia, Lithuania, The Balkans, Luxembourg, The Netherlands) feared to offend him. In France Nazi pressure was in part responsible for some of the post-Munich anti-democratic decrees. Fascism had intervened openly in Spain, had fostered a revolt in Brazil, was covertly aiding revolutionary movements in Rumania, Hungary, Poland, Lithuania. In Finland a foreign minister had to resign under Nazi pressure. Throughout eastern Europe after Munich the trend was toward less freedom, more dictatorship. In the U.S. alone did democracy feel itself strong enough at year's end to give Hitler his come-uppance.

The Fascintern, with Hitler in the driver's seat, with Mussolini, Franco and the Japanese military cabal riding behind, emerged in 1938 as an international, revolutionary movement. Rant as he might against the machinations of international Communism and international Jewry, or rave as he would that he was just a

Pan-German trying to get all the Germans back in one nation, Fuhrer Hitler had himself become the world's No. 1 International Revolutionist—so much so that if the oft-predicted struggle between Fascism and Communism now takes place it will be only because two revolutionist dictators, Hitler and Stalin, are too big to let each other live in the same world.

But Fuhrer Hitler does not regard himself as a revolutionary; he has become so only by force of circumstances. Fascism has discovered that freedom—of press, speech, assembly—is a potential danger to its own security. In Fascist phraseology democracy is often coupled with Communism. The Fascist battle against freedom is often carried forward under the false slogan of "Down with Communism!" One of the chief German complaints against democratic Czechoslovakia last summer was that it was an "outpost of Communism."

A generation ago western civilization had apparently outgrown the major evils of barbarism except for war between nations. The Russian Communist Revolution promoted the evil of class war. Hitler topped it by another, race war. Fascism and Communism both resurrected religious war. These multiple forms of barbarism gave shape in 1938 to an issue over which men may again, perhaps soon, shed blood: the issue of civilized liberty v. barbaric authoritarianism.

Lesser men of the year seemed small indeed beside the Fuhrer. . . .

HITLER'S RISE TO POWER

In religion, the two outstanding figures of 1938 were in sharp contrast save for their opposition to Adolf Hitler. One of them, Pope Pius XI, 81, spoke with "bitter sadness" of Italy's anti-Semitic laws, the harrying of Italian Catholic Action groups, the reception Italian dictator Benito Mussolini gave Hitler last May, declared sadly: "We have offered our now old life for the peace and prosperity of peoples. We offer it anew." By spending most of the year in a concentration camp, Protestant Pastor Martin Niemoller gave courageous witness to his faith.

It was noteworthy that few of these other men of the year would have been free to achieve their accomplishments in Nazi Germany. The genius of free wills has been so stifled by the oppression of dictatorship that Germany's output of poetry, prose, music, philosophy, art has been meagre indeed.

The man most responsible for this world tragedy is a moody, brooding, unprepossessing, 49-year-old Austrian-born ascetic with a Charlie Chaplin mustache. The son of an Austrian petty customs official, Adolf Hitler was raised as a spoiled child by a doting mother. Consistently failing to pass even the most elementary studies, he grew up a half-educated young man, untrained for any trade or profession, seemingly doomed to failure. Brilliant, charming, cosmopolitan Vienna he learned to loathe for what he called its Semitism; more to his liking was homogeneous Munich, his real home after 1912. To this man of no trade and few interests the Great War was a welcome event which gave him some purpose in life. Hitler took part in 48 engagements, won the German Iron Cross (first class), was wounded once and gassed once, was in a hospital when the Armistice of November 11, 1918 was declared.

His political career began in 1919 when he became Member No. 7 of the midget German Labor Party. Discovering his powers of oratory, Hitler soon became the party's leader, changed its name to the National Socialist German Labor Party, wrote its anti-Semitic, anti-democratic, authoritarian program. The party's first mass meeting took place in Munich in February 1920. The leader intended to participate in a monarchist attempt to seize power a month later; but for this abortive Putsch Fuhrer Hitler arrived too late. An even less successful National Socialist attempt—the famed Munich Beer Hall Putsch of 1923—provided the party with dead martyrs, landed Herr Hitler in jail. His incarceration at Landsberg Fortress gave him time to write the first volume of *Mein Kampf*, now a "must" on every German bookshelf. (Deputy Fuhrer Rudolf Hess helped write it. Imprisonment also gave Hitler time to perfect his tactics. Even before that time he got from his Communist opponents the idea of gangster-like party storm troopers; after this the principle of the small cell groups of devoted party workers.)

Outlawed in many German districts, the National Socialist Party nevertheless climbed steadily in membership. Time-honored Tammany Hall [Chicago political machine] methods of handing out many small favors were combined with rowdy terrorism and lurid, patriotic propaganda. The picture of a mystic, abstemious, charismatic Fuhrer was assiduously cultivated.

Not until 1929 did National Socialism win its first absolute majority in a city election (at Coburg) and make its first significant showing in a provincial election (in Thuringia). But from 1928 on the party almost continually gained in electoral strength. In the Reichstag [German parliament] elections of 1928 it polled 809,000 votes. Two years later 6,401,016 Germans voted for National Socialist deputies while in 1932 the vote was 13,732,779. While still short of a majority, the vote was nevertheless impressive proof of the power of the man and his movement.

The situation which gave rise to this demagogic, ignorant, des-

perate movement was inherent in the German Republic's birth
and in the craving of large sections of the politically immature
German people for strong, masterful leadership. Democracy in
Germany was conceived in the womb of military defeat. It was
the Republic which put its signature (unwillingly) to the humiliating Versailles Treaty, a brand of shame which it never lived
down in German minds.

That the German people love uniforms, parades, military formations, and submit easily to authority is no secret. Fuhrer
Hitler's own hero is Frederick the Great. That admiration stems
undoubtedly from Frederick's military prowess and autocratic
rule rather than from Frederick's love of French culture and his
hatred of Prussian boorishness. But unlike the polished Frederick, Fuhrer Hitler, whose reading has always been very limited,
invites few great minds to visit him, nor would Fuhrer Hitler
agree with Frederick's contention that he was "tired of ruling
over slaves.". . .

In bad straits even in fair weather, the German Republic collapsed under the weight of the 1929-34 depression in which German unemployment soared to 7,000,000 above a nationwide
wind drift of bankruptcies and failures. Called to power as
Chancellor of the Third Reich on January 30, 1933, by aged, se-
nile President Paul von Hindenburg, Chancellor Hitler began to
turn the Reich inside out. Unemployment was solved by: 1) a
far-reaching program of public works; 2) an intense re-armament
program, including a huge standing army; 3) enforced labor in
the service of the State (the German Labor Corps); 4) putting political enemies and Jewish, Communist and Socialist jobholders
in concentration camps.

What Adolf Hitler & Co. did to Germany in less than six years
was applauded wildly and ecstatically by most Germans. He
lifted the nation from post-War defeatism. Under the swastika
Germany was unified. His was no ordinary dictatorship, but
rather one of great energy and magnificent planning. The "socialist" part of National Socialism might be scoffed at by hard-&-
fast Marxists, but the Nazi movement nevertheless had a mass
basis. The 1,500 miles of magnificent highways built, schemes for
cheap cars and simple workers' benefits, grandiose plans for rebuilding German cities made Germans burst with pride. Germans might eat many substitute foods or wear ersatz clothes but
they did eat.

What Adolf Hitler & Co. did to the German people in that time
left civilized men and women aghast. Civil rights and liberties
have disappeared. Opposition to the Nazi regime has become
tantamount to suicide or worse. Free speech and free assembly

are anachronisms. The reputations of the once-vaunted German centres of learning have vanished. Education has been reduced to a National Socialist catechism.

Pace quickened. Germany's 700,000 Jews have been tortured physically, robbed of homes and properties, denied a chance to earn a living, chased off the streets. Now they are being held for "ransom," a gangster trick through the ages. But not only Jews have suffered. Out of Germany has come a steady, ever-swelling stream of refugees, Jews and Gentiles, liberals and conservatives, Catholics as well as Protestants, who could stand Naziism no longer. . . .

HITLER'S GERMANY: REPRESSION AND REPRISALS

Meanwhile, Germany has become a nation of uniforms, goose-stepping to Hitler's tune, where boys of ten are taught to throw hand grenades, where women are regarded as breeding machines. The most cruel joke of all, however, has been played by Hitler & Co. on those German capitalists and small businessmen who once backed National Socialism as a means of saving Germany's bourgeois economic structure from radicalism. The Nazi credo that the individual belongs to the state also applies to business. Some businesses have been confiscated outright, on others what amounts to a capital tax has been levied. Profits have been strictly controlled. Some idea of the increasing Governmental control and interference in business could be deduced from the fact that 80% of all building and 50% of all industrial orders in Germany originated last year with the Government. Hard-pressed for food-stuffs as well as funds, the Nazi regime has taken over large estates and in many instances collectivized agriculture, a procedure fundamentally similar to Russian Communism.

When Germany took over Austria she took upon herself the care and feeding of 7,000,000 poor relations. When 3,500,000 Sudetens were absorbed, there were that many more mouths to feed. As 1938 drew to a close many were the signs that the Nazi economy of exchange control, barter trade, lowered standard of living, "self-sufficiency," was cracking. Nor were signs lacking that many Germans disliked the cruelties of their Government, but were afraid to protest them. Having a hard time to provide enough bread to go round, Fuhrer Hitler was being driven to give the German people another diverting circus. The Nazi controlled press, jumping the rope at the count of Propaganda Minister Paul Joseph Goebbels, shrieked insults at real and imagined enemies. And the pace of the German dictatorship quickened as more & more guns rolled from factories and little more butter was produced.

In five years under the Man of 1938, regimented Germany had made itself one of the great military powers of the world today. The British Navy remains supreme on the seas. Most military men regard the French Army as incomparable. The biggest question mark is air strength, which changes from day to day, but most observers believe Germany superior in warplanes. Despite a shortage of trained officers and a lack of materials, the German Army has become a formidable machine which could probably be beaten only by a combination of opposing armies. As testimony to his nation's puissance, Fuhrer Hitler could look back over the year and remember that besides receiving countless large-bore statesmen (Mr. Chamberlain three times, for instance), he paid his personal respects to three kings (Sweden's Gustaf, Denmark's Christian, Italy's Vittorio Emanuele) and was visited by two (Bulgaria's Boris, Rumania's Carol—not counting Hungary's Regent, Horthy).

Meanwhile an estimated 1,133 streets and squares, notably Rathaus Platz in Vienna, acquired the name of Adolf Hitler. He delivered 96 public speeches, attended eleven opera performances (way below par), vanquished two rivals (Benes and Kurt von Schuschnigg, Austria's last Chancellor), sold 900,000 new copies of *Mein Kampf* in Germany besides selling it widely in Italy and Insurgent Spain. His only loss was in eyesight: he had to begin wearing spectacles for work. Last week Herr Hitler entertained at a Christmas party 7,000 workmen now building Berlin's new mammoth Chancellery, and told them: "The next decade will show those countries with their patent democracy where true culture is to be found."

THE RED ARMY'S LONG MARCH

DICK WILSON

In 1934, seeking safety from Chiang Kai-shek's Chinese Nationalists, Chinese Communists began a six-thousand-mile trek to northwestern China. A year later, under the leadership of Mao Tse-tung, they arrived at their destination. In the following selection, British journalist, author, and editor Dick Wilson focuses on the rigors of the *Changzheng*—Long March—which nearly half of the original marchers did not survive. Wilson recounts Chinese political commissar Hsiang Ying's tale of how the Red Army, forced to retreat into the forest, lost all contact with the outside world, as well as some of their best commanders, yet kept on going. According to Wilson, although some women went along on the march, they had to leave their young children behind in the care of peasant families and ended up losing all trace of them. For the duration of the Long March, claims Wilson, the level of discipline was high, most of the soldiers young, and the marching extraordinarily physically demanding.

M ost of the wounded . . . had to be left behind in the care of villagers, and a force of some 6,000 fit soldiers was assigned to stay in Kiangsi as a rearguard. . . .

Many of those who stayed behind were captured and killed—including Mao's younger brother Mao Tse-tan.

Red Army Commander Chu Teh explained afterwards: "We left many of our ablest military, political and mass leaders behind. . . .

"We also left behind about 20,000 of our wounded, scattered in mountain hospitals. After recovering, these men left the hospital

From *The Long March 1935: The Epic of Chinese Communism's Survival*, by Dick Wilson (New York: Viking, 1971). Copyright © 1971 by Dick Wilson. Reprinted with permission from the author.

and reported for duty. Maimed men were given money, sent to their homes, and allotted a pension of $50 a year. These pensions were paid out so long as our comrades in Kiangsi had money."

After several weeks the enemy occupied the chief base areas, but the rearguard enabled the main force to get out of the Kuomintang trap. . . .

IN RETREAT

Political Commissar Hsiang Ying told his story to [journalist] Edgar Snow in 1938: "We decided to decentralize our remaining forces, breaking them up into small partisan bands of several hundred men each, scattered over an extensive territory. . . .

"By the end of 1936 our forces were confronted with desperate odds. The enemy gave us no rest. We had some kind of skirmish at least once a week. New tactics deprived us of fighting with advantage or even on equal terms. At times we believed our Western armies had entirely perished. At night we dared not sleep in towns or villages for fear of surprise attack. We had to make our beds in the forests of the mountains. For nearly two years I never undressed at night, but slept with even my shoes on. So did most of our men. In that time I wore the same cotton uniform, which became ragged and faded and patched.

"We never had enough to eat. Had it not been for the help of the people we would have starved. Many of our smaller units, cut off by Nanking troops, were saved by the farmers, who hid their rifles. The farmers gladly shared with us what rice they had. . . .

"We lost all contact with the outside. We were like wild men, living and fighting by instinct. Many of our best commanders were killed, or died of disease. We had no medicines and no hospitals. Our ammunition ran very low. Many of our guns became useless; we had no arsenal and could not repair them. We could not even make bullets, and practiced extreme economy with those we had. Sometimes the farmers would smuggle in a little ammunition for us. But the blockade made this more and more difficult.

"At times we retired into the uninhabited forests. We learned the trails of Fukien and Kiangsi foot by foot. We knew every corner of the mountains. We learned to fast with nothing to eat for four or five days. And yet we became strong and agile as savages. Some of our look-outs practically lived in trees. Our young men could go up and down mountains with incredible speed. . . .

"The anti-Red forces narrowed the circle around us. The enemy built many new roads, blockhouses and fortifications. They depopulated many villages, burned them, and carried off all stocks of grain. They burned down thousands of trees on the mountains, and tried to trap us. Many of our scouts and couriers were captured.". . . .

Eventually a truce was struck, but the fighting resumed a year or two later.

Meanwhile the main force of the First Front Army that assembled near Yutu on October 15 and 16 to challenge the innermost line of Kuomintang blockhouses on the Anyuan-Hsinfeng-Kanchow road comprised some 85,000 regular soldiers and 15,000 officials of the soviet Government and Party. . . . The factories and military arsenal were stripped and most of the hardware and equipment buried, the rest being strapped on to the backs of mules and donkeys. Sewing machines, printing presses, heavy weapons, banknotes, gold bullion, silver dollars and thousands of documents were in the cavalcade. Mao Tse-min, the middle of the three Mao brothers, was in charge of this equipment and treasure, which held down the speed of the columns. "Mules, horses and luggage . . . crowded the narrow paths," wrote Liu Po-cheng afterwards. "Consequently, we could cover only one valley a night and we were very tired. Since the enemy used highways and marched at a great speed, we could not shake him off." The transport column used sometimes to lag behind by ten days' march, and in heavy rain could take five hours to complete one mile. . . .

ON THE MARCH

The retreating Communists behaved—at least in the early stages of the Long March—like a provisional government on the road.

"Each man," said the chief artillery engineer afterwards, "carried five pounds of ration rice and each had a shoulder pole from which hung either two small boxes of ammunition or hand grenades, or big kerosene cans filled with our most essential machinery and tools. Each pack contained a blanket or quilt, one quilted winter uniform, and three pairs of strong cloth shoes with thick rope soles tipped and heeled with metal.

"The people also gave us presents of dried vegetables, peppers, or such things. Each man had a drinking cup, a pair of chopsticks thrust into his puttees, and a needle and thread caught on the underside of the peak of his cap. All men wore big sun-rain hats made of two thin layers of bamboo with oiled paper between, and many had paper umbrellas stuck in their packs. Each man carried a rifle. . . .

"Everyone going on the Long March was dressed and equipped the same. Everyone was armed."

Swiss missionary Alfred Bosshardt [taken prisoner on route] recalled that the soldiers in his column had no leather shoes,

Soldiers in the Red Army defend a section of railroad track. The Red Army made a six-thousand-mile march to flee Chinese Nationalists.

only cloth sandals, shreds of twisted cloth bound on to the bare foot with string or straw. In the rain they would dissolve in a day, and so fresh sandals had to be plaited whenever there was a halt. Soldiers would weep in pain after a long stage of marching. The only European to undergo the entire March—Otto Braun or Li Teh—took size eleven shoes and could never get new ones big enough.

The sick and some of the leaders were able to ride on horseback, out there were very few horses and most of the men had to walk the entire way. . . .

Mao followed the style described by his batman a few years

earlier, during the Kiangsi campaigns: "He had only the simplest of belongings. Two cotton and wool mixture blankets, a sheet, two of the ordinary uniform jackets and trousers, a sweater, a patched umbrella, an enamel mug which served as his rice bowl, and a grey brief-case with nine pockets. On the march he used to carry the brief-case himself, and the umbrella, and I made a roll of the rest of the things. When we made camp I used to make up his bed with the blankets and sheet. He used the rest of his belongings as a pillow."

For the Long March itself Mao discarded his brief-case, but had acquired a proper enamel food container, a three-decker. He was still recovering from malaria when the journey started, and was described by one of his men as "thin and emaciated." Later he took to his feet, except for a period of relapse when he had to be carried on a stretcher. . . .

THE COURAGE OF THE WOMEN

Among the marchers were thirty-five women, the wives of the highest Government and Party officials. The rest of the women and all the children, including two of Mao's, had to be left behind. . . . Too young to go on the March, the children were placed out with peasant families and all trace was lost of them.

Despite careful and prolonged searches by the People's Liberation Army fifteen years later after the area was recaptured, none of these children was found. Mao's wife, Ho Tzu-chen, was several months pregnant when the March began, and was wounded in a low-flying bomber attack in Kweichow in the early stages of the March. It was said that she had twenty pieces of shrapnel in her body, yet she survived the ordeal and bore Mao yet another child in 1937. . . .

Mao offered the opinion afterwards that the women had been more courageous than the men. The most outstanding example, by common consent, was Kang Ke-ching, the wife of Chu Teh. She took her own weapons and knapsack on the March and was even said on one or two occasions to have carried a wounded soldier on her back. Chu, she explained, had an orderly to attend to his meals and clothes, and in any case "he did not like the idea of women devoting themselves only to domestic affairs." She had no time even to wash her own clothes on the March. "I always carried three or four rifles to encourage the others." Kang first took command in 1934 when visiting a village on Party work. "By chance," she afterwards explained, "we met the enemy and had to grab our guns and fight. I was temporarily elected commander by the 300 men there. I was the only woman. We fought for two hours; then the enemy retreated. I don't know whether I killed anyone or not—I couldn't see the results of my shooting—but I am a very good marksman. I must say this was a happy day for me.". . .

A RARE MIXTURE: CAMARADERIE AND DISCIPLINE

Snow, who knew China well, described the Red Army soldiers he saw in Shensi the year after their Long March as "perhaps the first consciously happy group of Chinese proletarians I had seen." Unlike most Chinese armies, they were not carefully segregated according to provincial origin, but mixed. "Their different provincial backgrounds and dialects did not seem to divide them, but became the subject of constant good-natured raillery.". . . They used to sing at the slightest pretext, and had a vast repertoire of propaganda and folk songs. But there were many moments on the March when no one could raise a tune to his lips.

An official history gives the proportion of peasants in the Red Army in April 1934, just before the March, as sixty-eight per cent: proletarian workers accounted for thirty per cent. Most of the soldiers were under twenty-three years old, the exact breakdown by age being given as one per cent below sixteen years, fifty-three per cent between sixteen and twenty-three years, forty-four per cent between twenty-four and forty years and four per cent over forty. Some twenty-eight per cent of the army were Communist Party members, and another seventeen per cent were Youth League members.

The level of discipline was high. When Snow was on the road with the Red Army in Shensi in 1936 he recorded that "When we passed wild apricot trees on the hills there was an abrupt dispersal until everyone had filled his pockets, and somebody always brought me back a handful. . . . But when we passed private orchards, nobody touched the fruit in them, and the grain and vegetables we ate in the villages were paid for in full.". . .

The rule was that the property of the rich—the landlords and the local officials—in the areas where the Red Army went could be confiscated, but only by order of the confiscation department of the Finance Commission . . . and only the appointed officers of this department were empowered to distribute such goods. The Marchers were generally hungry, but every now and again there was a feast. . . .

The marching was often strenuous beyond belief. The Ho Lung forces once marched for twenty-seven consecutive days without a single rest day, and twice they marched right through the night as well as through the preceding and following days, with only short halts: on one day they covered fifty miles.

Bosshardt remembers that on nights when torches were forbidden in case they were seen by the enemy, each soldier in Ho Lung's army marched with his hand on the shoulder of the man in front of him.

According to the official record, the main force of the First Front Army averaged almost one skirmish each day on the Long March, and had fifteen whole days of major pitched battle. They made 235 day marches and eighteen night marches, with a hundred days of halt (sometimes fighting) in between. But fifty-six of those days of halt were taken all at once in north-west Szechuan, and if the other forty-four are averaged out over the 6,000-mile route they mean one whole day's halt for every 114 miles.

The average daily coverage was thus seventeen miles over the whole year, or twenty-six miles if the eight-week recuperation in Szechuan is left out of the account. Commander Tso Chuan told Snow also that they crossed eighteen mountain ranges, five of them permanently snow-capped, twenty-four rivers and twelve provinces, and that they took sixty-two cities and towns along the route as well as breaking through the enveloping armies of no fewer than ten different provincial warlords.

THE SPANISH CIVIL WAR: THREE YEARS OF BARBARISM

MAX GALLO

The civil war that enveloped Spain between 1936 and 1939 toppled the elected government and ushered in the long-term dictatorship of Generalissimo Francisco Franco, who ruled Spain
with an iron hand until his death in 1975. In the view of many,
including French writer and academician Max Gallo, the author
of the following selection, the Spanish Civil War was a prologue
to World War II and Spain a testing ground for the strategies,
troops, and weapons of that war. Gallo describes the massacres
and executions that punctuated the war and writes that with the
Spanish Civil War "the age of barbarism had begun." Gallo contends that Franco's Nationalists would not have succeeded had
Fascist Italy and Nazi Germany refused to help Franco or had the
Western democracies intervened.

S pring 1938: that pitiless conflict, the Spanish Civil War, had
been raging for nearly two years. Since 1936, Europe, having countenanced the crushing of independent Ethiopia by
Fascist Italy, had seen war drawing closer. Hitler had remilita-
rized the left bank of the Rhine, and in defiance of the Treaty of
Versailles had brought back compulsory military service. Mussolini, after his triumph over the Negus, Haile Selassie, envisaged
with even greater arrogance Italian domination over the whole
Mediterranean. And when, on 17 July 1936, the troops of the
Spanish Legion of Morocco rose under the leadership of General

From *Spain Under Franco: A History*, by Max Gallo (New York: Dutton, 1974). Copyright
©1969 by Gerard & Cie. English translation © 1973 by E.P. Dutton & Co., Inc., and George
Allen & Unwin Ltd. Used by permission of the author.

Francisco Franco y Bahamonde, when the garrisons of the peninsula attempted, with varying degrees of success, to seize its cities,
when Italian aircraft enabled the Moroccan *Regulares* to cross
from Africa into Spain, when Fascist 'volunteers', side by side
with Nationalist troops, openly attacked the democratic forces of
the legal government, it became clear to all that war had come to
European soil.

French tourists, visiting the Basque country . . . looked across
into Spain at the explosions that marked the advance of an army
defying its own *Frente Popular* (Popular Front) government, duly
elected in February 1936. Through rented field-glasses, ensconced
under leafy bowers or sunshades, they watched war going on, as
though they were immune to its contagion.

In fact, from the first days of the fighting, Europe had been involved. Indeed, even before the opening of hostilities, before war
broke out in all its cruel reality, Mussolini had given advice and
financial aid to the Falangist and traditionalist elements which
were preparing their onslaught on a Republic still unsure of itself, torn by internal contradiction. . . . Italian aircraft intervened
from the start, followed by the German Condor Legion, then by
Italian troops, some 60,000 strong.

Italian submarines torpedoed those neutral or Russian ships
that ventured towards Spanish harbours, while the British and
French Governments, paralysed by their pacifism and by the
activity of Fascist sympathizers, and misled by the illusory
hope of possible compromise, adopted and clung to a policy of
non-intervention.

Meanwhile, however, volunteers from many countries had
come to Spain to fight by the side of the Republican troops. They
fired from the ruined buildings of the University City outside
Madrid, and from November 1936 onwards they triumphantly
resisted the assaults of Franco's forces, defeating the Italians on
the Guadalajara in March 1937. It was a bloody prefiguring of the
struggle which was to rend Europe a few years later; those who
cried *Arriba España* and those who replied *No pasarán* were acting out the prologue to the Second World War.

A STUDY IN BARBARISM

Spring 1938: the killing had been going on in Spain for two years.

Picasso has shown us that Spain, preyed on by monsters and
shattered by explosives, with despairing women lifting up their
arms and their eyes to heaven, from whence (as at [the Spanish
town] Guernica on 26 April 1937 [when it was bombed by the
Fascists]) came death. But these victims of air attacks (they numbered almost 12,000 by 1938) were not the only casualties. There

were wholesale massacres. In the bull-ring at Badajoz, in August 1936, 1,800 Republicans were executed in the space of twelve hours, and seven of their leaders were shot in the bull-pen before 3,000 spectators. At Málaga, which fell on 8 February 1937 into the hands of General Mario Roatta's Italian troops and the Nationalist forces, suspects were shot without trial from morning till night. In the other zone, priests, notables and landowners were being killed. Public squares, bull-rings, barracks yards, dirt roads in small villages and paved streets in cities, all were scenes of slaughter. The age of barbarism had begun. . . .

'A civil war is not a war but a disease,' said [French poet Antoine-Marie-Roger de] Saint-Exupéry. 'In a civil war the enemy is within, one is as it were fighting against oneself. And that, no doubt, is why this war assumes so terrible a form; there is more shooting than fighting; death here is like a quarantine camp—germ-bearers are liquidated. . . . They shoot men as though they were deforesting the land.' . . .

There were battles too, where often the tragedy of civil strife was heightened by the horror of summary executions by the roadside or in a field: soldiers in blue overalls and rope-soled sandals, ill-trained Republican soldiers who for a long time rejected all organization, heroic undisciplined anarchists, leaving the trenches at night to sleep in town, together with international fighters, sometimes . . . facing their compatriots on the other side. Fierce Moroccans recruited for a crusade, raping, plundering and killing; pitiless battles where nobody expected pity, where every man was aware of his fate—for the vanquished, usually death. Nationalist officers deliberately sought to inspire a 'salutary horror', and it is well known that at a ceremony in the great amphitheatre of the University of Salamanca, on 12 October 1936, General Millán Astray aimed his revolver at the old Basque philosopher Miguel Unamuno (who had in fact supported Franco's enterprise during the first few months), with the cry '¡Abajo la Inteligencia! ¡Viva la muerte!' The words and the action reflect the tone of the war that had been ravaging Spain for two years. 'You will win,' Unamuno replied, 'because you possess more brute force than you need.'

THE WAR (JULY 1936–SPRING 1938)

In fact, between July 1936 and the spring of 1938 the Nationalists strengthened their positions and the balance seemed likely to turn in their favour. True, their hope of a swift triumph had been shattered by the resistance of the people; true, Franco's troops advanced only thanks to the help of Fascist Italy and Nazi Germany, and thanks to the non-intervention of the democratic powers, which refused aid to the legal government in Madrid. Mexico remained loyal, the U.S.S.R. provided aircraft, tanks and men, but these two powers were remote; whatever the causes of Franco's successes, these were undeniable, and that was what mattered primarily.

Protected by Italian aircraft, Franco and his forces succeeded in crossing the Straits of Gibraltar, in spite of the fleet's loyalty to the Republic; but they failed to take Madrid, even with the help of German bombers, and meanwhile the Italians were defeated on the Guadalajara (March 1937). Although their advance was checked at the heart of Spain, the Nationalists took Málaga in the south (February 1937), and . . .—the bloodshed was appalling, 25,000 Republicans and 1,000 Nationalists were killed—Franco's troops gained possession of the Basque country (summer to October 1937): here the Republican defeat not only led to the repression, the summary executions which crowned the work begun at Guernica, but furthermore provided Franco's army with rich industrial provinces and created a Nationalist zone running from the south to the north of Spain, covering the west side of the peninsula, bordering on Portugal and touching the Mediterranean and the Atlantic. . . .

The superior power of the Nationalists was becoming evident. The sky was theirs, too: at midday on 20 January 1938, as crowds were leaving offices and factories, Italian aircraft attacked Barcelona, repeating the Guernica exploit with the same aim—terrorization. On 16 March, at three in the afternoon, there began a series of seventeen raids on the Catalan capital which continued uninterruptedly for some ten hours, killing 1,300 and wounding 3,000. Spain was unmistakably a testing-ground for the Second World War.

During this same spring of 1938, Nationalist troops, together with Italians of the *Corpo Truppe Volontarie*, broke through the Republican lines all along the south bank of the Ebro [River]. On 15 April the Nationalist troops of Alonso Vega reached the Mediterranean at Vinaroz: Republican Spain was cut in half. The central southern part was isolated from Catalonia. Nationalist and Italian soldiers might well shout for joy and throw their helmets in the air on the beach, while Moroccans went swimming; a decisive turning had been reached. Nationalists also attacked all along the Pyrenees, and refugees poured into France in their thousands; women, children and old men fled from Aragon, which was occupied by the troops of Generals Moscardo and Yagüe. Although the Republican soldiers reaching France were eager to go back to fight, fiercely raising clenched fists as they leaned out of the carriage windows, the Republic, now cut in half, was already faced with defeat.

Spring 1938: the fighting, the killing had been going on for two years, and the greatest battle was still to come, launched on 25 July by the Republicans, who with their surprise crossing of the Ebro broke up the enemy lines. 'The Italians have fallen into the Ebro, and only Republican flags now fly on its bridges'; so ran a popular song. The violence of the clash was something unparalleled in any civil war; and in fact this conflict had long been more than that. The Germans were there with their first Stukas, the Italians with their artillery, hundreds of tanks appeared, and opposite them the International Brigades under General Lister fought with relentless courage. . . .

The Republicans fought with an energy that amazed the whole world, half-trained soldiers resisting the strongest units of the Spanish, Moroccan, German and Italian armies, civilian-soldiers who knew that death was the only outcome.

THE MYSTERY OF AMELIA EARHART

WILLIAM H. STEWART

Aviatrix Amelia Earhart was the first woman to pilot an airplane across the Atlantic Ocean. In 1937, during an attempted world flight, she disappeared, never to be heard from again. Since that time, numerous theories have evolved about Earhart and her disappearance. The following selection focuses on the theory that Earhart was involved in espionage for the United States and was found by the Japanese, whose naval installations in the Marshall and Eastern Caroline Islands were the target of her aerial investigations. After explaining that this theory is based on two messages Earhart radioed to the Coast Guard cutter *Itasca*, William H. Stewart identifies different aspects of the theory. Stewart is a former foreign service officer in American Embassies of North Africa and Southeast Asia. He has served as a military historical cartographer and an American administrator of the former Japanese Mandated Islands (later known as the Trust Territory of the Pacific Islands of which the Northern Marianas (Saipan) and Marshall Islands were a part).

In the mystery surrounding the disappearance of Amelia Earhart and her navigator Fred Noonan, Saipan has featured prominently in the stories. On July 1, 1937, the famous aviatrix Amelia Earhart and her navigator, Fred Noonan, disappeared somewhere in the vicinity of the Phoenix Islands southwest of the Hawaiian Islands.

Many theories abound and those familiar with Saipan know that some believe that she was eventually found by the Japanese

Reprinted, with permission, from "Saipan and the Mystery of Amelia Earhart," by William H. Stewart, published as a special section of the *Commonwealth of Northern Mariana Islands (CNMI) Guide*, at www.cnmi-guide.com.

and brought to Saipan. The Japanese have consistently denied having any knowledge of the fate of Amelia Earhart. Some have theorized that she may have been engaged in espionage for the United States in an attempt to learn more about military activities in the Japanese Mandated Islands of Micronesia, particularly in the vicinity of Truk, which was believed at the time to be the site of a Japanese naval base. The theory rests upon the last message ever received from Earhart by the U.S. Coast Guard Cutter *Itasca* and whether or not the information received was a compass heading or a sun line. She radioed, "We are on a position 157 degrees—337 degrees, we will repeat this message on 6210 kilocycles.

"We are running north and south." The entire theory rests on two of several radio messages transmitted from her aircraft that provided flight information to the *Itasca*. One message being a position fix 5 hours after her departure from Lae, New Guinea, and a second message radioing either a heading on a compass or a sun line as she neared her destination.

For almost sixty years her disappearance has been a riddle wrapped in an enigma. Although it has been consistently denied by the United States Government, there must have been several high ranking officers within the American naval establishment who saw in Earhart's plan for a flight around the world a golden opportunity to reconnoiter the developments being carried out within the Truk Lagoon by the Imperial Japanese Navy. The mysterious disappearance of Amelia Earhart (Mrs. George P. Putnam) and her navigator, Fred Noonan (previously a Pan American Airways navigator), along with their Lockheed Electra -10 after the aircraft left Lae, the capital of the Australian Mandated Territory of New Guinea, is a puzzle that remains fascinating.

A FALSE POSITION?

It is not known if American intelligence officers ever bothered to read the annual reports the Japanese were required to submit to the League of Nations in the late thirties on their activities in the islands. If the United States authorities analyzed such reports they must have become curious as to the purpose of the imports of certain commodities listed in the statistical tables of the Annual Reports for 1936 –'37, which included 3.8 million tons of rice (enough to feed a huge naval establishment).

Did knowledge of these increasing imports prompt General Henry "Hap" Arnold, Army Air Corps Chief, to attempt to find out what had been taking place within the Japanese Mandated Islands beyond their wall of secrecy by ordering the flight of two B -24's to reconnoiter the area barely two weeks before the outbreak of war in the Pacific and attempt to learn what Earhart failed to do 4 years and 5 months earlier?

While the buildup of Truk as a great Gunko (naval base) had been kept a closely guarded secret, U.S. naval vessels were prohibited by the Japanese from entering the harbors of the Mandated Islands. By 1937, American naval authorities were becoming increasingly apprehensive of Japan's rearmament and the growing belligerency of its military. So much so that on Thanksgiving Day in 1941 (two weeks before the attack on Pearl Harbor), General Arnold ordered two B-24 aircraft stationed in San Francisco to fly to Manila. While enroute they were ordered to fly over Jaluit in the Marshall Islands and Truk in the Eastern Caroline Islands to photograph the naval installations there and attempt to find out what had been taking place at these locations within the Japanese Mandated Islands. Did the American military's curiosity about these islands prompt an earlier (1937) request of Amelia Earhart to also attempt to fly over the same islands for the same purpose but from a different direction? Did she do so?

The only serious problem with such a supposition is that a position report received from Earhart while in flight occurred at 5:20 P.M. (Lae time) and indicated her position at 04 degrees—33' south latitude by 159 degrees—06' east longitude, a fix which would place the aircraft in the vicinity of Nukumanu Island, northeast of Bougainville and in the area where it should have been assuming the original flight plan was being followed.

This fix would place the aircraft on a track from Lae to Howland Island some 742 nautical miles or about one-third the distance between the two points which are separated by 2,227 nautical miles. This radioed position is far to the southeast of Truk and almost due south of Ponape (Senyavin Island, now Pohnpei) and north of Guadalcanal. That the transmission was picked up in Lae is strange indeed, since the Electra's radio range was said to be (although not confirmed by this researcher) not much more than 400 miles. If this was in fact true—how is it that the signal was picked up from almost twice the distance?

Was it a hoax? Was it a deceptive position directed to confuse any Japanese radioman at Truk who might have been monitoring the much publicized flight path (presumed to be from Lae to Howland) and the radio frequency of 6210 KHz? If so, the report was received at Truk only a short time before the aircraft could have roared over the encircling reef at Truk to carry out its assignment of aerial espionage before turning east to fly toward Jaluit and beyond the International Date Line thence southeast to Howland. To intentionally radio a false position with the objective of disguising one's true position is a classic technique of deception. Had a Japanese been monitoring the radio at Truk, he could have plotted her position as a result of those coordinates and assumed she was outside the boundary of the Mandated Islands when in reality she could have been only an hour or so flying time south of Truk, bearing down on the Japanese anchorage, then zoom over the lagoon with enough light to observe the base before turning to fly east into the cover of the advancing evening darkness.

On July 2, 1937, Earhart departed Lae, New Guinea, with Howland Island, as her destination 2,227 nautical miles [n. mi.] distant on an azimuth of 79.8 degrees—almost due east. The aircraft was to rendezvous with the U.S. Coast Guard Cutter *Itasca*, which had been assigned by the U.S. Government to provide weather information and a directional beacon signal.

EARHART'S ROUTE IN QUESTION

Howland is a low island with the highest point not ten feet above sea level. It is located at 00 degrees—48' north latitude—176 degrees—38' west longitude, a mere dot on a Pacific chart.

It is interesting to note that on May 11, 1935, Fred Noonan replied to a letter from Navy Lt. Commander P.V.H. Weems, an authority on aerial navigation, in which Noonan wrote about certain equipment for the planned flight. He stated, "For reasons which I am certain you can understand, we are not permitted to discuss the particulars of the flight for dissemination among the general public."

For some time the aircraft identified as King - How - Able - Queen - Queen had been trying to communicate by radio with the American vessel. However, some of the signals received by the *Itasca*, and there were several, were at times either inaudible or incomprehensible. As the ship waited at Howland, its radio crackled shortly after 8 A.M., July 1st, with a woman's voice. "We are on the line of position 157 degrees—337 degrees—we will repeat this message on 6210 kilocycles wait listening on 6210 kilocycles—we are running north and south." This was the last message received by the *Itasca* from Earhart.

For sixteen days thereafter, eight United States Navy ships and sixty-four aircraft scanned 138,000 square miles of the Pacific for some evidence of the aircraft with the registry number 16020 and its crew of two. Nothing was found. Flying a heading of 79.8 degrees in a northeasterly direction would result in approaching Howland from the southwest. Flying a heading of 157 degrees (if this was in fact a compass heading rather than a sun line) would result in approaching the island from a northwestern direction. The question to be posed being—what would one have to do to approach Howland on a heading of 157 from the northwest? Could it be possible that Earhart, on a secret mission for the U.S. military, flew north from Lae over the Truk Lagoon to observe the installations and then anticipated a change in heading over Eten Island in the lagoon which would take her east over Jaluit in the Marshall Islands and then continued to fly east and cross the International Date Line to approach Howland from the northwest on a compass course of 157 degrees? If she did—then she was engaged in espionage—about that there can be no doubt. The distance in nautical miles from Lae to Truk is 888; from Truk to Jaluit—1,063; and from Jaluit to Howland (via Great Circle)—878 n. mi.

The total distance is 2,829 n. mi. as compared with 2,227 n. mi. when flying direct from Lae. The most direct route (Great Circle) from Jaluit to Howland is on a heading of 109.9 degrees for 878 n. miles. However, this route, while shorter, would require her to be in Japanese airspace and over several populated islands in the Marshalls for a longer period of time, which would afford the Japanese more time for interception should the flight be discovered.

Even so, the cover of darkness would provide added safety. Did she maintain an easterly heading of 090 degrees after passing over Jaluit to reach a (critical) point for a turn on the "western" side of the Dateline, then turn southwest on 157 degrees to reach Howland? The precise turning point on the U.S. side of the Dateline would be critical. If flying short—or flying beyond this critical point—a heading of 157 could still be flown—but the island would be missed in the empty expanse of the Pacific. One could indeed depart Lae for Howland on a heading of 79.8 degrees (the direct route), and without a functioning auto-pilot, drift off course either to the north or south of the intended tract and fly to a point southeast or northwest of Howland then turn the aircraft to 157 degrees or its reciprocal of 337 degrees either before or beyond the critical point in this area and miss the island. It is also quite possible that the islands were not accurately plotted on the charts of the period, which could account for a navigational error at the desired destination of the flight. She departed Lae at a time selected to result in arrival at Howland after sunrise for the obvious reason of being able to see the island and the crude, unlighted airstrip during daylight.

The United States Government certainly will never admit she was engaged in espionage, if in fact that was the case since the country was not at war at the time, and the Japanese have nothing to gain by admitting any knowledge of the fate of the two aviators. The mystery is left to the interested reader to ponder.

In the interest of objectivity it should be stated that professional navigators do not believe Earhart was involved in a reconnaissance flight over the Japanese Mandated Islands. This author bears full responsibility for any errors in the theory or calculations. However, one thing can be acknowledged, Amelia Earhart and Fred Noonan were two courageous pioneers in the true American spirit.

SIGHTINGS OF AN AMERICAN WOMAN

Forty years after the disappearance of Amelia Earhart, four Chamorro women were interviewed on Saipan by a Catholic Priest in November 1977. Their names have been intentionally omitted from this brief summary for obvious reasons. Their comments and recollections of the late thirties were provided to a U.S. Navy Admiral on Guam for forwarding to Washington. Summarizing the interviews, one woman stated that when she was a young girl, sometime around 1937 or '38, a foreign woman, thin in stature with brown hair—cut short similar to that of a man, would sometimes pass her house and on one occasion, looked sickly with one side of her body and one hand burned. The foreign woman, with whom the Chamorro lady could not communicate as she did not speak English at the time, was believed to be staying in a nearby building referred to by the local people as a hotel. This woman gave a ring with a "white" stone in it along with some pleasant-smelling balsam to the young Chamorro girl.

Later, two Chamorro girls were asked to make two wreaths and—when asked why—the girls were told that the "American" had died of "amoeba" (dysentery or diarrhea).

The Chamorro woman related that when the foreign woman was alive she was guarded. The other Chamorro woman recalled that as a child she remembered hearing that a plane had crashed "southwest of us" and the pilot was a woman. The Chamorro recalled that the Japanese were "very startled" because she was piloting the plane.

Still another Chamorro woman, when interviewed stated, "it could be 1939 or something like that when I first heard there was a woman spy who came to Saipan but they said she was most likely killed. But I did hear that an American woman was caught spying."

Still another Chamorro woman when interviewed recalled, "hearing about a plane that crashed, the topic of conversation in Saipan. I remembered going to church, I wanted to light a candle for my husband because a battleship was scheduled to come into port about 10 o'clock in the morning. The plane was exhibited and that was when the Japanese made an announcement to all the people that those who wanted to see an airplane may come and see it. That was the year 1937 or 1938."

"There were talks [sic.] about the plane having fallen down [sic.] in the island south of us in Micronesia. I know of a ring that belonged to that woman. I don't know what ever happened to it."

If the signals heard by Radio Nauru, Wake, Midway and Makapu Point originated from the Electra, then it could be assumed that Earhart did not crash in the sea but on an island, since sea water would have rendered the Electra's radio inoperable. Being on land and having been heard by Radio Nauru, it may be surmised that she survived a crash landing and was alive, and with the aircraft until 0948 (GMT) July 5, 1937. If so, this was the last signal ever received.

The possibility cannot be ignored that Earhart flew off course, strayed into airspace over the Japanese Mandated Islands, ran out of fuel and was picked up by the Japanese and taken to Saipan. If, on a heading from Lae of 79.8 degrees, it is possible that position report of 157–337 degrees is a navigation sun line. If so, the Truk theory may be incorrect.

Since the departure from Lae, Amelia Earhart was in flight 20 hours and 15 minutes, with 30 minutes of fuel remaining. It is not known for certain if she flew the Lae-Truk-Jaluit route, (2,829 n. miles) or the direct Lae-Howland route (2,227 n. miles). The difference between the two is 602 n. miles. The former route would require an average ground speed (g.s.) of 140 n.m.p.h., while the latter would require an average ground speed of 110 n.m.p.h. The take-off weight of the aircraft, length of the runway at Lae, and fuel capacity of the Electra are also critical factors to consider.

THE MYSTERY REMAINS UNSOLVED

Many bizarre stories have been advanced surrounding her disappearance. Among the strangest stories includes that of a United States soldier stationed on Saipan in 1944–'45, who claims to have seen the Lockheed Electra destroyed by American military in a damaged Japanese aircraft hanger at As Lito Field. Still another intriguing story concerns that of a bottle with its cork sealed with wax, which washed ashore on the coast of France in October 1938 with a note inside. The French language message stated that the writer had been a prisoner of the Japanese on Jaluit, where he claims to have seen Amelia Earhart and a male individual, both of whom were being held on the atoll for alleged spying on Japanese installations. The writer of the note stated he had been placed on a Japanese vessel bound for Europe and would throw the bottle overboard when the ship neared port.

This message is in the U.S. National Archives in Washington after having been given to American authorities at the U.S. Embassy in Paris.

Earhart's position report at 0720 hours GMT of 04 degrees–33 minutes south by 159 degrees–06 minutes east results in an approximate estimated time of arrival in the vicinity of Howland at approximately 2005 hours GMT, or two hours later than originally anticipated.

One might ask the reason for the continued interest in the Earhart saga. She was married to George P. Putnam, a public relations specialist (founder of Putnam Publishing Co.) who saw in the flight an opportunity to capitalize on the adventure, which was widely followed throughout the world. He actively promoted the attempt of an around-the-world flight in the news media. Amelia Earhart might be also recognized as being in the vanguard of what would later become known as the women's liberation movement. These factors have kept the issue before us through the years. The possibility cannot be ignored that Earhart flew off course, strayed into airspace over the Japanese Mandated Islands, ran out of fuel, and was picked up by the Japanese and taken to Saipan.

THE DEATH OF POLAND

WINSTON S. CHURCHILL

In 1939, Germany signed a pact with the Soviet Union in which the Soviets agreed not to defend Poland from the east if Germany attacked it from the west. A few days later, Nazi Germany invaded Poland, triggering World War II. In this excerpt from his six-volume work *The Second World War*, British prime minister Winston S. Churchill describes the invasion. According to Churchill, the Polish Army was outnumbered and totally outclassed by the German troops, and after only two weeks of fighting, its 2 million men no longer existed as an organized force. Within a month, writes Churchill, Poland was under Soviet and German control. In Churchill's view, the attack on Poland was the "perfect specimen" of modern blitzkrieg, or "lightning war."

A round the Cabinet table we were witnessing the swift and almost mechanical destruction of a weaker state according to Hitler's method and long design. Poland was open to German invasion on three sides. In all, fifty-six divisions, including all his nine armoured divisions, composed the invading armies. From East Prussia the Third Army (eight divisions) advanced southward on Warsaw and Bialystok. From Pomerania the Fourth Army (twelve divisions) was ordered to destroy the Polish troops in the Dantzig Corridor, and then move southeastward to Warsaw along both banks of the Vistula. The frontier opposite the Posen Bulge was held defensively by German reserve troops, but on their right to the southward lay the Eighth Army (seven divisions) whose task was to cover the left flank of

Excerpted from *The Gathering Storm*, by Winston S. Churchill. Copyright © 1948 by Houghton Mifflin Company; © renewed 1976 by Lady Spencer Churchill, the Honourable Lady Sarah Audley, and the Honourable Lady Soames. Reprinted by permission of Houghton Mifflin Company. All rights reserved.

the main thrust. This thrust was assigned to the Tenth Army (seventeen divisions) directed straight upon Warsaw. Farther south again, the Fourteenth Army (fourteen divisions) had a dual task, first to capture the important industrial area west of Cracow, and then, if the main front prospered, to make direct for Lemberg (Lwow) in southeast Poland.

Thus, the Polish forces on the frontiers were first to be penetrated, and then overwhelmed and surrounded by two pincer movements. . . . Those who escaped the closing of the Warsaw pincers would thus be cut off from retreat into Rumania. Over fifteen hundred modern aircraft was hurled on Poland. Their first duty was to overwhelm the Polish air force, and thereafter to support the Army on the battlefield, and beyond it to attack military installations and all communications by road and rail. They were also to spread terror far and wide.

TWO WEEKS TO DEFEAT

In numbers and equipment the Polish Army was no match for their assailants, nor were their dispositions wise. They spread all their forces along the frontiers of their native land. They had no central reserve. While taking a proud and haughty line against German ambitions, they had nevertheless feared to be accused of provocation by mobilising in good time against the masses gathering around them. Thirty divisions, representing only two-thirds of their active army, were ready or nearly ready to meet the first shock. The speed of events and the violent intervention of the German air force prevented the rest from reaching the forward positions till all was broken, and they were only involved in the final disasters. Thus, the thirty Polish divisions faced nearly double their numbers around a long perimeter with nothing behind them. Nor was it in numbers alone that they were inferior. They were heavily outclassed in artillery, and had but a single armoured brigade to meet the nine German Panzers, as they were already called. Their horse cavalry, of which they had twelve brigades, charged valiantly against the swarming tanks and armoured cars, but could not harm them with their swords and lances. Their nine hundred first-line aircraft, of which perhaps half were modern types, were taken by surprise and many were destroyed before they even got into the air.

According to Hitler's plan, the German armies were unleashed on September 1, and ahead of them his air force struck the Polish squadrons on their airfields. In two days the Polish air power was virtually annihilated. Within a week the German armies had bitten deep into Poland. Resistance everywhere was brave but vain. All the Polish armies on the frontiers, except the Posen group, whose flanks were deeply turned, were driven backward. . . . Only the Polish northern group was able to inflict a check upon the German Third Army. They were soon outflanked and fell back to the river Narew, where alone a fairly strong defensive system had been prepared in advance. Such were the results of the first week of the Blitzkrieg.

The second week was marked by bitter fighting and by its end the Polish Army, nominally of about two million men, ceased to exist as an organised force. . . . The two armoured divisions of the Tenth Army reached the outskirts of Warsaw, but having no infantry with them could not make headway against the desperate resistance organised by the townsfolk. Northeast of Warsaw the Third Army encircled the capital from the east, and its left column reached Brest-Litovsk a hundred miles behind the battle front.

It was within the claws of the Warsaw pincers that the Polish Army fought and died. . . . Although already virtually surrounded, the Polish Commander of the Posen army group, General Kutrzeba, resolved to strike south against the flank of the main German drive. This audacious Polish counter-attack, called the battle of the river Bzura, created a crisis which drew in, not only the German Eighth Army, but a part of the Tenth, deflected from their Warsaw objective, and even a corps of the Fourth Army from the north. Under the assault of all these powerful bodies, and overwhelmed by unresisted air bombardment, the Posen group maintained its ever-glorious struggle for ten days. It was finally blotted out on September 19.

In the meantime the outer pincers had met and closed. . . . There was no loophole of escape for straggling and daring individuals. On the twentieth, the Germans announced that the battle of the Vistula was "one of the greatest battles of extermination of all times."

POLAND: A VICTIM OF BLITZKRIEG

It was now the turn of the Soviets. What they now call "Democracy" came into action. On September 17, the Russian armies swarmed across the almost undefended Polish eastern frontier and rolled westward on a broad front. On the eighteenth, they occupied Vilna, and met their German collaborators at Brest-Litovsk. Here in the previous war the Bolsheviks, in breach of their solemn agreements with the Western Allies, had made their separate peace with the Kaiser's Germany, and had bowed to its harsh terms. Now in Brest-Litovsk, it was with Hitler's Germany that the Russian Communists grinned and shook hands. The ruin of Poland and its entire subjugation proceeded apace. Warsaw and Modlin still remained unconquered. The resistance of Warsaw, largely arising from the surge of its citizens, was magnificent and forlorn. After many days of violent bombardment from the air and by heavy artillery, much of which was rapidly transported across the great lateral highways from the idle Western Front, the Warsaw radio ceased to play the Polish National Anthem, and Hitler entered the ruins of the city. Modlin, a fortress twenty miles down the Vistula . . . fought on until the twenty-eighth. Thus, in one month all was over, and a nation of thirty-five millions fell into the merciless grip of those who sought not only conquest but enslavement, and indeed extinction for vast numbers.

We had seen a perfect specimen of the modern Blitzkrieg; the close interaction on the battlefield of army and air force; the violent bombardment of all communications and of any town that seemed an attractive target; the arming of an active Fifth Column; the free use of spies and parachutists; and above all, the irresistible forward thrusts of great masses of armour. . . .

The Soviet armies continued to advance up to the line they had settled with Hitler, and on the twenty-ninth the Russo-German Treaty partitioning Poland was formally signed. . . .

In a broadcast on October 1, I said:

> Poland has again been overrun by two of the Great Powers which held her in bondage for a hundred and fifty years, but were unable to quench the spirit of the Polish nation. The heroic defence of Warsaw shows that the soul of Poland is indestructible, and that she will rise again like a rock, which may for a time be submerged by a tidal wave, but which remains a rock.

1940–1945: A World at War

CHAPTER 4

HITLER JUSTIFIES MAKING WAR

ADOLF HITLER

Hitler's aggression did not stop with the 1939 invasion of Poland but continued with the invasions of Denmark, Norway, France, Belgium, Luxembourg, the Netherlands, and Romania. On April 6, 1941, the German army stood poised to invade yet two more nations: Yugoslavia and Greece. In Berlin that day, on behalf of his führer, Nazi propaganda minister Joseph Goebbels read the following Order of the Day to the German Army of the East. Hitler explains to the soldiers that Germany had made every effort to avoid war with Yugoslavia, but, thanks to the "warmonger" British, this was not possible. Yugoslavs, he claims, influenced by the British, secretly were mobilizing their army to go against the Germans. Greece, too, Hitler contends, had fallen under British influence. According to Hitler, Germany would not be satisfied until German soldiers beat their archenemy England in the Balkans, won freedom for "our German people," and secured "a living space for the German family."

S oldiers of the Southeast Front:
Since early this morning the German people are at war with the Belgrade Government of intrigue. We shall only lay down arms when this band of ruffians has been definitely and most emphatically eliminated, and the last Briton has left this part of the European Continent. These misled people realize that they must thank Britain for this situation, they must thank England, the greatest warmonger of all time.

The German people can enter into this new struggle with the

From "Order of the Day," a speech by Adolf Hitler, given April 6, 1941, Berlin, Germany.

inner satisfaction that its leaders have done everything to bring about a peaceful settlement.

We pray to God that He may lead our soldiers on the path and bless them as hitherto.

HITLER BLAMES ENGLAND

In accordance with the policy of letting others fight for her, as she did in the case of Poland, Britain again tried to involve Germany in the struggle in which Britain hoped that she would finish off the German people once and for all, to win the war, and, if possible, to destroy the entire German Army.

In a few weeks, long ago, the German soldiers on the Eastern Front swept aside Poland, the instrument of British policy. On April 9, 1940, Britain again attempted to reach its goal by a thrust on the German north flank, the thrust at Norway.

In an unforgettable struggle the German soldiers in Norway eliminated the British within a period of a few weeks.

What the world did not deem possible the German people have achieved. Again, only a few weeks later, [British prime minister Winston] Churchill thought the moment right to make a renewed thrust through the British Allies, France and Belgium, into the German region of the Ruhr. The victorious hour of our soldiers on the West Front began.

It is already war history how the German Armies defeated the legions of capitalism and plutocracy. After forty-five days this campaign in the West was equally and emphatically terminated.

Then Churchill concentrated the strength of his Empire against our ally, Italy, in Africa. Now the danger has also been banned from the African theater of the war through the cooperation of Italian and German units.

HITLER BLAMES THE YUGOSLAVS

The new aim of the British warmongers now consists of the realization of a plan that they had already hatched at the outbreak of the war and only postponed because of the gigantic victories of the German Army. The memory of the landing of British troops at Salonika in the course of the first World War also caught little Greece in the spider web of British intrigue.

I have repeatedly warned of the attempt by the British to land troops in Southeastern Europe, and I have said that this constitutes a threat to the German Reich. Unfortunately this warning went unheeded by the Yugoslav nation. I have further tried, always with the same patience, to convince Yugoslav statesmen of the absolute necessity for their cooperation with the German Reich for restoration of lasting peace and order within Yugoslavia.

After long effort we finally succeeded in securing the cooperation of Yugoslavia by its adherence to the Tripartite Pact without having demanded anything whatsoever of the Yugoslav nation except that it take its part in the reconstruction of a new order in Europe.

At this point the criminal usurpers of the new Belgrade Government took the power of the State unto themselves, which is a result of being in the pay of Churchill and Britain. As in the case of Poland, this new Belgrade Government has mobilized decrepit and old people into their inner Cabinet. Under these circumstances I was forced immediately to recall the German national colony within Yugoslav territory.

Members and officers of the German Embassy, employees of our consulates in Yugoslavia were daily being subjected to the most humiliating attacks. The German schools, exactly as in Poland, were laid in ruins by bandits. Innumerable German nationals were kidnapped and attacked by Yugoslavs and some even were killed.

THE GOAL: BEAT THE BRITISH IN THE BALKANS

In addition, Yugoslavia for weeks has planned a general mobilization of its army in great secrecy. This is the answer to my eight-year-long effort to bring about closer cooperation and friendship with the Yugoslav people, a task that I have pursued most fastidiously.

When British divisions were landed in Greece, just as in World War [I] days, the Serbs thought the time was ripe for taking advantage of the situation for new assassinations against Germany and her allies.

Soldiers of the Southeast Front: Now your zero hour has arrived. You will now take the interests of the German Reich under your protection as your comrades did a year ago in Norway and on the West Front. You will do just as well on the Southeast Front.

In doing this, your duty, you will not be less courageous than the men of those German divisions who in 1915, on the same Balkan soil, fought so victoriously. You will be humane only in those places where the enemy is humane toward you. Where the enemy confronts you with utter brutality you will beat them back with the same weapon.

The fight on Greek soil is not a battle against the Greek people, but against that archenemy, England, which is again trying to extend the war far into the Southeast Balkans, the same as he tried far in the north last year. For this reason, on this very spot in the Balkans, we shall fight shoulder to shoulder with our ally until the last Briton has found his Dunkerque in Greece.

If any Greeks support this British course, then those Greeks will fall at the same time as the British.

When the German soldier shall have proved himself, shall have proved that he is capable of beating the British in the Balkans, in the midst of snow and mountains, then also he will have proved that he can beat the British in the heat of the desert in Africa.

However, we will pursue no other ultimate aim than to win freedom for our German people and to secure a living space for the German family.

The prayers and thoughts, the very life of all Germans, are again in the heart of every German soldier.

THE PRIDE OF NAZI GERMANY: THE WEHRMACHT

OMER BARTOV

Many people believe that the German Wehrmacht cannot be held responsible for Nazi atrocities because its soldiers simply followed orders. In this selection, Omer Bartov, a professor of history, an author, and an internationally acclaimed scholar on the Holocaust, contends that the Wehrmacht willingly and efficiently supported the ideology espoused by the Hitler regime. He argues that the idea of the "professional" Wehrmacht truly is a myth. The soldiers and junior officers, who made up most of the Wehrmacht's combat troops, writes Bartov, believed in Hitler and his regime largely because they had been thoroughly indoctrinated in Nazi philosophy for most of their growing-up years. Bartov contends that the heavy prejudices and fears instilled in the ordinary Wehrmacht soldier relative to Jews, Russians, and Bolshevism was a major motivator of the Wehrmacht's especially vicious actions on the eastern front.

T he meticulous work done by German (and foreign) scholars . . . demonstrated that especially with the invasion of the Soviet Union on June 22nd, 1941, the Wehrmacht had not only paved the way for the regime's murder organisations, but had issued its own troops with a complex of what has been called 'criminal orders' which turned the Russian campaign into a war of murder and destruction on an unprecedented scale. The 'Barbarossa' decree, as the order for the attack on Soviet

Excerpted from "The Myths of the Wehrmacht," by Omer Bartov, *History Today*, April 1992. Reprinted with permission of *History Today*.

Russia was called, demanded the execution on the spot of all political commissars in the Red Army; curtailed martial law as regards the rights reserved for occupied populations; called for
the elimination of all partisans, political activists, and Jews; and
ordered the close collaboration of army units with the Einsatz-
gruppen, the extermination squads of the SS and SD. Moreover,
the army was ordered both to 'live off the land', which meant
that it supplied its needs by extensive plunder of the impoverished Russian population, and to assist in the ruthless exploita-
tion of the occupied lands in favour of the German population
in the rear.

Thus one cannot avoid the conclusion that the Wehrmacht
played a crucial role in making possible the occupation, exploita-
tion, and devastation by Nazi Germany of vast tracts of territory
in the East, as well as in the implementation of the 'Final Solution'.
This in turn was the direct result of the army's willingness wholly
to embrace Hitler's view of the war in the East not as one to be
fought according to the traditional rules of warfare, but as a
Weltanschauungs and Vernichtungskrieg, an ideological war of
total destruction in which there would be 'no comrades in arms'
and where none of the enemy must be spared. . . . The myth of the
'purely professional' soldiers had nothing to do with reality. As
far as their actions were concerned, the men of the Wehrmacht
were the willing and efficient instruments of the Nazi regime. Indeed, even during the last two years of the war, when under
growing Soviet pressure the army retreated from the East, the
soldiers took care to carry out a ruthless 'scorched earth' policy
which ensured that the liberated areas would suffer for many
years after the war from extreme hardship.

INDOCTRINATION AT AN EARLY AGE

If in Germany, and in some circles in the West, the myth of the
'professional' Wehrmacht was sustained long after the war, those
most viciously persecuted by the Nazis as the Reich's political
and 'biological' enemies by and large identified the German soldier with Hitler's regime. From their point of view, after all, with
the army came the occupation and all its horrors. The question
which still needs to be answered, however, is how did the German soldier conceive of himself, what were the ideals and concepts that motivated him, and what sort of memory have the surviving veterans retained from the war and disseminated in
post-war German society?

The soldiers and junior officers who formed the bulk of the
Wehrmacht's combat troops came to the army after years of extensive ideological preparation in a Nazified school system and

particularly in the Hitler Youth, whose impact on the mentality of German youngsters in the 1930s cannot be overestimated. As Gustav Koppke, a former soldier who had grown up in a working-class area, said during an interview in the early 1980s:

> Our workers' suburb and the HJ [Hitler Youth] were in no way contradictory . . . you shouldn't see it as if we young lads had to decide for something or against something; there was nothing else . . . and whoever wanted to become something belonged to it. . . . The HJ uniform was something positive in our childhood.

Not surprisingly, when explaining why he had later on volunteered to a Waffen-SS division, he added: 'I was raised then, in the National Socialist time, and had seen the world just as they had shown it to us'.

THE MYTH OF THE ENEMY

Once in the army, these young men were exposed to a massive propaganda and indoctrination campaign ranging from theoretical ideological sessions, to more subtle forms of persuasion by means of newspapers and army information sheets widely distributed among combat units, radio programmes directed at the soldiers who were given large numbers of receivers, orders of the day read out to the troops by their commanders, numerous 'educational' brochures on such subjects as history and geography, books collected in unit libraries, talks by visiting lecturers, and so forth.

Naturally, this indoctrination was most effective when it exploited already existing prejudices and anxieties, particularly in the case of the Jews, the Russians, and Bolshevism. What can hardly be doubted is that by the time the Wehrmacht marched into the Soviet Union, its troops were prepared to wage a campaign of the utmost ruthlessness and brutality against what they perceived to be a demonic enemy even before their first encounter with the Russians. Indeed, it is a measure of the efficacy of their indoctrination that when they did meet the enemy in the East, whether it was a Red Army soldier, a commissar, a Russian woman, or a Jew, they invariably perceived them as a living confirmation of their prejudices, that is as the embodiment of those diabolical qualities they had been taught to expect. Thus rather than accepting the myth of the Wehrmacht as an army which had remained aloof from ideological contamination, we should actually speak of the myth of the enemy which permeated the troops and powerfully motivated them on the battlefield. Here was indeed an explosive combination of hatred and fear, a sense that the Germans were fighting on the side of God, humanity, and justice, against an enemy representing Satan, subhumanity, and evil. Note, for instance, the following letter written by a soldier from the Eastern Front in July 1941:

> The German people owes a great debt to our Fuhrer, for had these beasts, who are our enemies here, come to Germany, such murders would have taken place that the world has never seen before. . . . What we have seen, no newspaper can describe, it borders on the unbelievable, even the Middle Ages do not compare with what has occurred here. And when one reads the 'Sturmer' [a Nazi newspaper] and looks at the pictures, that is only a weak illustration of what we see here and the crimes committed here by the Jews. Believe me, even the most sensational newspaper reports are only a fraction of what is happening here.

THE EASTERN FRONT WAS DIFFERENT

The myth of the Wehrmacht as a 'purely' professional army, accepted by so many military historians and soldiers in the West, had to do not only with ignorance, but also with the fact that in the West the Wehrmacht did behave differently, especially in the fighting of 1940. To be sure, in the latter stages of the war, and not least due to the fact that many soldiers fighting in France in 1944 had already served in Russia, its conduct became increasingly criminal. Nevertheless, the Eastern Front, where the lion's share of the Wehrmacht fought for most of the war, and where the back of the German army was broken, remained an essentially different experience.

This was so first and foremost due to Hitler's concept of the war in the East as a struggle for Lebensraum (living space) with a diabolical enemy, a notion transmitted to the troops by means of both orders and indoctrination, and widely accepted since it reflected both popular prejudices against Jews and Russians, and the deep and highly prevalent anxiety about Communism. The primitive conditions in which much of the Russian population was living, the cultural and linguistic gap, perceived as much greater than that separating Germany from the nations of Western Europe, all combined to create a perception of the enemy in the East as an Untermensch (subhuman). Add to this the ferocity of Russian resistance and the tremendous hardships of fighting in the East, and one comes closer to an understanding of the barbarous war conducted by Germany in the Soviet Union.

The consequent distorted perception of reality by the individ-

ual soldier against all available evidence is nevertheless quite
striking. The extent to which the Wehrmacht's troops perceived
the atrocities they themselves or their comrades had perpetrated
as evidence of the enemy's inhumanity is a painful reminder of
the manner in which people's minds can be moulded so as not
only to make them carry out criminal actions, but also to glorify
them as noble deeds aimed at eliminating evil. Thus, for instance,
Private Fred Fallnbigl wrote from the front in mid-July 1941:

> Now I know what war really means. But I also know
> that we had been forced into the war against the Soviet
> Union. For God have mercy on us, had we waited, or
> had these beasts come to us. For them even the most
> horrible death is still too good. I am glad that I can be
> here to put an end to this genocidal system.

THE RED ARMY DEHUMANISED

A lance-corporal writing in early August maintained that 'to
those in the homeland we soldiers can only say that he [Hitler]
has saved Germany and thereby the whole of Europe from the
Red Army by his decision. The battle is hard', he admitted, 'but
we know what we are fighting for, and with confidence in the
Fuhrer we will achieve victory'. And later that month another
soldier wrote from Russia:

> Precisely now one recognises perfectly what would have
> happened to our wives and children had these Russian
> hordes . . . succeeded in penetrating into our Fatherland.
> I have had the opportunity here to . . . observe these un-
> cultivated, multi-raced men. Thank God they have been
> thwarted from plundering and pillaging our homeland.

These sentiments were reiterated by numerous other soldiers,
Private Kurt Christmann exclaimed at the time:

> What would have happened to cultural Europe, had
> these sons of the Steppe, poisoned and drunk with a de-
> structive poison, these incited subhumans, invaded our
> beautiful Germany? Endlessly we thank our Fuhrer,
> with love and loyalty, the saviour and historical figure.

And in September Lance-Corporal O. Rentzch similarly asserted:

> It is good to know that this confrontation has already
> come. If otherwise those hordes had invaded our land,
> that would have . . . made for great bloodshed. No,
> now we want to shoulder ourselves all endeavours, in
> order to eradicate this universal plague.

Interestingly, while during the initial phase of the campaign in the East the dehumanised image of the enemy legitimised the barbarous policies of the Wehrmacht for the individual soldiers, by the time the Germany army was retreating and the Reich faced possible occupation by the Red Army, the same diabolical picture of the enemy was used to justify opposition to him at all cost. Indeed, vivid memories of atrocities committed by the Wehrmacht were now employed to threaten the troops with what they could expect of the Russians if they ever managed to conquer the German homeland. Fear of vengeance and knowledge of the pain and suffering of being occupied by a foreign army now combined to intensify German resistance. Note the following letter by a Wehrmacht captain written in mid-February 1943:

> May God allow the German people to find now the peace of mind and strength which would make it into the instrument needed by the Fuhrer to protect the West from ruin, for what the Asiatic hordes will not destroy, will be annihilated by Jewish hatred and revenge. The belief at the front is unshakable, and we all hope that, as [Hermann] Goring has said, with the rising sun the fortunes of war will again return to our side.

And in September 1944 one lieutenant wrote:

> Nothing may exist which could make us weak. Any German defeat would spell a total . . . destruction of all Germans. . . . We are the last bastion, with us stands and falls everything which has been created by German blood over the centuries.

THE MYTH LIVES ON

Myths do not disappear quickly, at least not as long as the cause of their growth is still present. The French still find it difficult to concede that the Wehrmacht was in fact not particularly superior technologically, that the training of its men was not significantly better, that the German command had committed some serious errors, and that the main military cause of the debacle was the blunders, not to say the stupidity, of their own generals. The Russians have similarly clung to the myth of a technologically superior Wehrmacht halted only by the courage and self-sacrifice of determined Soviet patriots (or Communists), and have refused for long to admit that in point of fact they had made exceptionally bad use of their own excellent equipment.

The Germans too prefer to remember what they perceive as their self-sacrificial, hopeless attempts to halt the Red Army from entering the homeland during the last months of the war, rather than linger on the memory of their years of conquest and subjugation of others. What the popular collective memory of Germans is reluctant to concede is both that they ended up defending themselves against a 'world of enemies' only because they had first tried to take over the world, and, even more importantly, that to the very end they were not fighting merely for the survival of Germany, but very much also for the continued existence of the Third Reich and all that it stood for.

THE BRITISH EMPIRE AND THE COMMONWEALTH: THEIR FINEST HOUR

WINSTON S. CHURCHILL

On June 14, 1940, the French capital, Paris, fell to the Germans. Four days later, in this speech to his nation's House of Commons, British prime minister Winston S. Churchill addresses the events in France, British capabilities, and the stance the British must take. Now that the Battle of France is over, he warns, the Germans will turn their sights to the British and the battle for Britain will begin in earnest. Churchill emphasizes that the British will keep fighting Nazi Germany, even if they have to do so alone. According to Churchill, army, navy, and air force advisers all agree that Britain should carry on the war and has "reasonable hope" of winning. Churchill proclaims his belief that the British people will face any challenge with which the enemy confronts them. Claiming that Adolf Hitler knows that if he does not break the British, he cannot win the war, Churchill contends that the survival of Christian civilization depends on the British.

T he disastrous military events which have happened during the past fortnight have not come to me with any sense of surprise. Indeed, I indicated a fortnight ago as clearly as I could to the House that the worst possibilities were open; and I made it perfectly clear then that whatever happened in France

From "Their Finest Hour," a speech by Winston Churchill to the British House of Commons, June 18, 1940. Reprinted with permission from Curtis Brown Ltd., London, on behalf of the Estate of Sir Winston S. Churchill. Copyright Winston S. Churchill, 1940.

would make no difference to the resolve of Britain and the British Empire to fight on, "if necessary for years, if necessary alone." During the last few days we have successfully brought off the great majority of the troops we had on the line of communication in France; and seven-eighths of the troops we have sent to France since the beginning of the war—that is to say, about 350,000 out of 400,000 men—are safely back in this country. Others are still fighting with the French, and fighting with considerable success in their local encounters against the enemy. We have also brought back a great mass of stores, rifles and munitions of all kinds which had been accumulated in France during the last nine months.

A Strong Military Prepared to Fight

We have, therefore, in this Island today a very large and powerful military force. This force comprises all our best-trained and our finest troops, including scores of thousands of those who have already measured their quality against the Germans and found themselves at no disadvantage. We have under arms at the present time in this Island over a million and a quarter men. Behind these we have the Local Defense Volunteers, numbering half a million, only a portion of whom, however, are yet armed with rifles or other firearms. We have incorporated into our Defense Forces every man for whom we have a weapon. We expect very large additions to our weapons in the near future, and in preparation for this we intend forthwith to call up, drill and train further large numbers. Those who are not called up, or else are employed during the vast business of munitions production in all its branches—and their ramifications are innumerable—will serve their country best by remaining at their ordinary work until they receive their summons. We have also over here Dominions armies. The Canadians had actually landed in France, but have now been safely withdrawn, much disappointed, but in perfect order, with all their artillery and equipment. And these very high-class forces from the Dominions will now take part in the defense of the Mother Country.

Lest the account which I have given of these large forces should raise the question: Why did they not take part in the great battle in France? I must make it clear that, apart from the divisions training and organizing at home, only 12 divisions were equipped to fight upon a scale which justified their being sent abroad. And this was fully up to the number which the French had been led to expect would be available in France at the ninth month of the war. The rest of our forces at home have a fighting value for home defense which will, of course, steadily increase every week that passes. Thus, the invasion of Great Britain would at this time require the transportation across the sea of hostile armies on a very large scale, and after they had been so transported they would have to be continually maintained with all the masses of munitions and supplies which are required for continuous battle—as continuous battle it will surely be.

Here is where we come to the Navy—and after all, we have a Navy. Some people seem to forget that we have a Navy. We must remind them. . . .

It seems to me that as far as sea-borne invasion on a great scale is concerned, we are far more capable of meeting it today than we were at many periods in the last war and during the early months of this war, before our other troops were trained, and while the B.E.F. [British Expeditionary Force] had proceeded abroad. . . .

BRITISH AIR POWER

This brings me, naturally, to the great question of invasion from the air, and of the impending struggle between the British and German Air Forces. It seems quite clear that no invasion on a scale beyond the capacity of our land forces to crush speedily is likely to take place from the air until our Air Force has been definitely overpowered. In the meantime, there may be raids by parachute troops and attempted descents of airborne soldiers. We should be able to give those gentry a warm reception both in the air and on the ground, if they reach it in any condition to continue the dispute. But the great question is: Can we break Hitler's air weapon? Now, of course, it is a very great pity that we have not got an Air Force at least equal to that of the most powerful enemy within striking distance of these shores. But we have a very powerful Air Force which has proved itself far superior in quality, both in men and in many types of machine, to what we have met so far in the numerous and fierce air battles which have been fought with the Germans. In France, where we were at a considerable disadvantage and lost many machines on the ground when they were standing round the aerodromes, we were accustomed to inflict in the air losses of as much as two and two-and-a-half to one. In the fighting over Dunkirk, which was a sort of no-man's-land, we undoubtedly beat the German Air Force, and gained the mastery of the local air, inflicting here a loss of three or four to one day after day. . . .

During the great battle in France, we gave very powerful and continuous aid to the French Army, both by fighters and bombers; but in spite of every kind of pressure we never would allow the entire metropolitan fighter strength of the Air Force to be consumed. This decision was painful, but it was also right, because the fortunes of the battle in France could not have been decisively affected even if we had thrown in our entire fighter force. That battle was lost by the unfortunate strategical opening, by the extraordinary and unforseen power of the armored columns, and by the great preponderance of the German Army in numbers. Our fighter Air Force might easily have been exhausted as a mere accident in that great struggle, and then we should have found ourselves at the present time in a very serious plight. But as it is, I am happy to inform the House that our fighter strength is stronger at the present time relatively to the Germans, who have suffered terrible losses, than it has ever seen; and consequently we believe ourselves possessed of the capacity to continue the war in the air under better conditions than we have ever experienced before. I look forward confidently to the exploits of our fighter pilots—these splendid men, this brilliant youth—who will have the glory of saving their native land, their island home, and all they love, from the most deadly of all attacks.

There remains, of course, the danger of bombing attacks, which will certainly be made very soon upon us by the bomber forces of the enemy. It is true that the German bomber force is superior in numbers to ours; but we have a very large bomber force also, which we shall use to strike at military targets in Germany without intermission. I do not at all underrate the severity of the ordeal which lies before us; but I believe our countrymen will show themselves capable of standing up to it, . . . and will be able to stand up to it, and carry on in spite of it, at least as well as any other people in the world. Much will depend upon this; every man and every woman will have the chance to show the finest qualities of their race, and render the highest service to their cause. For all of us, at this time, whatever our sphere, our station, our occupation or our duties, it will be a help to remember the famous lines: *He nothing common did or mean, Upon that memorable scene.*

I have thought it right upon this occasion to give the House and the country some indication of the solid, practical grounds upon which we base our inflexible resolve to continue the war. There are a good many people who say, "Never mind. Win or lose, sink or swim, better die than submit to tyranny—and such a tyranny." And I do not dissociate myself from them. But I can assure them that our professional advisers of the three Services unitedly advise that we should carry on the war, and that there are good and reasonable hopes of final victory. . . .

Britain Must Stand Firm

We may now ask ourselves: In what way has our position worsened since the beginning of the war? It has worsened by the fact that the Germans have conquered a large part of the coast line of

Western Europe, and many small countries have been overrun by them. This aggravates the possibilities of air attack and adds to our naval preoccupations. It in no way diminishes, but on the contrary definitely increases, the power of our long-distance blockade. Similarly, the entrance of Italy into the war increases the power of our long-distance blockade. We have stopped the worst leak by that. We do not know whether military resistance will come to an end in France or not, but should it do so, then of course the Germans will be able to concentrate their forces, both military and industrial, upon us. . . .

If Hitler can bring under his despotic control the industries of the countries he has conquered, this will add greatly to his already vast armament output. On the other hand, this will not happen immediately, and we are now assured of immense, continuous and increasing support in supplies and munitions of all kinds from the United States; and especially of aeroplanes and pilots from the Dominions and across the oceans coming from regions which are beyond the reach of enemy bombers.

I do not see how any of these factors can operate to our detriment on balance before the winter comes; and the winter will impose a strain upon the Nazi regime, with almost all Europe writhing and starving under its cruel heel, which, for all their ruthlessness, will run them very hard. We must not forget that from the moment when we declared war on the 3rd September it was always possible for Germany to turn all her Air Force upon this country, together with any other devices of invasion she might conceive, and that France could have done little or nothing to prevent her doing so. We have, therefore, lived under this danger, in principle and in a slightly modified form, during all these months. In the meanwhile, however, we have enormously improved our methods of defense, and we have learned what we had no right to assume at the beginning, namely, that the individual aircraft and the individual British pilot have a sure and definite superiority. Therefore, in casting up this dread balancesheet and contemplating our dangers with a disillusioned eye, I see great reason for intense vigilance and exertion, but none whatever for panic or despair.

During the first four years of the last war the Allies experienced nothing but disaster and disappointment. That was our constant fear: one blow after another, terrible losses, frightful dangers. Everything miscarried. And yet at the end of those four years the morale of the Allies was higher than that of the Germans, who had moved from one aggressive triumph to another, and who stood everywhere triumphant invaders of the lands into which they had broken. During that war we repeatedly asked ourselves the question: How are we going to win? and no one was able ever to answer it with much precision, until at the end, quite suddenly, quite unexpectedly, our terrible foe collapsed before us, and we were so glutted with victory that in our folly we threw it away.

We do not yet know what will happen in France or whether the French resistance will be prolonged, both in France and in the French Empire overseas. The French Government will be throwing away great opportunities and casting adrift their future if they do not continue the war in accordance with their Treaty obligations, from which we have not felt able to release them. The House will have read the historic declaration in which, at the desire of many Frenchmen—and of our own hearts—we have proclaimed our willingness at the darkest hour in French history to conclude a union of common citizenship in this struggle. However matters may go in France or with the French Government, or other French Governments, we in this Island and in the British Empire will never lose our sense of comradeship with the French people. If we are now called upon to endure what they have been suffering, we shall emulate their courage, and if final victory rewards our toils they shall share the gains, aye, and freedom shall be restored to all. We abate nothing of our just demands; not one jot or tittle do we recede. Czechs, Poles, Norwegians, Dutch, Belgians have joined their causes to our own. All these shall be restored.

What [French] General [Maxime] Weygand called the Battle of France is over. I expect that the Battle of Britain is about to begin. Upon this battle depends the survival of Christian civilization. Upon it depends our own British life, and the long continuity of our institutions and our Empire. The whole fury and might of the enemy must very soon be turned on us. Hitler knows that he will have to break us in this Island or lose the war. If we can stand up to him, all Europe may be free and the life of the world may move forward into broad, sunlit uplands. But if we fail, then the whole world, including the United States, including all that we have known and cared for, will sink into the abyss of a new Dark Age made more sinister, and perhaps more protracted, by the lights of perverted science. Let us therefore brace ourselves to our duties, and so bear ourselves that, if the British Empire and its Commonwealth last for a thousand years, men will still say, "This was their finest hour."

LIFE AND DEATH DURING THE BLITZ

LEONARD MOSLEY

The late British-born journalist, military historian, and acclaimed biographer Leonard Mosley was a war correspondent during World War II, covering the campaigns in India, the Middle East, Italy, and Germany. In London and on the cliffs of Dover in 1940 during the Battle of Britain, he returned to London numerous times during the blitz, the German aerial bombardment of England. In the following selection, Mosley describes the devastation created by German bombs in the London East End slum of Silvertown in September 1940. He explains that the area's local council had refused to allocate funds to build air-raid shelters because its members did not believe there would be a war. Mosley describes the chaotic scene as German bombs dropped continuously on Silvertown and how the buses that were supposed to evacuate the people failed to come.

C hief Superintendent Reginald Smith of the [London] Metropolitan Police picked up the telephone as it rang in his office on the morning of September 12, 1940, and tried to concentrate on what the voice at the other end was saying. He had not been out of his clothes for more than four days and had snatched only catnaps during that time. His body was crying out for sleep and a bath, and his heart was sick.

Ever since the big raid of September 7 the Germans had been concentrating on the East End. He and his policemen had done what they could by clearing the way for firemen and ambulances, working with air-raid wardens and shepherding people

From *Backs to the Wall: The Heroic Story of the People of London During World War II*, by Leonard Mosley (London: Weidenfeld & Nicolson, 1971). Copyright © 1971 by Leonard Mosley. Reprinted with permission.

from their wrecked and burning homes, helping demolition squads dig for broken beings whimpering underneath the rubble. Five of his men had died in the line of duty during these days: one by flinging himself on top of a baby just as a bomb dropped fifty yards away; one while trying to activate the sprinklers in a burning warehouse; another by drowning in a Thameside lock covered with blazing oil; a fourth underneath the walls of a collapsing factory; and a fifth blown against a building in Canning Town. Those who survived had worked night and day, and in most places they had brought some sort of succor and comfort to the populace.

THE SITUATION IN SILVERTOWN

But not in Silvertown. In Silvertown they had failed, and its inhabitants' nerves had cracked.

Silvertown was one of London's worst slum areas. Most of its people lived three and four to a room in row after row of insalubrious ramshackle houses. The name came from the biggest factory in the district, S.W. Silver and Company, which employed a large force of young women in the manufacture of rubber goods and waterproofing materials. There were fertilizer and soap factories nearby, and the air of the district curdled with a mixture of appalling smells, which the natives had long since ceased to notice. In addition to factory workers, there was also a large population of seamen and dockers, for Silvertown was surrounded on all sides by the docks and wharves of the Pool of London, and these waterways cut the area off from neighboring West Ham, to which it was administratively attached.

When Superintendent Smith had made his first tour of K Division after being posted there in the spring of 1940, his police guide saved Silvertown for the last. As they drove through the neighborhood, the man said, "This is the place you'll have to watch out for, Reg. It's not the people—they're all right. Typical Cockneys, friendly lot. Get a bit drunk on Saturdays. Did you know there are more pubs in Silvertown than in any other equivalent district in London? They use 'em, too, but they don't do any real harm. No, it's the West Ham Council. Real lot of Bolshies, if you ask me. Won't do a thing about the war."

Superintendent Smith was to discover that, though he used the language of a die-hard Tory, his guide had truth on his side. Not that the councilors of West Ham *were* Bolshies; they were simply stubborn, short-sighted old men. Their average age was over sixty, and they refused to listen or to learn. West Ham was a stronghold of the Labour party, and most of the members who filled the safe seats on the council were party hacks who had slavishly followed the party line all through the nineteen-thirties. That line was to express loathing and abhorrence of Hitler, the Nazi party and Fascist Germany, but to do nothing to help rearm Britain so that she could face up to the inevitable enemy. When the government instructed local councils throughout Britain to start building air-raid shelters for their people in 1937, 1938 and 1939, the old men of West Ham refused. They stubbornly insisted that war was not necessary and therefore would not come, so why waste money on protecting people from it? When . . . pressed . . . they had tried blackmail. They would build shelters, they said, if the government would pay for them—but not unless. That will show those Tories they can't bully us, they told each other gleefully.

Unfortunately, the government didn't try to bully them. If the Socialists of West Ham wanted to leave their people unprotected, that was their concern.

DISASTER FALLS FROM THE SKIES

When the enemy planes came over on September 7, Silvertown seemed to get more than its share from the start. Silver and Company was soon on fire, and black smoke from the burning rubber billowed up, acting as a target for the second, third and fourth waves of bombers, and high explosives and incendiaries rained down on the houses surrounding it. The trek of refugees had begun; people fled with what belongings they could gather across the swing bridges to the higher ground on the other side. Police, firemen and air-raid wardens were glad to see them go, because Silvertown was no longer a place for anyone to stay in. Those who remained behind were either the dead, the sick and infirm, the wounded or those stubborn souls who refused to leave their damaged houses and life's possessions.

In the early hours of Sunday morning, September 8, Superintendent Smith had managed to get through to Silvertown from his headquarters to see the situation for himself. Even today he does not like to talk much about the journey. Bombs were dropping almost continuously, roads were barred by bomb craters or collapsed buildings, firemen were battling great fires everywhere, and several times his car had to be helped over great piles of crisscrossing firehoses leading down to the pumps on the Thames. There was too much noise from the fires and the bombs to talk, and in any case, everyone was wearing a face mask against the appalling stench from the wrecked fertilizer factory.

In the center of Silvertown, Smith found a local clergyman trying to control the situation. All air-raid wardens were either dead or had fled with the refugees. The Reverend Walter Paton had taken over and was trying to round up women and children from the ruins and get them to some sort of shelter. His own church and home had been hit; indeed, there was barely a house standing in three square miles, save for one semibombed school into which he had crammed nearly seven bundled men, women and children. Their state was pitiful. They sat on their baggage, stunned out of their minds by shock, the continual noise and the bombs, waiting to be rescued from the inferno. "You've got to get them out, you've got to get them out," the reverend kept saying.

Smith had vowed that he would. Somehow he made his way to a police station that was still functioning and went to work on the telephone. Yes, he was told, the situation in Silvertown was known; yes, it was clear that the people were in desperate straits; yes, a convoy of buses had been sent to get the people out of the school; and yes, it was understood that the school was vulnerable not only to bombs but to blast.

A Case of Misunderstood Directions

Later on Sunday morning Reginald Smith had received confirmation that a convoy of buses was on its way to Silvertown to rescue the homeless. After that, the multiplicity of his other tasks had made him forget those miserable, stunned people sitting on their luggage in that forlorn school, waiting amid the crescendo of bombs to be taken away to safety. That is, he forgot until Monday morning when his secretary said, "Isn't it terrible about Silvertown, sir? They had a direct hit on a school there—four hundred and fifty people killed. A lot of women and kids among them."

Smith cried, "But they shouldn't have been there! They were sending buses for them. What happened to the buses?"

What had happened to the buses was that the drivers had been told to assemble at a pub called The George and then drive in to collect the refugees. But the convoy leader had taken them to a pub of the same name on the other side of the river. By the time they reached the school, the sirens had started again; deciding that Silvertown was no place to stay while bombs were falling, the drivers had retreated back across the river. Some hours later, when they returned, the school was gone along with most of the people in it.

No wonder the few survivors of Silvertown were bitter. As for Superintendent Smith, he was sick at the thought of what he might have done.

Despair Underground in London

Now, as the voice on the telephone had just been reminding him, Smith was faced by another problem of people in shelters, and this time there were thousands, not hundreds, involved. By this time what came to be known as the Blitz had really begun, at least in the East End. There were three or four raids every day and alerts all through the night. Desperate for some place to hide, Cockneys were searching for any place which looked deep and safe. One sanctuary they had found was an unfinished stretch of the London Underground just beyond Stratford Broadway Station.

"You'd better come and have a look," his sergeant said. "You won't believe your eyes, or your nose."

When he got there it was two o'clock in the morning and there was a raid on. He and his companion stumbled over the last stretches of railway lines leading out of Stratford Broadway Station until they came to a black mass ahead which was impossible to see as a shape but easy to identify from the great wafts of hot air and the sounds which came pulsing out of it. "I'd put your hankie over your face if I was you, sir," the sergeant said. Smith, who got queasy on boats, felt the blood draining from his face.

"The first thing I heard," he recalls, "was the great hollow hubbub, a sort of soughing and wailing, as if there were animals down there moaning and crying. And then, as we went on, this terrible stench hit me. It was worse than dead bodies, hot and thick and so fetid that I gagged and then vomited. About fifty yards in I stopped. Ahead of me, I could see faces peering towards me lit by candles and lanterns, and it was like a painting of hell. There were young voices singing and old voices wailing and babies crying. And everywhere these faces staring out of the flickering darkness."

His sergeant said, "There's all sorts in there, I can tell you—white and black and yellow, though most of them are so filthy you can't tell the difference. Some of them haven't been out for days, and they refuse to leave. Some of the old folks are dying, but we won't know how many until they bring the bodies out. You can't tell from the smell. They do everything in there. No sanitation and no shame, I can tell you."

The sergeant started to walk farther in, but Smith was suddenly overwhelmed; four days of sleeplessness, bombing and responsibility had taken their toll at last. He began vomiting again. "I can't go on," he said. "I've got to get out of here. But something's got to be done, it's got to be done." He turned and hurried away to the light at the entrance to the tunnel.

HIROHITO AND THE CONDUCT OF WORLD WAR II

HERBERT P. BIX

Historians continue to explore the extent of Japanese emperor Hirohito's role during World War II. In this selection, historian Herbert P. Bix, most recently a professor in the Graduate School of Social Sciences at Hitotsubashi University in Tokyo, maintains that Hirohito knew the truth about the war. In Bix's view, Hirohito also knew that the Japanese people were being misled—and, to a certain degree, brainwashed—by their own officials. Bix writes that although bureaucrats often kept information from Hirohito to avoid being scolded or asked "inconvenient" questions by him, from 1941 on Hirohito had access to almost all military intelligence as well as other highly informative sources. Officials spent so much time making sure Hirohito was well informed, contends Bix, that their primary duties—operations and strategic planning—did not get the attention required.

F ollowing the outbreak of the German-Soviet war in the summer of 1941, the Japanese army and navy chiefs of staff, together with the emperor's other main advisers, began to spend more and more of their workdays at court. Hirohito's command prerogatives were changing quickly, and he was about to become a commander in chief in every sense of the word. The liaison conference, which had been formed in November 1937 and suspended two months later until July 1940, was revived, convened with greater frequency, and gradually strengthened. The

Excerpted from *Hirohito and the Modern Making of Japan*, by Herbert P. Bix. Copyright © 2000 by Herbert P. Bix. Reprinted by permission of HarperCollins Publishers, Inc.

president of the Planning Board and the home minister became permanent constituent members of the liaison conference, and in the course of a year, it developed into the most important regularly convened body for deciding national policies and guidelines for policies.

The liaison conference also moved its deliberations from the prime minister's official mansion to the palace. It eclipsed the cabinet, usurped its decision-making function, and became, in effect, a forum for debates and arguments that had to be resolved, ultimately, by the emperor himself. Between September 27, 1940, and November 1941, there were scores of liaison conference meetings. Many more followed thereafter. . . .

Final decisions of the liaison conference continued to be formally disclosed through imperial conferences, which now began to convene more frequently. The Imperial Headquarters was also reorganized, and new agencies or sections added until 1945. . . . By May 1945 the headquarters staff, some working within the palace compound but the overwhelming majority outside, had grown to more than 1,792.

HIROHITO IS IN CHARGE

Certain key features of the high command structure, and Hirohito's way of working within it, remained unchanged, however. The independent bureaucratic interests of the emperor's military and civil advisory organs continued to shape policy. Guidelines for the conduct of the war continued to be drafted far down the military chain of command and moved upward through a process of negotiation and consensus building. And the ever-wary Hirohito continued to search out contradictions and discrepancies in whatever reported to him. Thus, whenever the army and navy chiefs of staff or top cabinet ministers made formal reports that were in conflict, and sometimes when they were quite consistent or nearly identical, if Hirohito was not convinced by the argument put forward, he would reject them.

As the danger of war with the United States and Britain drew nearer, and as senior general staff officers . . . acquired a better understanding of Hirohito's character and the breadth of his military knowledge, the middle-echelon officers who prepared his briefing and background materials learned how their immediate superiors could avoid his scoldings and inconvenient questions. One cannot dismiss altogether the possibility that at least some materials intended for the emperor's study in ratifying (or rejecting) command decisions may have been shaped if not distorted by interservice maneuverings. . . .

On the other hand Hirohito understood very well how the policy deliberation process worked. He knew the names and careers of the most important bureau, department, and section chiefs of the Army, Navy, and Foreign Ministries, and their tendencies. His chief aide-de-camp's office in the palace was connected by a hot-line telephone to the offices of the Army and Navy Operations Sections and their First Departments so that his aides could im-mediately convey imperial questions or raise queries of their own. Hirohito knew who headed the First Department of the Imperial Headquarters—Army, charged with the development of opera-tions plans and troop deployments; and who within the First De-partment was in charge of the Twentieth Group (grand strategic planning) and the Second Section (operations). More important, he was familiar with the step-by-step bureaucratic procedures that led directly to the drafting of the "national policy" documents deliberated at the liaison conferences and studied by him.

HIROHITO WAS WELL INFORMED

From 1941 onward, the high-command machinery steadily be-came more elaborate. The emperor widened and deepened his access to include just about all military intelligence. Detailed question-and-answer materials were compiled by staff officers in the Operations Sections, and war situation reports reached him on a weekly, daily, and sometimes twice-daily basis. Monthly and annual state-of-the-war evaluations were also compiled for the emperor's perusal; and, as historian Yamada Akira documented, Hirohito routinely received drafts of developing war plans and full explanations of operations, accompanied by detailed maps, informing him why an operation should be mounted and the units that would be carrying it out.

Battle reports and situation reports were delivered to the palace daily and, after the Pacific war started, shown to the emperor at any time of the day or night. These included itemization of com-bat losses and their causes, places where Japanese troops were do-ing well or not so well, and even such details as where cargo ships had been sunk and what matériel had been lost with them. Some-times "even telegrams coming into the Imperial Headquarters from the front lines" were shown to Hirohito by his three army and five navy aides-de-camp, serving around the clock on rotat-ing shifts. Among the many duties of these aides was the regular updating of Hirohito's operations maps. In addition, throughout the Pacific war the chief of the Navy General Staff sent the em-peror formal written reports, titled "Explanatory Materials for the Emperor Concerning the War Situation." These, added to his other sources of information, kept the emperor extraordinarily well informed. But a flaw in this intelligence system was that the army and navy prepared and presented their secret information to him separately, so that only the emperor himself ever knew the entire picture, especially in respect to losses.

When the "facts" reported from the front lines were inaccurate, Hirohito's "information" was misinformation. Still, Yamada observes, the emperor's briefers "believed in what they reported." Certainly their intentions were not to deceive him but to present accurate figures on the losses in personnel and armaments sustained by Japanese forces, as well as the damage inflicted by them. The materials he received were timely, detailed, and of high quality—as indeed they had to be, for the emperor was not only directing the grand strategic unfolding of the war, but pressing for solutions to the inevitable mishaps and miscalculations of his staff and field commands.

A FACTOR OF DEFEAT

In addition, to check on the accuracy of the reports he was receiving, Hirohito would often send his army and navy aides, as well as his own brothers, on inspection tours to various fronts to gather information outside routine channels. According to Ogata Kenichi, Hirohito's army aide-de-camp from March 1942 to November 1945, the emperor "sent his aides as close to the front lines as possible and chose the seasons when the troops were suffering most. When they returned, the emperor received them as though he valued their reports more than anything else." When questioning his ministers of state and the chiefs of the general staffs, Hirohito frequently quoted from these reports. In this way too, he kept his imperial eye constantly on his commanders.

Finally Hirohito continued his practice of viewing domestic and foreign newsreels and movies, screened for him at the palace, usually two or three times a week. He continued to read the censored Japanese press daily, and often pointedly questioned his military leaders about the news he found there. Thus he not only knew the truth about the war, he was also aware of the slanted versions or even outright "brainwashing" the Japanese people were receiving.

As early as the eve of Pearl Harbor, this enormous, time-consuming effort by the high command to be sure Hirohito was fully informed had begun to detract from the efficiency of key officers involved in operations and strategic planning. Because the First Department head, for example, spent so much of his time keeping the emperor abreast of developments, he often could not immerse himself fully in his main duties, which were the planning of operations and strategies. Imoto Tokuma, who served on the Army General Staff during 1941, believed that this unintended consequence of the monarchy's modus operandi became a factor in Japan's defeat. Keeping Hirohito informed was a Herculean effort that forced department heads to delegate their top-level work down to "section chiefs and their subordinates," who soon became drawn into "the war leadership activities of the department heads. When that confusion occurred, officers who might still be able to handle routine administrative affairs were quite unable to meet the Imperial Headquarters operational planning responsibilities."

Pearl Harbor: One Man's Story

John McGoran

On December 7, 1941—described by President Franklin D. Roosevelt as a "date which will live in infamy"—the Japanese air force attacked the U.S. naval base at Pearl Harbor, Hawaii. One of the survivors of the surprise attack was John McGoran, a U.S. Navy seaman on the battleship USS *California*. In the following selection, McGoran relates what happened when his ship was hit by Japanese torpedoes. He describes his experiences at his battle station in the powder-handling room and his foray with two other seamen to his sleeping quarters to investigate a reported break in the ship's anti-aircraft ammunition supply line. McGoran goes on to recount the rescue of a shipmate and the devastation and deaths he encountered as a member of a ten-man work party sent out into the ruins of Battleship Row to search for anti-aircraft ammunition.

The morning of December 7, 1941 was typical of any Sunday morning aboard the battleship USS *California*. My billet for meals was the Marines' casemate #8 (an armored enclosure for a gun) located portside midship, just where the forecastle breaks and a ladder leads down to the quarter-deck. Breakfast over, I took my dirty dishes to the scullery below. Lamentably, that's the way peace ended. Just then a sailor ran by crazily singing, "The Japs are coming—hurrah, hurrah!" I don't remember the alarm that sounded General Quarters. I only know that suddenly I joined in a rush to battle stations, in No. 3 turret's lower powder handling room.

From "Pearl Harbor Remembered," by John McGoran, published at www.execpc.com/~dschaaf/mcgoran.html. Reprinted with permission from the author.

THE *CALIFORNIA* IS HIT

When hurrying to our battle stations, to reach the decks below, we were trained to jump down the hatch—instead of using it's ladder—(ladder is ship talk and most often refers to a steep iron stairway). Then, grab onto a bar attached to the overhead (ceiling) of the deck below and swing one's body into a run in the lower passageway. That's roughly the way I arrived at my battle station in the "lower powder handling room" where a First-class petty-officer named Allen was in charge.

Allen was one of those old-time petty officers referred to as "The backbone of the Fleet." Now, he was busily giving orders we couldn't carry out because no one had the keys to the powder magazines (room).

Suddenly, a violent lurching shook us all, tossing us around like so many unmuscled puppets as the ship seemed to rise up a foot, then settle back. Allen grabbed at his ear phones. "We're hit," he cried. "A torpedo!"

"So what!" I thought foolishly. "Enjoy it!" The armor plating around the USS *California* was at least a foot thick.

My idiot elation was brief. A torpedo had hit us. (Three in all hit below the armor plating and made huge holes.) The fuel tank next to our port magazine ignited in flames and there we were, surrounded on three sides by powder-filled magazines.

Immediately orders came to check the temperature of the bulkhead (wall) separating the magazine from the fuel tank. We forced the lock on the magazine door and opened it. With that accomplished we discovered the covers had shaken off some of the cans containing the 14-inch powder bags and the aisle was strewn with ripped open bags of gunpowder.

Anxiously, I entered, walking carefully over the debris to feel the bulkhead. I returned and reported to Allen that the bulkhead was cool. Allen in turn passed the reassuring word over the mouthpiece of his headset to the bridge.

A LIFE SAVED

Whatever reply came back over the phones was reflected in the strain on Allen's face. He couldn't seem to comprehend, perhaps he didn't want to believe. He turned to us and almost in a whisper said, "The *Oklahoma*! It has capsized!" Frighteningly, our ship was beginning to list dangerously.

Allen received a report that our anti-aircraft ammunition supply line had broken down from an explosion. The break was reported to be in "CL" compartment, my sleeping quarters, and when the call came, I said I'd go. Two other seamen also volunteered for the job.

As I stood there looking into "CL" compartment, my companion, a seaman named "Smitty," called to me. I turned to see him on the opposite side of the conveyor trying to help a shipmate whose back was against the bulkhead, but who was slowly slipping to the deck (floor). His eyes were rolled back into his head. He looked like he was dying.

"This one is still alive," Smitty said calmly. Smitty was a small fellow but he managed to wrestle the wounded shipmate to me and I pulled his limp body over the conveyor into the passageway. If on December 6th anyone had asked me to help save the life of this offensive guy, I would have answered, "To hell with him." I had known this fellow since boot-camp, and he was one of the most overbearing individuals I had ever met. But now, unconscious, he had no personality; his was a life to be saved.

The USS California was one of the many ships very badly damaged when the Japanese attacked Pearl Harbor, the event that drew the United States into WWII.

To reach the first-aid station, Smitty and I back-tracked aft on the starboard side. Now and then, we had to stop and lay him down, so we could rest. Catching our breaths, we moved on again. As we trudged along, we had to again open and close the watertight bulkhead doors while making our way back through the passageway to a ladder up, which was near the man-hole down to number three lower handling, from where we started.

The hatch-cover at the top of the ladder was dogged down—another Navy term for closed and watertight. But, it was the nearest escape to the decks above. We undogged the hatch and pushed it open. Smitty took the injured man's legs and started up the ladder; I got him under the arms again and just as I'd taken a second or third step up the ladder an explosion again rocked the ship.

Suddenly, a steam pipe nearby blew out. In a stunning moment of chaos that followed, I heard the cry, "Gas!" Unquestioningly, I held my breath until I could fit my gas-mask to my face. The gas mask was very uncomfortable and it was difficult to cope with. Finally, I lifted it a bit to sniff the air to determine whether or not it smelled safe to breathe; it did.

Smitty and I debated whether to try to escape by going back to "CL" compartment and try a ladder there, or opening this hatch again and trying to escape here. Hesitatingly, we again tackled this ladder. We again opened the hatch cover and saw no evidence of damage from the explosion.

A ROOM FULL OF VICTIMS

What actually happened was a bomb penetrated the decks above and exploded in front of the ship's store, several feet forward of the ladder. It killed "Boots," one of the masters-at-arms (ship's policeman). It bent a heavy steel hatch-combing flush with the deck.

We picked up our injured shipmate and carried him up. This time, we were lucky and got him to the first-aid station.

Some station! It was normally the crews' recreation room, but now a state of incredible confusion prevailed. We laid our shipmate on the deck. A chief petty officer, whom I recognized as one of the "black-gang" (engine room crew), came over and with great authority asked if he was alive. "We think so," I said. "Then get him out of the way," ordered the chief. "Slide him under the table where nobody will trip over him." (Later in the week, I learned that the fellow's back had been broken, but he would recover.) Then the chief went back to directing and sorting the living from the dead. As men brought in casualties, the chief would say, "Dead or alive? If they're dead, take them into the other room and throw them on the dead pile." He repeatedly made rounds of the room inspecting bodies. "This man is dead—Get him out of here." Normally this cold, hard manner would have been resented. Now, I could only feel admiration for his efficiency.

As I stood, trying to comprehend all of this, someone handed me a bottle of root-beer and a sandwich. Ordinarily I would have retched at the sight of so much blood, but I ate and drank, completely amazed at my appetite under such conditions and decided it was all incomprehensible.

IN SEARCH OF AMMUNITION

While I was in the first-aid station, word came to abandon ship. Whether or not this was an official order, I don't know. But instead, the Chief Petty Officer in charge and a Warrant Officer named Applegate formed a work-party of ten men to search for anti-aircraft ammunition, since ours could not be reached, due to a bomb explosion.

Our work-party first went aft to the door which exited onto the starboard quarter-deck. We were about to proceed across the quarter-deck to board a motor launch when someone warned us that a wave of strafing Japanese planes was passing over. The planes came in low, firing their machine guns. Between sorties, men from nearby battle stations raced out on the quarter-deck and dragged to shelter those who had been struck by the machine gun fire. Then, as soon as we felt it was safe, we ran for the motor launch, which was waiting for us at the port quarter dry docks. She seemed to be out of the channel; perhaps she had turned to avoid a bomb.

Our coxswain took our launch into the space between the capsized *Oklahoma* and the port side forecastle of the *Maryland*. Shouting up to sailors on the *Maryland*'s forecastle, we tried to convey to them that we needed ammunition, but we could rouse no support. Their problems were far greater to them than what we were shouting up to them from our motor launch. Had we spoken to an officer there, we might have been more successful.

Once it became clear that we could expect no help from this quarter, we gave up trying to board the *Maryland*. The coxswain maneuvered the motor launch from between the two battleships and motored around the whale-shaped hull of the capsized *Oklahoma* and went to the USS *West Virginia*.

By this time, the *West Virginia* had sunk deep enough so that it was with little effort that Warrant Officer Applegate, and the five men he picked . . . clambered aboard. I watched as they crossed the ship's forecastle, walking under the barrels of the 16-inch guns, and walk aft on the starboard side. We never saw them again.

Within minutes the forecastle shot up in smoke and flames. (It may have been the bomb that hit the turret of the *Tennessee*.) An officer in his white uniform appeared engulfed in the fire. Someone on board shouted, "Get out of there. The ship can blow up any minute."

The explosion frightened us terribly. The coxswain began backing the launch away from the burning battleship. Suddenly, I saw that the coxswain was not aware of the danger immediately behind our launch; we were backing straight for one of the large propellers of the capsized *Oklahoma* sticking high out of the water.

I yelled at the coxswain, "Reverse your engines." At the same time, two of us clambered to the tiller-deck, and scrambled over the taffrail. With one hand grasping the taffrail, we reached with our legs—spread eagle-like—and with our feet, shoved against the propeller. Unquestionably, our effort prevented the motor launch from being damaged; but we just did what the situation required.

The coxswain now had the launch underway forward. Then we saw a man struggling in the water near the midships section of the *West Virginia*. "We're going in after him," he told us. The coxswain maneuvered in to pick up the man from the water, bringing him dangerously close to the perimeter of the burning oil that was closing in.

By now I was overwhelmed by all that was happening around us and for the life of me, I can't recall whether that man made it into the boat. We headed for 1010 dock at the Navy shipyard.

And there was, indeed, reason to feel overwhelmed. On every side were almost unbearable sights. Battleship Row was devastated. From the direction of the dry docks, an explosion shook the harbor. This was the destroyer *Shaw.* Just two weeks before, I had visited my brother's ship in that same dry dock.

The *St. Louis* was gaining speed, but we were able to come alongside her starboard quarter . . . , where we tried to clamber aboard the gangway which was still hanging over the side. An officer on deck denied us permission to come aboard. Frustrated, we abandoned the attempt to board the *St. Louis* and headed for 1010 dock at the Naval Ship Yard, where everyone went their individual ways.

Only one who was there can fully appreciate what took place. As a Pearl Harbor Survivor who was at ground zero on "Battleship Row" the morning of December 7, 1941, I feel, "if you didn't go through it, there's no words that can adequately describe it; if you were there, then no words are necessary."

AMERICA'S SHAME: JAPANESE INTERNMENT CAMPS

DONALD H. ESTES AND MATTHEW T. ESTES

In April 1942, afraid that the Japanese living on the West Coast might help Japan invade the United States, the U.S. government forced more than 100,000 Japanese Americans, most of them American citizens, into relocation camps located farther inland. In the following selection, academicians Donald H. and Matthew T. Estes relate how the government decision affected California's San Diego County Nikkei community—that is, Japanese and Americans of Japanese ancestry. According to the authors, fifteen hundred San Diego County Japanese of all ages—with no idea of where they were being taken and allowed to bring only what they could carry—were loaded onto two trains by military police officers. The authors go on to describe the substandard conditions that the Japanese were forced to endure once they arrived at their final destination. The Japanese, the authors demonstrate, were made to live out the war years isolated behind a barbed-wire fence, denied most common amenities, and accorded only restricted interaction with the world outside their camp.

O n April 1, 1942, time ran out not only for the young Nisei, but the whole local Nikkei community. On that day General [John G.] DeWitt issued Civilian Exclusion Order Number 4, and it was definitely not a case of April's Fool. In an interesting turn of the English language the order announced that: "All persons, both alien and non-alien, will be evacuated

From "Further and Further Away: The Relocation of San Diego's Nikkei Community, 1942," by Donald H. Estes and Matthew T. Estes, *Journal of San Diego History*, vol. 39, nos. 1–2 (Winter/Spring 1993). Reprinted by permission of the San Diego Historical Society.

from the designated area by 12:00 noon, Wednesday April 8, 1942." DeWitt, the Army, and the government of the United States still could not quite bring themselves to say that they were detaining and removing American citizens. This particular group of American citizens had, by military fiat, become "non-aliens."

For purposes of the evacuation the Army initially interpreted "Japanese" to mean a resident of the prohibited zones with any ascertainable trace of Japanese blood. Later, it was discovered that a wide range of persons ranging from Japanese women married to Caucasian males through individuals with varying degrees of Japanese ancestry down to as little as one-sixteenth had been caught up by the Army's order. After the fact, the military initiated procedures to allow specific categories of persons of Japanese ancestry and individuals identified by the Army as being of "mixed-blood" to apply for deferments and exemptions from their detention, and be released from the assembly centers.

The seven days that followed that fateful April Fool's Day were ones of intense, anxiety-filled activity as the local Nikkei began to prepare for their diaspora. Everyone, from the very old to the very young prepared to leave. Since the evacuation order specifically limited their baggage to items that could be carried, what could not be stored with friends or sold, was simply abandoned. . . .

THE EVACUATION GETS UNDERWAY

On the morning of Wednesday, April 8, 1942, over fifteen hundred men, women, and children gathered at the Santa Fe Depot where they were met by armed military police and two waiting trains. . . .

At around four in the afternoon the Military Police began to load the trains according to an alphabetical list that had been previously prepared. At five o'clock in the afternoon, right on schedule, the first train pulled out. Even at this point in the evacuation the destination of the trains was unknown to those aboard.

Twelve-year-old Ben Segawa, whose family farmed in [San Diego's] Mission Valley, remembered, "As the train began to move, armed Military Police came through cars ordering everyone to pull the shades down so we could not see out. It was hot and cramped and people could hardly move."

The second train—scheduled to follow the first—experienced a series of delays. To compound the problem, the train also carried the sick and families with infants. By eight o'clock in the evening the train had still not departed and many of the young mothers were concerned about getting milk warmed for their babies.

Dr. [Roy] Tanaka, the physician in charge of the families, recalled this hectic first night of exile:

Around eight o'clock in the evening mothers started coming up to me saying "We can't feed the babies." We did have prepared milk, but we didn't have any way to warm it.

I asked one of the guards. . . . He was an elderly man, and I said to him, "Sir, we are having a problem. These mothers have babies that need to be fed, but we need some warm milk. Where can I get some hot water?" He said, "That's a problem isn't it." So I said, "Maybe we can use the men's restroom, maybe there's enough hot water in there." So that was all I was doing. Commuting back and forth. There was enough hot water . . . just lukewarm. . . . So I warmed the bottles as best I could and gave them to the mothers, and someone else would hand me their bottles to be warmed. At least the infants ate that night, I don't think I did.

Finally, with shades drawn, the second train got underway at one o'clock in the morning. The 125 mile trip to Los Angeles took seven hours. . . . For whatever the reasons, the prison train was sidetracked throughout the trip north to allow trains with higher-priority cargos a clear line. One advantage that the second train did have over the first was that it was not stoned along the way.

A City Encased by Barbed Wire

Arriving in Los Angeles the exiles were given a breakfast consisting of a sandwich and a piece of fruit and then were loaded on to busses for the next stage of their journey. Their destination—the newly designated Santa Anita Assembly Center, at the Santa Anita Racetrack in Arcadia, California. On the track's infield the Army had begun to build the tarpaper and wood barracks that would eventually house over 18,500 men, women, and children and, for a time, become California's thirty-second most populous city, a city completely surrounded by barbed wire.

Once off the busses the former San Diegans passed through an initial checkpoint where their luggage was searched for "contra-band." Seized immediately were all cameras, radios, and knives of any type. Doctor's bags were taken, and later returned minus all medications and registered narcotics. Although receipts for the confiscated narcotics were requested from Center authorities, they were never provided.

Since they were among the first detainees to arrive, many of the San Diego families were assigned to horse stables that had been converted into living spaces of eight feet by twelve feet. Tarpaper had been spread on the ground and the walls freshly whitewashed. This did little to cover the reeking smell of manure and horse urine, and the toadstools that regularly bloomed from the straw-covered dirt floors. Partitions of tarpaper were also used to separate the stalls, but they did not extend all the way to the ceiling. . . .

Since the number of stables was limited, the remaining families were moved into the tarpaper barracks almost as soon as they were completed. What rose up on the infield were row after row of uniform, black-tarpaper–covered barracks. At first, finding one's residence proved a problem for some:

> We have been busy getting established in our new homes, which were formally horse stables. We have been given good army beds and blankets. The food is getting better as the cooks become more experienced.

> There are just rows and rows of similar houses and we get lost trying to find our own. My girl friends got lost in a blackout which occurred our first night here.

These barrack-style buildings were typically partitioned into two rooms measuring twenty by eight feet and assigned to families of two or three individuals. Four rooms measuring twenty by twelve feet were assigned to families composed of four to six persons.

Each army "bunk" initially came with a single military wool blanket and a straw tick which served in place of a mattress. For sanitary reasons the tick was to be washed each month. New straw for the tick was provided every two weeks, but because it was normally deposited in the middle of the street, cleanliness remained a challenge for most residents.

A LACK OF PRIVACY AND AMENITIES

Lighting at the Center was inadequate at best. Each room was allotted a single line with an accompanying forty watt bulb. Almost immediately problems developed with overloaded circuits and blown fuses. The intensity of the issue became serious enough for the civilian manager of the Center, H. Russell Amory, to react officially. In special bulletins issued on April 15, and later on May 1, he requested that the use of all electric heaters, irons, stoves, boilers, heating pads, and curling irons be discontinued at once. In response to a corollary irritant, residents were further warned that: "The Utility section will refuse to replace blown fuses between 5 P.M. and 8 A.M.". . . .

Toilet facilities were crude. Inconveniently separated from their living quarters, residents discovered that little provision had been made for comfort, and none for modesty. The facilities consisted of "ten seats lined up: hard, fresh-sawed unsandpapered wood; automatic flushing about every fifteen minutes." Because of the lack of partitions many women initially were reluctant to use the exposed toilets, and a number of them were eventually admitted to the Center medical facility with bowel disorders. Ben Segawa, recalling his Santa Anita experiences noted:

> I remember every time I had to go to the bathroom at night I had to go to another building that was about fifty feet away. The minute I left our barracks, that search-light would hit you and follow you right to where you were going. The light would wait there until you came back out and the light hit you and followed you right back to your barracks again. They kept track of every move we made. I was only twelve years old, what could I do?

Later, residents raided a scrap lumber pile and were able to build some temporary partitions for the toilets.

COLOR-CODED MESS HALLS AND BAD FOOD

For Nikkei families meals were traditionally times when the family came together not only for sustenance but for serious social interaction as well. Now, along with the other forced changes, this facet of their culture was all but destroyed. At Santa Anita meals were eaten in six communal mess halls that seated from seven hundred and fifty people to a phenomenal five thousand. To accommodate this volume the grandstand of the track was converted into a mess hall. Even then, all meals were scheduled in shifts.

The six mess halls were designed by color: Blue, Green, White, Orange, and Yellow. Residents were issued colored buttons for admittance and numbers to designate their shift.

On July 29, 1942, the Center newsletter, the *Pacemaker*, reported that rice was the largest single item of food consumed by Center residents. The White mess hall alone used three tons of rice per week. Until experienced food preparers were either identified among the residents or trained, the quality of the food varied widely.

San Diegan Tets Hirasaki wrote at the time:

> Now that we have a number of San Diego men working in the kitchens the food has improved a bit, especially the salads. I heard we are to receive meat soon, but I think it will mostly be stew meat, because we are not al-lowed knives, only spoons and forks as eating utensils.

Another former San Diegan, Masaaki Hironaka, recalls:

I clearly remember early on they were serving some
meat. It really looked wonderful, so I asked for a second
slice, and that was my first encounter with beef heart. I
still can't really stomach it. Even to this day.

According to Dr. Tanaka, diarrhea periodically became en-
demic to certain mess halls, prompting the Center to rigidly enforce sanitation standards. The hospital at Santa Anita was a
seventy-five bed facility headed by Dr. Norman Kobayashi. Dr.
Tanaka remembers months of twelve-hour days, seven days a
week, with a twenty-four hour hospital duty tour every fifth day.
The hospital was set up in the paddock area and had none of the
conveniences of a modern hospital.

We did some surgery in the hospital. We eventually got
the equipment, but it was a while before we could do
surgery at all. Before we had the equipment we would
send an ambulance to take them to the [Los Angeles]
County Hospital.

We used to make house calls for people who couldn't
make it to the hospital. There was a couple with only
one boy from someplace up north. I remember I was
the first to see this boy when he got sick. I told the
couple, "This child is awfully sick. Why don't you take
him to the hospital?" And, the father said, "I'm not going to take my kid to a Goddamn horse hospital." I
said, "You and I are more or less in the same boat. Sure
that's not a hospital, but it's better than staying in a
horse stable. At least we could probably do something
for him. Take blood samples, things like that." He said,
"Absolutely not."

Three other doctors looked at the boy, and when the
fourth saw him, he looked so bad that the doctor insisted the boy be brought to the hospital. We had to give
the child a transfusion but we had no way to crossmatch
the blood. We sent him to L.A. County but he died there.

FIGHTING OFF THE BOREDOM

As in most cases of institutionalization, boredom set in quickly,
particularly on the young adult population. While the salaries set
by the [War Relocation Board] were low, ranging from eight dollars a month for unskilled or semi-skilled labor through twelve
dollars for skilled labor, with top salaries available to residents of
sixteen dollars a month for professional or supervisory jobs, there
was a high demand for any type of job. Some of the younger res-

idents, like Tets Hirasaki, who was a messenger during the day, wrote friends requesting that the tools of their former trade being held in storage be shipped to them. Shortly after his tonsorial equipment arrived, Hirasaki began operating as a barber in the evenings.

Young women, too, sought meaningful activity at the Center. In a letter, Yoshiko Kubo wrote:

> Tomorrow, the recreation center for children between the ages of five and ten years of age opens, and that will take care of the younger children. I hope to start working as a waitress in one of the cafeterias or as a helper in the children's recreation department.

As the assembly Center began to take on the form of a medium-sized city it acquired its own local paper—the *Santa Anita Pacemaker*. First published on April 21, 1942, the newsletter appeared at varying intervals, usually twice a week, until the Center's closure in October, 1942. . . .

Because temples and churches had historically been mainstays of the Nikkei community they were among the first institutions to be reorganized at Santa Anita. . . .

Another pre-war activity that was established with alacrity was a softball league. The premier issue of the *Pacemaker* reported that the San Diego Falcons had scored their second straight victory, much to the delight of their coach, Yas Nakamoto, who immediately issued a challenge to take on all comers. A band, an orchestra, choirs, Cub Scout Packs and Boy Scout Troops all followed in relatively short order. . . .

The earliest contacts with the world outside the barbed wire were made largely through the fence at the Center's Baldwin Avenue gate on an almost daily basis. Because of the volume of activity around the gate, and a perceived security risk, formal visitor regulations were issued by Center manager Amory on April 20. These initial regulations limited outside contacts to blood relatives (an interesting category since most Nikkei were already detained or in the process of being detained), and business agents. Passes had to be obtained from the Center administration with the designated visiting hours being limited to 2 P.M. to 4 P.M. daily.

In late June a Visitor's House was completed, allowing non-Nikkei friends to meet with the internees. Visitor's permits and strict regulations governing the conditions of the visits were still enforced, and guests were limited to a single thirty-minute period. . . .

On July 22 the Center newsletter reported that an average of one hundred visitors were coming each weekday and three hundred per weekend, further commenting that "the Visitor's house is one of the Center's top morale builders." The same story quoted Susumu Yamanaka, a Center auxiliary policeman, as saying, ". . . residents often cry with joy when their pets are brought in by friends to visit."

THE AMERICAN WAR EFFORT

FRANKLIN DELANO ROOSEVELT

On October 12, 1942, shortly after his return from an inspection tour of U.S. military camps, training stations, and factories, President Franklin Delano Roosevelt addressed the American people via radio to let them know what he had learned about the American war effort. In the speech, Roosevelt declares that America was fast becoming one united fighting force and commends the American people on their unbeatable spirit. He explains that although American industry has expanded to meet the increased wartime production needs, manpower has become a challenge—a matter not of sufficiency but of distribution. Especially problematic, he avers, is the scarcity of farm labor in many places. Roosevelt states definitively that America is fighting in this war to restore faith, hope, and peace worldwide and to so completely destroy the military power of Germany, Italy, and Japan that it will not resurface in the future to threaten the freedoms and lives of the next generation.

T his whole nation of one hundred and thirty million free men, women and children is becoming one great fighting force. Some of us are soldiers or sailors, some of us are civilians. Some of us are fighting the war in airplanes five miles above the continent of Europe or the islands of the Pacific—and some of us are fighting it in mines deep down in the earth of Pennsylvania or Montana. A few of us are decorated with medals for heroic achievement, but all of us can have that deep and permanent inner satisfaction that comes from doing the best we

From a radio address of Franklin Delano Roosevelt, October 12, 1942.

know how—each of us playing an honorable part in the great
struggle to save our democratic civilization.

Whatever our individual circumstances or opportunities—
we are all in it, and our spirit is good, and we Americans and
our allies are going to win—and do not let anyone tell you anything different. . . .

AMERICAN INDUSTRY EXPANDS TO MEET THE NEED

There are now millions of Americans in army camps, in naval
stations, in factories and in shipyards. . . .

In the last war, I had seen great factories; but until I saw some
of the new present-day plants, I had not thoroughly visualized
our American war effort. Of course, I saw only a small portion of
all our plants, but that portion was a good cross-section, and it
was deeply impressive.

The United States has been at war for only ten months, and is
engaged in the enormous task of multiplying its armed forces
many times. We are by no means at full production level yet. But
I could not help asking myself on the trip, where would we be
today if the Government of the United States had not begun to
build many of its factories for this huge increase more than two
years ago, more than a year before war was forced upon us at
Pearl Harbor?

We have also had to face the problem of shipping. Ships in
every part of the world continue to be sunk by enemy action. But
the total tonnage of ships coming out of American, Canadian and
British shipyards, day by day, has increased so fast that we are
getting ahead of our enemies in the bitter battle of transportation.

In expanding our shipping, we have had to enlist many thousands of men for our Merchant Marine. These men are serving
magnificently. They are risking their lives every hour so that guns
and tanks and planes and ammunition and food may be carried
to the heroic defenders of Stalingrad and to all the United Nations' forces all over the world. . . .

As I told the three press association representatives who accompanied me, I was impressed by the large proportion of
women employed—doing skilled manual labor running machines. As time goes on, and many more of our men enter the
armed forces, this proportion of women will increase. Within less
than a year from now, I think, there will probably be as many
women as men working in our war production plants.

I had some enlightening experiences relating to the old saying
of us men that curiosity—inquisitiveness—is stronger among
woman. I noticed, frequently, that when we drove unannounced

down the middle aisle of a great plant full of workers and machines, the first people to look up from their work were the men—and not the women. It was chiefly the men who were arguing as to whether that fellow in the straw hat was really the President or not.

So having seen the quality of the work and of the workers on our production lines—and coupling these firsthand observations with the reports of actual performance of our weapons on the fighting fronts—I can say to you that we are getting ahead of our enemies in the battle of production.

THE PROBLEM OF MANPOWER MUST BE FACED

And of great importance to our future production was the effective and rapid manner in which the Congress met the serious problem of the rising cost of living. It was a splendid example of the operation of democratic processes in wartime. . . .

In order to keep stepping up our production, we have had to add millions of workers to the total labor force of the Nation. And as new factories came into operation, we must find additional millions of workers.

This presents a formidable problem in the mobilization of manpower.

It is not that we do not have enough people in this country to do the job. The problem is to have the right numbers of the right people in the right places at the right time.

We are learning to ration materials, and we must now learn to ration manpower. The major objectives of a sound manpower policy are:

First, to select and train men of the highest fighting efficiency needed for our armed forces in the achievement of victory over our enemies in combat.

Second, to man our war industries and farms with the workers needed to produce the arms and munitions and food required by ourselves and by our fighting allies to win this war.

In order to do this, we shall be compelled to stop workers from moving from one war job to another as a matter of personal preference; to stop employers from stealing labor from each other; to use older men, and handicapped people, and more women, and even grown boys and girls, wherever possible and reasonable, to replace men of military age and fitness; to train new personnel for essential war work; and to stop the wastage of labor in all non-essential activities. . . .

The school authorities in all the states should work out plans to enable our high school students to take some time from their school year, to use their summer vacations, to help farmers raise and harvest their crops, or to work somewhere in the war industries. This does not mean closing schools and stopping education. It does mean giving older students a better opportunity to contribute their bit to the war effort. Such work will do no harm to the students.

People should do their work as near their homes as possible. We cannot afford to transport a single worker into an area where there is already a worker available to do the job.

In some communities, employers dislike to employ women. In others they are reluctant to hire Negroes. In still others, older men are not wanted. We can no longer afford to indulge such prejudices or practices.

Every citizen wants to know what essential war work he can do the best. He can get the answer by applying to the nearest United States Employment Service office. There are four thousand five hundred of these offices throughout the Nation. They form the corner grocery stores of our manpower system. . . .

FARMERS MUST PRODUCE

Perhaps the most difficult phase of the manpower problem is the scarcity of farm labor in many places. I have seen evidences of the fact, however, that the people are trying to meet it as well as possible.

In one community that I visited a perishable crop was harvested by turning out the whole of the high school for three or four days.

And in another community of fruit growers the usual Japanese labor was not available; but when the fruit ripened, the banker, the butcher, the lawyer, the garage man, the druggist, the local editor, and in fact every able-bodied man and woman in the town, left their occupations, went out gathering the fruit, and sent it to market.

Every farmer in the land must realize fully that his production is part of war production, and that he is regarded by the Nation as essential to victory. The American people expect him to keep his production up, and even to increase it. We will use every effort to help him to get labor; but, at the same time, he and the people of his community must use ingenuity and cooperative effort to produce crops, and livestock and dairy products.

THE AGE LIMIT MUST BE LOWERED

It may be that all of our volunteer effort—however well intentioned and well administered—will not suffice wholly to solve this problem. In that case, we shall have to adopt new legislation. And if this is necessary, I do not believe that the American people will shrink from it.

In a sense, every American, because of the privilege of his citizenship, is a part of the Selective Service.

The Nation owes a debt of gratitude to the Selective Service Boards. The successful operation of the Selective Service System and the way it has been accepted by the great mass of our citizens give us confidence that if necessary, the same principle could be used to solve any manpower problem.

And I want to say also a word of praise and thanks to the more than ten million people, all over the country, who have volunteered for the work of civilian defense—and who are working hard at it. They are displaying unselfish devotion in the patient performance of their often tiresome and always anonymous tasks. In doing this important neighborly work they are helping to fortify our national unity and our real understanding of the fact that we are all involved in this war. . . .

All of our combat units that go overseas must consist of young, strong men who have had thorough training. An Army division that has an average age of twenty-three or twenty-four is a better fighting unit than one which has an average age of thirty-three or thirty-four. The more of such troops we have in the field, the sooner the war will be won, and the smaller will be the cost in casualties.

Therefore, I believe that it will be necessary to lower the present minimum age limit for Selective Service from twenty years down to eighteen. We have learned how inevitable that is—and how important to the speeding up of victory.

I can very thoroughly understand the feelings of all parents whose sons have entered our armed forces. I have an appreciation of that feeling and so has my wife. I want every father and every mother who has a son in the service to know—again, from what I have seen with my own eyes—that the men in the Army, Navy and Marine Corps are receiving today the best possible training, equipment and medical care. And we will never fail to provide for the spiritual needs of our officers and men under the Chaplains of our armed services. . . .

We . . . will continue to leave the plans for this war to the military leaders. The military and naval plans of the United States are made by the Joint Staff of the Army and Navy which is constantly in session in Washington. . . . They meet and confer regularly with representatives of the British Joint Staff, and with representatives of Russia, China, the Netherlands, Poland, Norway, the British Dominions and other nations working in the common cause. . . .

As I have said before, many major decisions of strategy have been made. One of them—on which we have all agreed—relates to the necessity of diverting enemy forces from Russia and

China to other theaters of war by new offensives against Germany and Japan. . . .

We are mindful of the countless millions of people whose future liberty and whose very lives depend upon permanent victory for the United Nations.

There are a few people in this country who, when the collapse of the Axis begins, will tell our people that we are safe once more; that we can tell the rest of the world to "stew in its own juice"; that never again will we help to pull "the other fellow's chestnuts from the fire"; that the future of civilization can jolly well take care of itself insofar as we are concerned.

But it is useless to win battles if the cause for which we fight these battles is lost. It is useless to win a war unless it stays won.

We, therefore, fight for the restoration and perpetuation of faith and hope and peace throughout the world.

The objective of today is clear and realistic. It is to destroy completely the military power of Germany, Italy and Japan to such good purpose that their threat against us and all the other United Nations cannot be revived a generation hence. We are united in seeking the kind of victory that will guarantee that our grandchildren can grow and, under God, may live their lives, free from the constant threat of invasion, destruction, slavery and violent death.

HITLER'S "FINAL SOLUTION": PERSECUTION BEYOND CONCEPTION

ARTHUR M. SCHLESINGER JR.

World-acclaimed historian and political activist Arthur M. Schlesinger Jr. is a Pulitzer Prize-winner; the holder of numerous awards, including the National Humanities Medal; and a former special assistant to U.S. presidents John F. Kennedy and Lyndon B. Johnson. In this selection, Schlesinger offers insights into why the American and British governments did not do more to save the Jews of Europe. According to Schlesinger, although both governments had hints of the Final Solution in mid-to-late 1942, it was not really a subject of discussion, largely because those who did know about it thought in terms of increased persecution, not genocide. Schlesinger argues that it is unfair to blame President Roosevelt for America not doing more to help. Roosevelt, he contends, was more pro-Jewish than any other American president, but given the general tendency toward anti-Semitism at the time, he could not risk losing American support for the war by characterizing it as one to save Jews.

I n the Eighties and Nineties, a furious controversy erupted over the supposed failure of the American and British governments to do more to save the Jews of Europe. One wonders why this controversy suddenly exploded so many years af-

Excerpted from *A Life in the Twentieth Century*, by Arthur M. Schlesinger Jr. Copyright © 2000 by Arthur M. Schlesinger Jr. Reprinted by permission of Houghton Mifflin Company. All rights reserved.

ter the fact. The word 'holocaust' was not even applied to Hitler's extermination of the Jews till the Sixties; it did not acquire a capital letter until the Seventies. . . .

The controversy turned in part on the extent of knowledge in Washington and London about the Nazi decision, taken in 1941, to change the anti-Semitic policy from expulsion to extermination. I have asked myself and I have asked R&A [Research-and-Analysis] colleagues when any of us first became aware of a program of mass murder as something qualitatively different from the well-recognized viciousness of the concentration camps. OSS [Office of Strategic Services] presumably received the best possible intelligence, and German-Jewish refugees would have been the last people inclined to ignore or discount reports of a Final Solution.

Yet my recollection is that, even in the summer of 1944 as we received with horror the mounting flow of information about the camps, most of us were still thinking of an increase in persecution rather than a new and barbaric policy of genocide. This was certainly the line of the *PW Weekly* and I cannot find R&A colleagues who recall a moment of blazing revelation about the Final Solution. Nor do I recall the question of rescue operations coming up.

In his excellent study *Foreign Intelligence: Research and Analysis in the Office of Strategic Services, 1942–1945* (1989), Barry M. Katz writes of the Central European analysts, "Although they had reported regularly on incidences [sic] of official violence and terrorism, on mass deportations, and on the network of Nazi concentration camps, their papers prior to [1945] . . . yield no unambiguous evidence that they had grasped these as elements of a systematic policy of genocide." Neither Felix Gilbert nor Bill Langer even mentioned the Holocaust in their memoirs. "In retrospect," wrote Stuart Hughes in his memoir, "what amazes me is how little heed I had paid to the 'Final Solution.'"

A WIDESPREAD MYOPIA ABOUT THE HOLOCAUST

Yet the American and British governments had intimations of the Final Solution as early as August 1942. That November, after the confirmation of dread reports by Undersecretary of State Sumner Welles, Rabbi Stephen Wise went public in a dramatic press conference. WISE SAYS HITLER HAS ORDERED 4,000,000 JEWS SLAIN IN 1942 was the headline in the next day's *New York Herald Tribune*. On December 17 Roosevelt and [British prime minister Winston] Churchill issued a joint statement condemning the "bestial policy of cold-blooded extermination." Edward R. Murrow, broadcasting from London, dismissed the term 'concentration camp' as "obsolete. . . . It is now possible to speak only of 'extermination camp.'" American newspapers carried stories of the Nazi program of mass murder.

Why did R&A analysts not make more of this ghastly development? Some may have been diverted by Franz Neumann and what he called "the spearhead theory of anti-Semitism." Franz saw Hitler's war against the Jews not as an end in itself but as a way of whipping up mass support in order to attain a larger end—"the destruction of free institutions, beliefs, and groups." His "personal conviction," he even wrote in [his analysis,] *Behemoth*, was that "the German people are the least anti-Semitic of all." Marxists . . . tended to regard anti-Semitism not as an all-devouring Nazi obsession, but rather as a cynical tactic used to steer the masses away from the class war.

Myopia was widespread. Non-Marxists were equally oblivious. OWI's [Office of War Information] Voice of America employed many European Jews in foreign language broadcasts. Yet VOA's [Voice of America] historian, Holly Cowan Shulman, whose father . . . Lou Cowan ran the Voice in the last years of the war, went through file after file of VOA papers and found no mention of the Holocaust and little about the plight of the European Jews. She was astonished by "the yawning silence with which the Voice of America treated the persecution and ultimate destruction of European Jewry."

Forty years after, she asked the French-Jewish journalist . . . Michel Gordey, of the wartime VOA's French desk, how they all could have ignored the Holocaust. If there had been an OWI directive not to mention the massacre of the Jews, Gordey told her, he would have resigned. "The only conclusion I can draw is that I did not know about the Holocaust."

GENOCIDE IS NOT BELIEVED

When Jan Karski came out of Poland and brought Washington the news of the extermination policy, Felix Frankfurter refused to believe it. "I do not mean that you are lying," he told Karski. "I simply said I cannot believe you." "We knew in a general way that Jews were being persecuted," said William J. Casey, the head of SI/OSS in Europe, ". . . but few if any comprehended the appalling magnitude of it. . . . The most devastating experience of the war for most of us was the first visit to a concentration camp." Although the Roosevelt-Churchill declaration of December 17, 1942, was "front-page news," Telford Taylor, an American intelligence officer destined to be a major prosecutor at the Nuremberg trials, later wrote, "[I]t made astonishingly—indeed shamefully—little impact on the public mind. I myself did not become aware of the Holocaust until my exposure to the relevant documents and witnesses at Nuremberg." The correspondent William Shirer had broadcast from Berlin in the Thirties and published his best-selling *Berlin Diary* in 1941. Asked later how he had reacted to reports that a whole people were being systematically obliterated, Shirer replied, "I couldn't believe it. . . . I did not get the story, really, until the war-crimes trial at Nuremberg."

Daniel Lerner, of Russian-Jewish extraction and the chief editor in the Intelligence Branch of the Psychological Warfare Division, in his 1949 book *Sykewar: Psychological Warfare Against Germany, D-Day to VE-Day* is oblivious to the Final Solution. "The full horrors of [the concentration camps] Auschwitz and Buchenwald," wrote George Ball, co-director of the United States Strategic Bombing Survey, later undersecretary of state, "made a deep impression only after the documented revelations of Nuremberg. It was only then that I became fully and sickeningly aware of the atrocious persecution of Jews and Slavs." "Even we refugees from Germany," wrote Max Frankel of the *New York Times*, "were predisposed to disbelieve the reports of genocide. Did the Nazis persecute the Jews? Yes, of course, we knew that. . . . But gas chambers? Ovens? . . . Unbelievable. Unimaginable." The *Pocket Guide to Germany*, issued by the War Department for the instruction of the army of occupation, did not mention the death camps.

The British were equally unknowing. Brian Urquhart, an intelligence officer advancing with his unit into Germany, later the great international civil servant of his (my) generation, recalled, "The actual extermination of millions of people was simply unimaginable. We were completely unprepared for [the concentration camp] Belsen." "It took some time," my Cambridge friend Noel Annan, another intelligence officer, has written ". . . for the enormity of Germany's crimes against the Jews to sink in. In intelligence we knew of the gas ovens, but not of the scale, the thoroughness, the bureaucratic efficiency with which Jews had been hunted down and slaughtered. No one at the end of the war, as I recollect realised that the figure of Jewish dead ran into millions." Isaiah Berlin, a Zionist and an intimate friend of the Jewish leaders Chaim Weizmann and Nahum Goldman, writing his weekly political reports in the British Embassy in Washington, told me in later years that he knew nothing about the Holocaust until 1945.

The formidable political philosopher Raymond Aron, a French Jew working for [the Free French Forces leader Charles] de Gaulle in London, thought that the murder of a whole category of humanity was inconceivable. He was not aware of the Holocaust, he said, until allied armies liberated the death camps in

1945. Even [Zionist] David Ben-Gurion read reports of the Final Solution with disbelief and busied himself not with rescue plans for European Jews but with postwar plans for Palestine. "As far as overall Zionist priorities were concerned," Peter Novick writes, "it is clear that working for the creation of a Jewish state took precedence over working to save Europe's Jews."

RIGHTEOUSNESS IN RETROSPECT

How does one reconcile two clashing impressions? One is that from late 1942 on everyone, more or less, had heard about the Final Solution. The other is that many people in a position to be informed and with a predilection to care, people who listened to Ed Murrow and read about Rabbi Wise's press conference and the Roosevelt-Churchill statement of December 17, 1942, still did not comprehend the actuality of the Final Solution. How could both things have been true?

In his *Grammar of Assent,* Cardinal Newman distinguishes between notional and real assent. Notional assent is assent to abstractions; real assent is assent to things. Notional assent does not affect conduct; real assent does. This distinction applies, I think, to perceptions of the Holocaust. "To have read about it in the papers," Holly Cowan Shulman writes, "and to incorporate that knowledge into one's being are two different things." Abstract knowledge is not enough.

We now know that the Holocaust was terribly real, and latter-day critics castigate those who failed to see it as terribly real at the time. But knowing how it all came out confers a considerable advantage. At the time, faced by an uneven flow of uncertain and speculative reports, many Americans—many refugees too—were honestly puzzled and, reluctant to accept the most pessimistic possibilities, found persuasive reasons for postponement or denial.

People remembered the phony atrocity stories of the Great War only thirty years before—Germans invading Belgium, children with their hands cut off, mass rapes and executions, all attested by such authorities as Lord Bryce. Later these stories turned out to be inventions of allied propaganda. Recalling this, skeptical newspaper editors rarely put stories about Nazi atrocities on the front page. For most Americans who read about it at the time, the Final Solution commanded notional rather than real assent.

"Perhaps we were so preoccupied with the squalid menace of the war," wrote George Ball, "we did not focus on this unspeakable ghastliness. It may also be that the idea of mass extermination was so far outside the traditional comprehension of most Americans that we instinctively refused to believe its existence.". . .

FDR Is Not to Blame

The blame-lovers of the Nineties, while inert before the holocausts of their own day, became virulent critics of Franklin D. Roosevelt and accused him of betraying the Jews.

Actually, FDR was probably the most pro-Jewish of all American presidents. No president up to this time had so many Jews in his inner circle or appointed so many to high office. Opponents called it the "Jew Deal." And FDR well knew how strong anti-Semitism was in America during the Great Depression. The Swedish economist Gunnar Myrdal, imported in the late Thirties to study the Negro question, observed in his great work *An American Dilemma* that anti-Semitism in America "probably was somewhat stronger than in Germany before the Nazi regime."

FDR perfectly understood that it would be fatal to let the war against Hitler be defined as a war to save the Jews. He knew that he must emphasize the large and vital interest all Americans had in stopping Hitler. Anti-Semitism actually increased as the war wore on. In 1945 Hadley Cantril's Office of Public Opinion Research at Princeton reported that 64 percent of Americans believed that "Jews have too much power and influence in the United States."

Yet for all that, FDR repeatedly protested the slaughter of the Jews. In his presidency, Gerhard Weinberg, that fine historian of the Second World War, reminds us, "The United States accepted about twice as many Jewish refugees as the rest of the world put together: about 200,000 out of 300,000." FDR's priority quite properly was winning the war, and he had no doubt that this was the best way to save the Jews, and everybody else.

Professor Weinberg, recalling the daily death toll in the extermination camps, asks us to consider "how many Jews would have survived had the war ended even a week or ten days earlier—and, conversely, how many more would have died had the war lasted an additional week or ten days." The number, he concludes, would be greater than the total number of Jews saved by the various rescue efforts of 1944–45. Was winning the war as quickly as possible really such a bad idea?

Harry Truman and the Decision to Unleash the Atomic Bomb

Harry S. Truman

On August 5, 1945, the United States dropped an atomic bomb on the Japanese city of Hiroshima, causing massive destruction and more than fifty thousand deaths. Four days later, more than forty thousand people were killed when the Americans released a second atomic bomb, this time on the Japanese city of Nagasaki. In the following selection, Harry S. Truman, president of the United States at the time, explains how he arrived at the decision to unleash the bomb. According to Truman, he did not find out such a bomb existed until the evening of April 12, 1945, after President Franklin D. Roosevelt died. Truman explains that although he made the decision to drop the bomb, he did not do it alone. He writes that he had no choice in the end. He was convinced, he reports, that the Japanese would keep refusing to surrender and that an additional hundreds and thousands of lives would be lost if the United States continued using only conventional weaponry.

Just about all the fighting in the world is caused by the lack of enough to eat and enough to wear and the lack of a good place to live, but if atomic energy is used the way it ought to be, it can save the whole world from fighting each other to get what's

Excerpted from *Where the Buck Stops*, edited by Margaret Truman. Copyright © 1989 by Margaret Truman. Reprinted with permission of Warner Books, Inc.

necessary for people to have. It can do unbelievable good for the world, truly a world of good, if people can be persuaded to get along by looking at examples of the times they didn't get along and were wiped out and destroyed because they couldn't get along. The same thing can happen now, except this time it will wipe out the whole population of the world if we go to war with this atomic energy, which we turned loose.

THE MOST TERRIBLE WEAPON KNOWN

I was the president who made the decision to unleash that terrible power, of course, and it was a difficult and dreadful decision to have to make. Some people have the mistaken impression that I made it on my own and in haste and almost on impulse, but it was nothing like that at all.

If I live to be a hundred years old, I'll never forget the day that I was first told about the atomic bomb. It was about 7:30 P.M. on the evening of April 12, 1945, just hours after Franklin Roosevelt had died at 3:35 P.M., and no more than half an hour after I was sworn in as president at 7:09 P.M. Henry L. Stimson, who was Roosevelt's secretary of war and then mine, took me aside and reminded me that Roosevelt had authorized the development of a sort of superbomb and that that bomb was almost ready. I was still stunned by Roosevelt's death and by the fact that I was now president, and I didn't think much more about it at the time. But then, on April 26, Stimson asked for a meeting in my office, at which he was joined by Major General Leslie Groves, who was in charge of the operation that was developing the bomb, the Manhattan Project. The meeting was so secret that Groves came into the White House by the back door. And at the meeting, Stimson handed me a memorandum that said, "Within four months we shall in all probability have completed the most terrible weapon ever known in human history, one bomb which could destroy a whole city."

Stimson said very gravely that he didn't know whether we could or should use the bomb because he was afraid that it was so powerful that it could end up destroying the whole world. I felt the same fear as he and Groves continued to talk about it, and when I read Groves's twenty-four-page report. The report said that the first bomb would probably be ready by July and have the strength of about five hundred tons of TNT, and even more frighteningly, it went on to say that a second bomb would probably be ready by August and have the strength of as much as twelve hundred tons of TNT. We weren't aware then that that was just the tip of the iceberg. That second bomb turned out to have the power of twenty thousand tons of TNT, and the hydro-

A large mushroom cloud rose to the sky after the United States dropped the atomic bomb on Hiroshima, Japan, on August 5, 1945. More than fifty thousand people were killed by the bomb.

gen bomb that eventually followed it had the explosive power of twenty million tons of TNT.

Stimson's memo suggested the formation of a committee to assist me in deciding whether or not to use the bomb on Japan, and I agreed completely. The committee, which we called the Interim Committee, was formed at once and consisted of Stimson as

chairman, James F. Byrnes, who later became my secretary of
state, as my representative on the committee, James B. Conant,
who was the president of Harvard, Karl T. Compton, who was
the president of the Massachusetts Institute of Technology, and
Vannevar Bush, who was the head of our Office of Scientific Research and Development. The Interim Committee in turn called
in, for advice and information, the scientists who developed the
bomb: Arthur H. Compton, who was Karl Compton's brother,
Enrico Fermi, Ernest O. Lawrence, and J. Robert Oppenheimer.

DROPPING THE BOMB WAS THE ONLY CHOICE

Then, on May 8, my sixty-first birthday, the Germans surrendered, and I had to remind our country that the war was only
half over, that we still had to face the war with Japan. The winning of that war, we all knew, might even be more difficult to accomplish, because the Japanese were self-proclaimed fanatic war-
riors who made it all too clear that they preferred death to defeat
in battle. Just a month before, after our soldiers and Marines
landed on Okinawa, the Japanese lost 100,000 men out of the
120,000 in their garrison, and yet, though they were defeated
without any question in the world, thousands more Japanese soldiers fell on their own grenades and died rather than surrender.

Nevertheless, I pleaded with the Japanese in my speech announcing Germany's surrender, begging them to surrender, too,
but was not too surprised when they refused. And on June 18, I
met with the Joint Chiefs of Staff to discuss what I hoped would
be our final push against the Japanese. We still hadn't decided
whether or not to use the atomic bomb, and the chiefs of staff
suggested that we plan an attack on Kyushu, the Japanese island
on their extreme west, around the beginning of November, and
follow up with an attack on the more important island of Hon-
shu. But the statistics that the generals gave me were as fright-
ening as the news of the big bomb. The chiefs of staff estimated
that the Japanese still had five thousand attack planes, seventeen
garrisons on the island of Kyushu alone, and a total of more than
two million men on all of the islands of Japan. General [George
C.] Marshall then estimated that, since the Japanese would unquestionably fight even more fiercely than ever on their own
homeland, we would probably lose a quarter of a million men
and possibly as many as a half million in taking the two islands.
I could not bear this thought, and it led to the decision to use the
atomic bomb.

We talked first about blockading Japan and trying to blast
them into surrender with conventional weaponry; but Marshall
and others made it clear that this would never work, pointing out

that we'd hit Germany in this way and they hadn't surrendered until we got troops into Germany itself. Another general also pointed out that Germany's munitions industries were more or less centralized and that our constant bombings of these facilities never made them quit, and Japan's industries were much more spread apart and harder to hit. Then, when we finally talked about the atomic bomb, on July 21, coming to the awful conclusion that it would probably be the only way the Japanese might be made to surrender, quickly, we talked first about hitting some isolated area, some low-population area where there would not be too many casualties but where the Japanese could see the power of the new weapon. Reluctantly, we decided against that as well, feeling that that just wouldn't be enough to convince the fanatic Japanese. And we finally selected four possible target areas, all heavy military-manufacturing areas: Hiroshima, Kokura, Nagasaki, and Niigata.

"I Did What I Thought Was Right"

I know the world will never forget that the first bomb was dropped on Hiroshima on August 5, at 7:15 P.M. Washington time, and the second on Nagasaki on August 9. One more plea for surrender had been made to the Japanese on July 29, and was rejected immediately. Then I gave the final order, saying I had no qualms "if millions of lives could be saved." I meant both American and Japanese lives.

The Japanese surrendered five days after the bomb was dropped on Nagasaki, and a number of major Japanese military men and diplomats later confirmed publicly that there would have been no quick surrender without it. For this reason, I made what I believed to be the only possible decision. I said something to this effect in a letter to my sister, Mary: "It was a terrible decision. But I made it. And I made it to save 250,000 boys from the United States, and I'd make it again under similar circumstances." I said the same thing at somewhat greater length in a speech at a university in 1965:

"It was a question of saving hundreds of thousands of American lives. . . . You don't feel normal when you have to plan hundreds of thousands of . . . deaths of American boys who are alive and joking and having fun while you're doing your planning. You break your heart and your head trying to figure out a way to save one life. . . . The name given to our invasion plan was Olympic, but I saw nothing godly about the killing of all the people that would be necessary to make that invasion. The casualty estimates called for seven hundred and fifty thousand American casualties— two hundred and fifty thousand killed, five hundred thousand maimed for life. . . . I couldn't worry about what history would say about my personal morality. I made the only decision I ever knew how to make. I did what I thought was right."

I still think that. But God knows it underlines the need for an organization like the United Nations to prevent another and probably final world war.

THE BIRTH OF THE UNITED NATIONS OF THE CIVILIZED WORLD

KENNETH S. DAVIS

Today the United Nations, originally formed as a successor to the ineffectual League of Nations, includes virtually all the countries in the world, with 189 member nations. In the selection that follows, the late American historian and biographer Kenneth S. Davis explains that in the early 1940s the public welcomed the possibility of a union of international powers, one that was much stronger than a mere alliance. According to Davis, President Franklin D. Roosevelt originally suggested—and continued to press for—the preparation and signing of the Declaration by United Nations, issued on January 1, 1942, by the twenty-six nations fighting the Axis powers. Among the difficulties that had to be resolved before the document was signed, Davis writes, was the order in which the signatures were to appear, the absence of a reference to religious freedom, and the use of the term *Authorities* after the word *Governments* in the first sentence of the declaration.

The joint press conference and the two [Prime Minister Winston] Churchill addresses, especially his address to [the U.S.] Congress, along with the Atlantic Charter and [President Franklin D.] Roosevelt's public emphasis upon the closeness of the personal bond between him and His Majesty's first minister, had by the end of 1941 encouraged a popular belief that what was now [1942] happening at the Washington Conference,

Excerpted from *FDR: The War President, 1940–1943*, by Kenneth S. Davis. Copyright © 2000 by The Kenneth S. Davis and Jean S. Davis Revocable Trust. Reprinted by permission of Random House, Inc.

code-named Arcadia, was something more than the shaping of another international military alliance. An alliance is a linkage between sharply defined sovereign powers. The powers have space between them; their alliance is but a narrow bridge, generally a flimsy one, cast across this space for a limited time. But now in Washington, or so the more thoughtful and idealistic among the populace were encouraged to believe, a considerable portion of this separateness, this international space, was in process of being annihilated. There appeared to be occurring a limited pooling of sovereignty in a new supranational organism, an organism radically different from the failed League of Nations insofar as it was, to the extent of this pooling, not a league but a union—a making of one out of many. The end of the process, attainable, perhaps, within the lifetime of millions who now struggled on the battlefields of Europe and Asia and Africa, might be a United States of the civilized world!

THE JOINT DECLARATION IS ISSUED

This public perception was sharpened and clarified on New Year's Day 1942 when barely twenty-four hours after Churchill's return to Washington from Ottawa [Canada], there was signed in the Oval Room of the White House a joint declaration by the twenty-six nations who were at war with Axis powers. It was headed DECLARATION BY UNITED NATIONS, and its full text appeared in the newspapers of January 2 as follows:

> *A Joint Declaration by The United States of America, The United Kingdom of Great Britain and Northern Ireland, the Union of Soviet Socialist Republics, China, Australia, Belgium, Canada, Costa Rica, Cuba, Czechoslovakia, Dominican Republic, El Salvador, Greece, Guatemala, Haiti, Honduras, India, Luxembourg, Netherlands, New Zealand, Nicaragua, Norway, Panama, Poland, South Africa, Yugoslavia.*

> The Governments signatory hereto,

> Having subscribed to a common program of purposes and principles embodied in the Joint Declaration of the President of the United States and the Prime Minister of the United Kingdom of Great Britain and Northern Ireland, dated August 14, 1941, known as the Atlantic Charter.

> Being convinced that complete victory over their enemies is essential to defend life, liberty, independence, and religious freedom, and to preserve human rights and justice in their own lands as well as in other lands,

and that they are now engaged in a common struggle against savage and brutal forces seeking to subjugate the world, DECLARE:

Each Government pledges itself to employ its full resources, military or economic, against those members of the Tripartite Pact and its adherents with which such Government is at war.

Each Government pledges itself to cooperate with the Governments signatory hereto, and not to make a separate armistice or peace with the enemies.

The foregoing Declaration may be adhered to by other nations which are, or which may be, rendering material assistance and contributions in the struggle for victory over Hitlerism.

Done at Washington

January First, 1942

A MATTER OF PROTOCOL

Like the Atlantic Charter, this document was prepared at the instigation of Roosevelt, who proposed the enterprise to Churchill on December 23. Like the Atlantic Charter, it was in its final form a revised blend of two drafts originally prepared separately by Roosevelt and Churchill. And, even more than in the case of the charter, its preparation was marvelous for the speed with which it was accomplished. For this last, too, Roosevelt was largely responsible; he pressed for a New Year's Day publication of the document because he was anxious to offset the effect upon the public mind of the horrendous news that was pouring night and day out of the Far East. Finally, it was Roosevelt who had come up with "United Nations" as a replacement for the dull-sounding "Associated Nations" in the Declaration's heading. "Allies" being ruled out because the word had treaty implications, and a treaty had to be ratified by the U.S. Senate. (Plausible legend has it that Roosevelt was so excitedly pleased by his "United Nations" inspiration that he hurried to communicate it to Churchill, wheeling himself into the latter's quarters without knocking and finding the Prime Minister emerging stark naked from the bathtub. He began to retreat, with an embarrassed apology. "Think nothing of it," Churchill said airily. "The Prime Minister of Great Britain has nothing to conceal from the President of the United States.") A number of difficulties had to be overcome. In what order, for instance, was the document to be signed? In the first joint draft, the United States signed first, the United Kingdom second, then four British Dominions and Commonwealths (Australia, Canada, New Zealand, South Africa), then the other nations in alphabetical order. India was omitted at the behest of Churchill and the British war cabinet. But this was clearly unsatisfactory. It placed the Union of Soviet Socialist Republics far down the list, though the USSR was the chief of Hitler's fighting opponents; it ignored the fact that Indian troops were the major component of the British forces now fighting the Japanese. The problem was solved by listing with the United States and Britain the other two of what Roosevelt called the "Big Four," namely, the USSR and China, and then listing the others alphabetically, India being finally included after both [British Ambassador Edward Frederick Lindley Wood, Lord] Halifax and [British foreign secretary Anthony] Eden had vehemently protested her exclusion.

Another problem arose when [special assistant to Roosevelt Harry] Hopkins, reviewing the first joint draft, remarked the absence from it of any reference to religious freedom, a subject whose omission from the Atlantic Charter had exposed that document to much adverse criticism. Hopkins strongly recommended that "every effort" be made "to get religious freedom in this document" and that, since atheistic Communist Russia might object, Roosevelt press the point with Maxim Litvinov, who had just replaced the abrasive [Constantine A.] Oumansky as Soviet ambassador in Washington. Roosevelt did so when he lunched with the new ambassador, and with Hopkins, on December 27. Litvinov, the failed architect of a united front against Hitler in the 1930s, had lived in poverty, disgrace, and a fully justified fear for his life after his replacement by [Vyacheslav] Molotov as Soviet foreign minister in 1939. He knew that [Russian leader Joseph] Stalin suspected him of excessively pro-Western, pro-democratic sympathies; he was acutely aware that such suspicion, if he did anything to confirm it in Stalin's mind, could be fatal to him. He was consequently extremely reluctant to seek Stalin's approval of the proposed insertion in the draft document he had already cabled to Moscow. At last, fearfully, he did so. Whereupon, to quote Churchill's memoirs, Stalin accepted the insertion "as a matter of course."

Litvinov's palpable fear of Stalin also worked against the inclusion of the words "and Authorities" after the word "Governments" in the first sentence of the declaration. Churchill proposed doing so in order to permit the listing of Free France as a declaration signer. Roosevelt had initially no objection to this, and the Free French would certainly have been delighted to sign. But Litvinov said that he, as an official of the Soviet Foreign Office, had no authority to approve the slightest textual change in a document that committed the whole of the Soviet government and that had already received Moscow's approval. If the word "Authorities" were inserted, he would be unable to sign the declaration unless and until Moscow had specifically authorized his doing so. And since it was impossible to obtain such permission, assuming it were forthcoming, without delaying the ceremonial signing beyond the New Year's Day deadline, the insertion was not made. ". . . Litvinov is a mere automaton, evidently frightened out of his wits after what he has gone through," a disgusted Churchill cabled Clement Attlee, head of Britain's Labour Party and, by that token, generally regarded as Britain's Deputy Prime Minister. But, Churchill went on, "This can be covered by an exchange of letters making clear that the word 'Nations' covers authorities such as the Free French, or insurgent organizations which may arise in Spain, in North Africa, or in Germany itself. Settlement was imperative because . . . President was . . . very keen on January 1."

FOR FURTHER RESEARCH

Frederick Lewis Allen, *Only Yesterday: An Informal History of the Nineteen-Twenties.* New York: Harper & Row, 1931.

Frederick Lewis Allen, *Since Yesterday: The 1930s in America September 3, 1929–September 3, 1939.* New York: Harper & Row, 1968.

Benjamin Appel, *The People Talk: American Voices from the Great Depression.* New York: Simon and Schuster, 1981.

Antony Beevor, *The Spanish Civil War.* New York: Penguin USA, 2001.

Nicholas Bethell, *The War Hitler Won: The Fall of Poland, September 1939.* New York: Holt, Rinehart and Winston, 1972.

Herbert P. Bix, *Hirohito and the Making of Modern Japan.* New York: HarperCollins, 2000.

Bruce Bliven, "Flapper Jane," *The New Republic,* September 9, 1925.

Piers Brendon, *The Dark Valley: A Panorama of the 1930s.* New York: Alfred Knopf, 2000.

Tom Brokaw, *The Greatest Generation.* New York: Random House, 1998.

Tom Brokaw, *The Greatest Generation Speaks.* New York: Random House, 1998.

Daniel Allen Butler, *The Lusitania: The Life, Loss, and Legacy of an Ocean Legend.* Mechanicsburg, PA: Stackpole Books, 2000.

Howard Carter and A.C. Mace, *The Discovery of the Tomb of Tutankhamen.* New York: Dover Publications, 1977 replication of Volume I of the work *The Tomb of Tut•Ankh•Amen Dis-*

covered by the Late Earl of Carnarvon and Howard Carter, originally published by Cassell, London, 1923.

Winston S. Churchill, *The Second World War: The Gathering Storm.* Boston: Houghton Mifflin, 1948.

Alfred W. Crosby, *America's Forgotten Pandemic: The Influenza of 1918.* New York: Cambridge University Press, 1989.

Kenneth S. Davis, *FDR: The War President 1940–1943 A History.* New York: Random House, 2000.

John W. Dower, *Embracing Defeat: Japan in the Wake of World War II.* New York: W.W. Norton, 1999.

Max Gallo, *Spain Under Franco: A History.* New York: E.P. Dutton, 1974.

John A. Garraty, *The Great Depression: An Inquiry into the causes, course, and consequences of the Worldwide Depression of the Nineteen-Thirties, as seen by contemporaries and in the Light of History.* San Diego, CA: Harcourt Brace Jovanovich, 1986.

G.S. Graber, *Caravans to Oblivion: The Armenian Genocide, 1915.* New York: John Wiley & Sons, 1996.

Mark Jonathan Harris and Deborah Oppenheimer, *Into the Arms of Strangers: Stories of the Kindertransport.* Bloomsbury Publishing, 2000.

John Keegan, *The First World War.* New York: Alfred A. Knopf, 1999.

Ian Kershaw, *Hitler: 1889–1936 Hubris.* New York: W.W. Norton, 1999.

Lord Kinross, *Ataturk: A Biography of Mustafa Kemal, Father of Modern Turkey.* New York: Quill William Morrow, 1964.

Gina Kolata, *Flu: The Story of the Great Influenza Pandemic of 1918 and the Search for the Virus that Caused It.* New York: Farrar, Straus and Giroux, 1999.

William Edward Leuchtenburg and Daniel J. Boorstin, *The Perils of Prosperity 1914–1932.* Chicago: University of Chicago Press, 1993.

David McCullough, *The Path Between the Seas: The Creation of the Panama Canal 1870–1914.* New York: Simon and Schuster, 1977.

David McCullough, *Truman*. New York: Simon and Schuster, 1992.

Donald E. Miller and Lorna Touryan Miller, *Survivors: An Oral History of the Armenian Genocide*. Berkeley and Los Angeles, CA: University of California Press, 1993.

Leonard Mosley, *Backs to the Wall: The Heroic Story of the People of London During World War II*. New York: Random House, 1971.

Benito Mussolini, *My Autobiography*. New York: Charles Scribner's Sons, 1928.

Donald Neff, "Britain Issues the Balfour Declaration," *Washington Report on Middle East Affairs*, October/November 1995.

Allan Nevins and Frank Earnest Hill, *Ford: Expansion and Challenge 1915–1933*. New York: Charles Scribner's Sons, 1957.

Geoffrey Perrett, *America in the Twenties*. New York: Simon and Schuster, 1982.

Doris L. Rich, *Amelia Earhart: A Biography*. Washington, DC: Smithsonian Institution Press, 1996.

Bernat Rosner, Frederic C. Tubach, and Sally Patterson Tubach, *An Uncommon Friendship: From Opposite Sides of the Holocaust*. Berkeley and Los Angeles, CA: University of California Press, 2001.

Harrison E. Salisbury, *Russia in Revolution 1900–1930*. Austin, TX: Holt, Rinehart and Winston, 1978.

Arthur M. Schlesinger Jr., *A Life in the Twentieth Century: Innocent Beginnings, 1917–1950*. Boston: Houghton Mifflin, 2000.

Monica Itoi Sone, *Nisei Daughter*. Seattle, WA: University of Washington Press, 1979.

Mark Sullivan, *Our Times: The United States 1900–1925*. New York: Charles Scribner's Sons, 1935.

Charles W. Sweeney with James A. Antonucci and Marion K. Antonucci, *War's End: An Eyewitness Account of America's Last Atomic Mission*. New York: Avon Books, 1997.

Edmond Taylor, *The Fall of the Dynasties: The Collapse of the Old Order 1905–1922*. Garden City, NY: Doubleday, 1963.

John M. Taylor, "Fateful Voyage of *Lusitania*," *Quarterly Journal of Military History*, vol. 11, no. 3, Spring 1999.

Margaret Truman, ed., *Where the Buck Stops: The Personal and Private Writings of Harry S. Truman*. New York: Warner Books, 1989.

Dick Wilson, *The Long March 1935: The Epic of Chinese Communism's Survival*. New York: Viking Press, 1971.

Stanley A. Wolpert, *Gandhi's Passion: The Life and Legacy of Mahatma Gandhi*. Oxford, UK: Oxford University Press, 2001.

INDEX